Contents

The interviews

Leaders

Classic entrepreneurs

Leadership and Entrepreneurship in the Hospitality Industry

**Chris Sheppardson and
Heather Gibson**

NORWICH CITY COLLEGE

Stock No	247468	
Class	647.94068 SHE	
Cat.		Proc	IWL

247 468

 Goodfellow Publishers Ltd

Published by Goodfellow Publishers Limited,
Woodeaton, Oxford, OX3 9TJ
http://www.goodfellowpublishers.com

British Library Cataloguing in Publication Data: a catalogue record for
this title is available from the British Library.

Library of Congress Catalog Card Number: on file.

ISBN: 978-1-906884-49-9

Copyright © Chris Sheppardson and Heather Gibson 2011

All rights reserved. The text of this publication, or any part thereof,
may not be reproduced or transmitted in any form or by any means,
electronic or mechanical, including photocopying, recording, storage in
an information retrieval system, or otherwise, without prior permission
of the publisher or under licence from the Copyright Licensing
Agency Limited. Further details of such licences (for reprographic
reproduction) may be obtained from the Copyright Licensing Agency
Limited, of Saffron House, 6–10 Kirby Street, London EC1N 8TS.

 Design and typesetting by P.K. McBride, www.macbride.org.uk

Cover design by Cylinder, www.cylindermedia.com

Printed by Marston Book Services, www.marston.co.uk

'Leadership and learning are indispensable to each other.'
JFK

Corporate entrepreneurs

Preface

In difficult times, the issue of leadership and entrepreneurship always comes to the fore and is a popular area of debate. This is natural as they are both key to economic performance and being able to see the light at the end of the tunnel. In today's climate, there is much money being invested into leadership development courses. The intentions behind these are very good and it is important to understand the topic so that we develop an understanding of leadership, but what does lie at the heart of the success of both leaders and entrepreneurs?

We pose this question as so much lies within the mindset and approach that these individuals bring to their business. So many leaders and entrepreneurs have a mental picture that other people just cannot see. Many times we have heard an entrepreneur make a statement 'other people might think it was a huge risk, but I thought there was an opportunity'. Peter Lederer (Chairman, Gleneagles) will often be heard asking 'what does success look like?' He is asking whether the end destination can be clearly visualised. Marc Verstringhe (founder of Catering and Allied Services International) would often describe his role as being to stand at the top of a mountain and have a clear vision across the valley below so that he could guide his team. Others in the team would stand at various points lower down on the mountain and their views would be naturally more impaired. A nice description, but the reality is that there are many, even at CEO level, who do not have a clear view. It is far harder to gain than many realise and some are in need of either glasses or a telescope. It is those with clear vision that do stand apart.

It has recently become a cliché that successful people in all fields – whether business or sport – 'play what is in front of them'. They are able to adapt to changing markets and conditions. They are able to handle setbacks and find a way forward. Why? Because they possess a clear vision of the destination that they are trying to reach and do not take their eye off this goal. Great sportsmen will often talk about visualing winning prior to playing a game. They are often trained to visualise every possibility of what could go wrong during the course of a game or race and are able to adapt to the setback and still win. It creates a positive mentality that allows them to handle situations because they are psychologically prepared. It is rare to find business people who do this to the same extent and most would laugh at the thought, but whether they realise it or not, they do it naturally and instinctively, and travel a similar road. Leaders and entrepreneurs see a picture that the others simply cannot.

Of course, it is not just about visualisation and positive mental attitude. This is too simple. It takes some very special traits. Often very talented individuals never fulfil their potential for the reason that they do possess the most important inner traits – courage, conviction, or work ethic. Many can talk a good line and be strategic, but few can deliver in reality.

The following text asks: What are the stories that stand behind successful leaders and entrepreneurs and what can be learn from their stories? The hospitality industry is an excellent forum for reviewing this question, for so many of its leaders are self-made; characters that have built great careers from humble beginnings.

This book is about the psychology that lies behind leaders and entrepreneurs, for without the right mindset, all theoretical concepts on the subject become less valid. The book illustrates that the stories of successful leaders and entrepreneurs are often down to their personal qualities: hard work, tenacity, courage, passion that creates a mental picture of the world. Above all, these people are individuals: human, but flawed at the same time; compassionate, inspirational individuals. These characteristics are especially a feature of people in the hospitality industry and there are many lessons in the individual stories we tell, and common themes that we can draw from all of them.

The following is the result of over 100 conversations with industry leaders and entrepreneurs, and the key message lies with their individual stories.

Acknowledgements

This book is the culmination of several years of discussion with some of the hospitality industry's most successful leaders and entrepreneurs, largely through interviews in EP Business in *Hospitality* magazine (formerly *En Passant* magazine). During this time many people have been involved in contributing articles which are featured in this book, and the authors wish to thank: Sally Houston, David Coubrough, Rachel Brown, Christian Delteil, Jennifer Miller and Mark Lederer.

For their images we wish to thank Susannah Fields and Joanne Aldridge.

Finally, the authors wish to acknowledge the ongoing support 'behind the scenes' of Suzanna Hunter, Nick Sheppardson, Karl Schorman and Nick Metcalfe.

Structure of this book

This book has two main sections: *Leaders* and *Entrepreneurs*. Each section has an introductory outline of the authors' view on leadership and entrepreneurialism, followed by a series of real-life profiles and interviews with hospitality professionals. The profiles are a combination of those specifically written for this book and interviews adapted from *EP Magazine*. The book ends with a section, *The leader and the entrepreneur*, which concludes the lessons that can be learnt from the profiles.

Introduction

So many admire, and aspire to be, leaders and entrepreneurs. This is understandable and as natural as it can be. Leaders and entrepreneurs set the tone of society. It is easy to admire those that possess courage and conviction. Their lives appear – rightly or wrongly – to have more meaning and to be able to leave a legacy that others will remember. It is natural for everyone to want their lives to have a positive impact.

So what does it require?

Much has been written over the years about leadership and entrepreneurship. Some has been thought provoking and insightful. But often the studies are misleading. There is an old belief that 90% of people are frightened of failure and this creates barriers that prevent real success. Maybe it is as straightforward and simple as this – that leaders and entrepreneurs stand in the 10% but if this is the case, why is it that they are able to find the courage the lack of which hinders others? Of course, the reality is more complex and this will be illustrated in the featured case studies.

There are many people who possess natural talent but are unable to turn that into something meaningful. Why? The hard truth is that they do not have the necessary character traits needed that allows them to reach the pinnacle. We can write and discuss leadership and entrepreneurship. We can aspire to the qualities required but very, very few are able to achieve this status for it requires some very rare qualities.

The aim of the following study is to look at exactly what is required. What is it that drives leaders and entrepreneurs? Are they natural or created?

Once we have completed the following journey, I suspect we will find that success is determined by character traits that are not unique to either leaders or entrepreneurs but are important traits that serve to determine success.

So why is there a need for another book on the subject? There are two good reasons.

First, many of the theories are exactly that – theories, but leadership and great entrepreneurship is not theoretical. It is real and our journey is to discover the reality of leadership and entrepreneurship. It cannot be taught and few can turn themselves into either leaders or entrepreneurs.

What these two groups possess is something that makes them stand apart and this is worth truly understanding. The following is based on over 100 conversations with some of the greatest and best from the hospitality industry.

Second, the leaders and entrepreneurs that live within the hospitality arena are quite special characters. This book will look at the characters that stand behind the real achievements.

The hospitality industry is made up of all types of leader. There are those that have risen from the lowest levels through hard work and a high work ethic. Often these are larger than life characters, flawed but real. There are also those that have come via more traditional routes – universities and business schools. But wherever they have come from, they have had to lead businesses that rely on the skills of its people, not just the asset base.

Food is an emotive business. A great restaurant relies on a great chef. This cannot be manufactured. It relies on skill. What makes a great restaurant manager is how they make their customer feel and the service delivered. It is hard to train. It requires empathy and subtlety. A great hotel relies on groups of varied, skilled individuals who come together as one. Leaders, therefore, need to harness teams.

The hospitality industry is also no longer a Cinderella business. It is now world class. London is seen by many as the leading culinary city in the world. It possesses some of the greatest hotels, chefs, sommeliers, and companies that can compete with any. There are lessons to be learnt from this industry and some very good case studies and examples. In the following, we will look at the personal stories of some of the best. As the old saying goes, 'it is always best to learn from the best'.

1 Leadership

Never to be underestimated

The importance of leadership cannot be underestimated.

As a society we are almost obsessed with the concept. Our leaders are core to the way we view life and how we feel about ourselves. We expect so much – whether it is the Prime Minister, the captain of a national sports team or the leader of a company. They are held responsible for the performance and wellbeing of whatever entity they lead.

It is no coincidence that the last UK General Election (2010) evolved more around the performance of the three leaders than about real policy issues. It is no coincidence that the lifespan of corporate CEOs is short, as can be the careers of our sporting icons once they have become captain. It is a harsh reality and in truth, it is often only a matter of time before even the best leaders are exposed to failure.

In the last election, Nick Clegg and Gordon Brown were almost polar opposites but they turned the British General Election of 2010 on its head. It can be argued that David Cameron, who everyone thought would shine as a natural speaker, was placed under unexpected pressure by the performance of Nick Clegg in the leadership debates. At the same time, Gordon Brown's leadership style split many. It was only near to the end of the campaign that we came to see the real man, and his honest approach won more admiration than is often credited.

> 'I know that Labour hasn't done everything right and I know, really I know, I'm not perfect.' (Gordon Brown)

Leaders are supposed to never display vulnerability but it can be argued that Brown's approach did not lose the election but saved Labour from a large defeat. He had been the iron Chancellor who had never seemed at ease as PM. Suddenly we saw a man with real emotions rather than the intense, almost self-orientated version we had seen up to that point. History may well be kinder to his performance as leader than many were at the time.

To understand how important leadership is, it may be worth just looking at a couple of high profile examples.

Winston Churchill will go down as one of the finest Prime Ministers that the country ever had. His leadership during the Second World War is still referred to as awe-inspiring. He is often described as the greatest Briton of the 20th century. Yet this was a man who, five years earlier, was viewed as difficult, almost maverick, and dangerous.

This was a man whose personal habits would not have been tolerated without the success he showed. However, these traits were forgiven as he inspired trust and courage from the country at a time when all appeared lost. And yet he still lost the General Election of 1946, when Clement Attlee came to power. In contrast, Attlee's government arguably created more lasting change (such as the creation of the NHS) than almost any other government and yet lasted only one term. Why? Was it due to the quiet, managerial manner of Attlee himself? Many historians believe that Attlee's achievements were under-rated but that is the fickle nature of leadership. It is not just about competence but how confident others feel.

The JFK story is remarkably similar to Churchill's. This is a man who enjoys a status well beyond what he actually achieved. This is a man whose personal faults were forgiven as he too inspired a generation. It can be correctly noted that JFK's faults came out more after his death, but all the journals of his close colleagues – who must have known of his personal ways – display loyalty and respect. Why? What generated this in those around him?

Bill Clinton is often better known for his personal faults and yet often it was commented that the world was safer under his tenure than under George W. Bush. It is also commented that even though Clinton faced impeachment charges and was proven to be less than candid at times, he would still have won the 2000 Presidential election. Leaders do not need to be perfect but they do need to be able to inspire and to be liked.

Sometimes sport throws up the clearest examples and the one that particularly stands out is the story of Ian Botham and Mike Brearley as captains of the England cricket team in 1980–81. What makes this story was interesting is that it is three-sided as it also involves the leadership of the Australian captain, Kim Hughes.

In 1979, Ian Botham was the star player who was thrust in the captain's role with little preparation. It was understandable that he struggled as so much rested on his shoulders. In the summer of 1981, the Australians came to play an Ashes series. They were a highly regarded team who boasted the talents of Dennis Lillee, Rodney Marsh, Allan Border and Terry Alderman. It was always going to be a tough series to win and England lost the first match. After the second Test Match, Botham walked off the turf at Lords as though he was a disgraced player. As is now famous, the pavilion members remained disrespectfully silent as he left the arena. It was too harsh a reaction but the truth is that the crowd had turned against him and he was not even afforded almost the most basic of courtesies.

Botham resigned straight after the match and Mike Brearley – the successful former captain – returned to the role. The following three Test matches saw the star player return to form with performances that captured the hearts of the nation and inspired almost legendary status back on the player. Brearley took the plaudits for his leadership and, following his retirement, went onto to write a best selling book – *The Art of Captaincy*. It is a very good book but it is doubtful that it would have been a best seller without success in that summer series.

Brearley, as a player, was not worth his place in the team but he knew how to motivate and lead a team. He was also incredibly lucky as England went on to win the series 3–1; a series they should have lost 3–1 if anything normal had taken place.

What had changed in Botham? Simply, the pressures of expectation had been taken away and he was free to be the true player that he was. Botham was not a natural captain. He was a brilliant player but arguably understood little about those he had to lead. Brearley in contrast understood his players.

Just as it was fascinating to observe Brearley's leadership and the change in Botham, their success also resulted from a dramatic fall in confidence within the much heralded Australian team. It has been much commented that the Australians became psychologically damaged during that series as they lost match-winning positions. Their captain, Kim Hughes, came under increased criticism both externally and within the team itself. The players lost confidence in their captain and looked towards to the other senior players – Rod Marsh and Dennis Lillee. His ability to lead was broken and it was little surprise that he resigned a few short months later.

Did Kim Hughes's captaincy contribute to Botham's success? Maybe, but undoubtedly the Australians certainly looked like a side playing with fear, which was very unlike their normal approach. Brearley and Botham took the plaudits but there is as much a story in the lack of inspiration that Hughes provided to his team at moments of crisis.

Tim Yeo, the Conservative MP, wrote of Brearley:

> 'Brearley's skill was in motivating his team and commanding respect, despite his own limited abilities. While Bobby Moore was as skilful a player as a captain, the impact of Mike Brearley's leadership was far greater than his playing skills.

In his book, Brearley's analysis of the captain's importance received attention across the academic spectrum. In his introduction to the second edition, published in 2001, Brearley described the similarity between a team captain and an NHS manager.

> Both must absorb and understand the anxieties of colleagues and team members.

Brearley concluded:

> 'There is no substitute for the leader's capacity to bring people together in a common task, so that people come to take pleasure in their joint and individual work.'

With a test batting average of just 22, Brearley was only a moderately skilled international cricketer – but he was a great captain, able to motivate, innovate, persist and inspire. These are essential skills for great managers and leaders of individuals.

Leadership is important. We hear of great leaders every day but interestingly, there is a view that we are seeing fewer and fewer leaders come to the fore as high profile figures have less freedom to express themselves in the modern world. One comment out of place or one mistake is now not forgiven in a world that is 24/7. It is an irony – we need and desire leaders and yet we hinder their development. Of course, leadership will continue to exist and be required but it will arguably be forced to change.

One example that is becoming well cited is that of Tony Hayward, the former CEO of BP who during the height of the Deepwater Horizon oil spill on America's Gulf Coast was quoted as saying 'I just want my life back' and was pictured spending some relaxation time on a sailing boat. One can be empathetic and understand that Hayward had been under intense pressure as leaders in the USA turned on BP, but what was required was a comment that showed understanding, confidence and maybe some level of humility – not a self-orientated comment. He was lost from that moment.

The unfair question this leads to is whether Hayward was a true leader or a manager in a leadership role? What is the difference? It will become clear as the book progresses but there has been a growing momentum in the debate over whether or not companies are becoming ever more dominated by management processes and systems and whether that, as a result, we are witnessing a decline in real examples of business leaders who are inspiring others to grow and become the leaders of tomorrow.

Maybe, maybe not. It is certainly a time of change and the result is that leadership will change in style, but it is unlikely to require different content, for people throughout the ages have been inspired by the same traits.

At a future point of time, when experts review the last decade, it is likely to be seen to be a period that has changed business as radically as any point of time in living memory. All the technological advances, the rise of social media and generational changes have impacted on the way work is viewed and business is conducted. There is a pattern of change that is seeing business relationships and conduct become increasingly more open and transparent. In many ways this is no bad development but how is this pattern impacting?

Leadership style alone has changed quite startlingly. Visible leadership from the front has become almost viewed as being old school and there is ever less room for the maverick in today's organisations. Companies often ask for 'entrepreneurial spirit' but find it very difficult to accommodate as entrepreneurs are often wilful characters and lateral thinkers who can be hard to manage. As already stated, any misquote or wrongful action is now communicated and circulated so widely and at speed which makes it very hard to manage and it is understandable that organisations have responded accordingly. As communication becomes easier, faster and more open; the less open will be leaders – of all types – as any error is hard to control and the impact on an organisation can be out of proportion to what was actually said. There are many, many examples.

It is no coincidence that research has shown that middle managers today can name very few of the hospitality industry's leading CEOs compared to the number 15 years ago when senior players would have been well known and clear, visible role models for aspiring talent. Is it wrong? Is it right? It does not matter – it is just different.

There has been much research over the last decade that has looked into the changing psychology of the generations X,Y and Z – how these generations are more insular, self-focused and achievement orientated – so it is hardly little surprise that corporate psychologies are changing as the new begin to replace the old. The problem is that change is hard at the best of times but with the speed of change today, it is especially difficult to keep up.

Business today is far less personal and far more factual. There is less trust in 'gut feel'; more emphasis is placed on statistics and measurements. There is less focus on teams and more on what each individual specifically brings to the table. There is less collective accountability and far more individual accountability. Of course, this creates an irony in that CEOs are less visible and yet more accountable.

In some ways this change is sad but in others it is good. As this process of change continues, then it is logical that all historical barriers to progression will fall away.

Is there any merit to this view?

Undoubtedly, the demands that are now placed upon business leaders are high and intense. It can be no coincidence that research tells us that fewer and fewer executives aspire to a CEO position. It is just worth recalling the response of Don Davenport (former CEO of the Compass Group UK) to a question on whether or not CEOs are given enough time to develop success.

> 'I think that shareholders are more demanding and they need to see growth and for that growth to come through in cash. One only has to pick up the financial press and someone is getting hammered for something. It is just more aggressive. Businesses are more transparent today – far more honest than ever before and mistakes cannot be hidden.'

We also know that the emerging generations possess a very different value set to those of previous generations. Will leadership be viewed in the same way in 2020?

Are managers becoming leaders?

It is a great debate but hardly new. One only has to recall the Attlee v. Churchill debate. However, there is a value just looking at the various schools of thought that circulate; all have some degree of merit, but none is complete.

Why does it have value then? Because it does raise some fair points for consideration but also serves to illustrate why there is a gulf between reality and theory.

Let's examine some of the key points that are made:

Modern business culture runs the risk of alienating the leaders of tomorrow

There is a prevalent school of thought that puts forward the case that industry does not possess the clear leadership and vision of past eras and that the modern business climate is not encouraging the leaders of tomorrow to come to the fore. The argument is that too much importance is being attached to corporate branding and internal processes, which allows management to flourish and that potential leadership material find themselves becoming pushed away from the core. There is, it is argued, less and less room for the 'free spirit'/maverick within the corporate organisation.

The CEO Lifespan

Recent research has also indicated that only one in four board directors now aspire to become a CEO because of the pressures and dangers that come with the role. It is also often stated that the average lifespan of a CEO of a major concern is becoming shorter and shorter (average tenure is reputedly 32 months) and that, as a result, the full focus of anyone holding such a position has to be on shareholder value, as there is simply no time allowed for the implementation of a new vision. This leads to the question as to whether or not the art of leadership is valued anymore. Maybe this is the heart of the debate, as one school of thought will argue that as a CEO's tenure is so short that all they can focus upon is the financial performance of a business whilst another will argue that those businesses that do not focus upon its people will never be able to sustain prolonged periods of profitable growth as it requires a highly motivated internal culture.

Therefore, should a CEO be a leader or a manager? An industry innovator or an accountant?

Is too much expected of CEOs, if the reputed average lifespan is so short?

These are all valid questions to be considered as often prolonged success in any discipline comes as a result of a strong workforce coupled with a talented management team. As many will state, strong teams often come from spending long periods together, and often as a result of keeping their nerve through tough times. There is an old adage that 'good teams are created in adversity'.

There is also the view that companies, especially those that are quoted, have to be far more transparent than in previous times. There is far less room for error and as a result, it has developed a safety first approach.

There is conflict between leadership vision and shareholder value

The decline in leadership is directly related to the growth in importance of financial institutions within the industry. It is argued that the change began in the early 1990s when hospitality companies began to covet the respect of City institutions who had arguably previously viewed the hospitality and leisure sectors with suspicion. The view is that these sectors do now command respect as well-run businesses that can deliver good shareholder value but perhaps something has been lost along the way.

Increased sophistication of management systems

Conversely, the counter argument is that the reason that financial institutions are now so involved in the sector is that the industry has become far more sophisticated in its managerial systems and processes, which has built greater trust in the viability of the long-term profitability of businesses. Financial institutions will always feel more comfortable with businesses that possess sound infrastructures that can support managers rather than those businesses that rely on inspirational leadership.

'If you obey all the rules, you miss all the fun.'
Katherine Hepburn

Consumer trust of the brand

We have all heard the view that 'the customer has learnt to trust a brand and for this to occur, it needs to be completely consistent in order to build the level of consumer trust required.' There is a view that has been put forward that leaders can be inspirational but that they can also be maverick, which will influence organisations both positively and negatively. With the demands of the modern business world, perhaps this is too haphazard and it is better to possess a 'safer' management methodology that focuses on the product and the market rather than any vision – especially within public quoted concerns. After all, the shareholder wants a return on their investment, rather than inspiration.

Leadership and people

Where the debate grows in importance is over how it inspires and develops the people of tomorrow. One view is that as businesses have become more sophisticated in terms of processes and systems that the reliance on good management has become less.

There is a question mark over whether managers today are as skilled in all disciplines as was the case a decade ago. It can be argued that businesses have had to create greater systems and processes to support management as the much-discussed skills shortages have bitten. Many businesses never replaced management lost in the 1990–94 recession and learnt to live without many positions. The roles undertaken by these lost management positions were either divided between colleagues or replaced via systems and procedures.

The lack of talent has meant greater investment in processes and this is another important factor in the whole debate. The industry is under strain as it is working to often low margins with a market that is expecting ever higher standards. Against this backdrop there is great expectation on profit generation and growth. At the same time, we know that the skills shortages have meant a highly competitive employment market where there are greater and greater options for middle management who are far more mercenary than in previous eras.

Increasing innovation in a low margin economy

Critics of the above view will point out that although the industry may be struggling to attract talent, it is no less innovative or creative as can be seen by rising standards, and the way that customer choice has vastly expanded and exploded within the market. Just look at the examples from the casual dining sector where prices per head are no greater than a decade ago – in fact they have fallen – and yet the overall standard offered is of a higher quality. The belief is that this has occurred through a mix of excellent management coupled with good leadership as shown by the examples of James Horler, Ian Neill, and Tony Hughes, who have all 'broken the mould' in different ways during the last ten years.

'Excellence is not an accomplishment. It is a spirit, a never-ending process.'

Lawrence Miller

The flaw in the above views?

Do we believe that this is all new?

One of the great truths about all leaders is that they 'play what is in front of them'. These issues and constraints are not new. There may be differences but these will be subtle rather than great. Throughout history, life has not been perfect and leaders still emerge. Churchill had little time when he became PM to ensure the country was energised to defend against invasion.

One cannot imagine that historical leaders such as Napoleon, Genghis Khan, Alexander the Great asking for time to build a team. They simply played what stood in front of them.

Hitler is one of the most controversial leaders in history. Understandably he is condemned for his crimes but he came to power as he offered Germany a vision of how to find wellbeing again after the difficulties they faced in the 1930s. If anything, the example of Hitler shows how people will follow any vision that appears to offer social prosperity and wellbeing to them.

Leaders will emerge in any time, however small or large the struggle.

Many of the above schools of thought emerged during the boom years when leadership was less important. Leadership comes to the fore during the difficult days. It is in these periods when people look for someone to provide them with a solution; a way forward that will deliver the feel good factor.

Visualisation

One of the key traits possessed by leaders but that is often misunderstood is the word 'vision'.

So many leaders have a mental picture that other people just cannot see.

Vision is really about a clear view of an objective and clarity of thought. Many times we have heard an entrepreneur make a statement 'other people might think it was a huge risk, but I thought there was an opportunity'. Peter Lederer (Chairman, Gleneagles) will often be heard asking: 'What does success look like?'. He is asking whether the end destination can be clearly visualised. Marc Verstringhe (founder of Catering and Allied Services International) would often describe his role to stand at the top of a mountain and have a clear role across the valley below so that he could guide his team. Others in the team would stand at various points lower down on the mountain and their views would naturally be more impaired. A nice description but the reality is that there are many even at CEO level, who do not have a clear view. It is far harder than many realise to gain and some are in need of either glasses or telescopes. It is those with clear vision that do stand apart.

It has recently become a cliché that successful people in all fields – whether business or sport – 'play what is in front of them'. They are able to adapt to changing markets and conditions. They are able to handle setbacks and find a way forward. Why? Because they possess a clear vision of the destination that they are trying to reach and do not take their eye off this goal. Great sportsmen will often talk about mentally visualising winning, prior to playing a game. They are often trained to visualise every possibility of what could go wrong during the course of a game or race and are able to adapt to the setback and still win. It creates a positive mentality that allows them to handle situations because they are psychologically prepared. It is rare to find businessmen who do this to the same extent and most would laugh at the thought but whether they realise it or not, they do it naturally and instinctively and travel a similar road. Leaders and entrepreneurs do see a picture that the normal person just cannot see.

Of course, it is not just about visualisation and positive mental attitude. This is too simple. It takes some very special traits. Often very talented individuals never fulfil their potential for the reason that they do possess the most important inner traits – courage, conviction, or work ethic. Many can talk a good line and be strategic but few can deliver in reality.

Leadership in 2011

On saying all this, what makes 2011 so fascinating – maybe one of the most fascinating periods – is that either existing leaders are going to need to adapt and change or new leaders will emerge; or most likely, both.

The world is changing at such speed. One week's worth of *New York Times* carries more information than a person would have had in a lifetime 100 years ago. Knowledge and information is immediately available and means that everyone is receiving increased amounts of information. The result is that much that is communicated does not reach its target audience as they are receiving too much each day. It means that we all need to learn new ways to communicate.

Is it a coincidence that in January 2011, the Roffey Park Institute launched a report that stated 'Company directors [are] cocooned in a boardroom bubble – out of touch with reality and alienating employees'?

Certainly a melodramatic comment but arguably off target. Why?

The report is the result of a comprehensive survey of over 1500 managers. The controversial aspect of it is that it points towards a growing gulf between the perception and understanding of performance by board directors and middle management. The report notes that whilst 83% of board directors feel redundancies within their organisations have been handled well or very well; just 44% of managers on grades below them hold the same view.

The report found that board directors were considerably more positive than middle management. They:

- were more secure in their jobs (60% compared to 41% of management)
- were more confident of finding work elsewhere (45% compared to 32%)
- were more certain of progressing their careers (63% to 41%)
- were more optimistic about the future (67% to 48%)
- were more positive about their organisation's leadership (89% compared to 70%)

- had a stronger collective sense of purpose (74% to 47%)
- had good or very good wellbeing (77% to 55%)
- were less stressed (31% to 46%)
- were happier with work–life balance (56% to 46%).

The gap in perception is quite noticeable. It can be argued that this is natural in recession years when it can be hard going and maybe only the board possess a full view of how a company is placed. However, Jo Hennessy – Director of Research at Roffey Park – noted:

> 'The *Management Agenda 2011* findings suggest that many senior executives are living in their own world, which has a distinctly rosy hue, for their positive view is out of sync with the concerns and challenges of managers reported by managers beneath them.'

(http://www.roffeypark.com/press/Pages/ManagementAgenda2011.aspx)

There is no doubt that many directors would disagree with this comment and point to the fact this has not only been one of the severest recessions in which to guide their boats through but that it is becoming ever more difficult and complex to communicate effectively throughout businesses.

However, the report does note that an increasing number of management believe that their leadership teams are effective. The fact that 70% of managers are positive about their company's leadership is a good result.

One of the key issues that the report tries to address is that wellbeing at work does relate directly to a manager's general happiness. Jo Hennessy notes:

> 'The message to business is that wellbeing or happiness at work really does matter: it's not just ethical, it has bottom line impact and makes good business sense. The *Management Agenda 2011* findings echo previous research by Roffey Park showing it is those organisations that are steadfastly driven by their purpose, not their shareholders, which are the most financially successful.'

She notes:

> 'Indeed, the financial crisis has shown how conventional, finance-orientated measures of business can mask extreme failings and, as the

board level findings of our research show, insulate senior executives from the real concerns facing employees in their business.'

Again, many directors will be cynical about this viewpoint and maybe it is questionable to discuss the concept of happiness at a time when many businesses are simply seeking to survive. However, it does point towards a new challenge that is facing all companies as there is a need to learn about the social change that is happening in every organisation of all sizes.

This Management Agenda report proves evidence of the gap between leadership and management that most organisations are aware of. It also indicates that the leadership teams are learning but there is clearly still much to be done yet.

It will be fascinating to see how the report changes in 2012 and 2013 as new leadership talent emerges and boards continue to adapt.

What is leadership?

Most people define leadership as the ability to set the direction of a business, organisation or entity. However, is there more to it than just that?

There is an old Chinese proverb which states: 'He who thinks he leads and has no one following him is only taking a walk'. The point is that many believe that leadership lies in the position of leader itself but the key is how the leader attracts 'followers' to support them. Those that possess a loyal team committed to fulfilling a vision display real leadership.

However, very few possess the skill set for being a leader and yet many do believe that they possess the skills for the role. This is understandable as it is not a skill set that can be taught or developed. Many have tried to become leaders but have failed as it is not a natural trait and they have tried to be something that is not within them. So what is leadership? Do we understand it? There are so many different aspects to leadership that it is hard to capture.

At this point I always recall the story of a senior civil servant who served both Churchill and Attlee between 1940 and 1950. He is reputed to have stated that one of them was completely organised, knew exactly what he was doing and why he was doing it. He knew every detail and had a grasp of every fact. The other, he stated, was often instinctive, often disorganised and hugely frustrating to work with as he was often changing his mind. Which was which? Many would assume that the former was Churchill when actually it was Attlee, and yet Churchill did inspire a nation. Isn't it strange, as we now know that those that harboured the most doubts over Churchill's leadership were those who perhaps worked closest to him and yet the people at large developed a great affection for their lead er?

There is a similar story rcounted about Margaret Thatcher from a civil servant who served both Thatcher and Shirley Williams, who in the 1970s was seen as the more likely to become the first female Prime Minister. The story is that the civil servant would take an idea to Shirley Williams who would answer very positively and yet do nothing with the idea, which was highly frustrating. With Thatcher, she would more often than not say an immediate 'no' to an idea but then, once she had considered the proposal, she would act on it if she felt it had merit, which was highly motivational for the civil servant. Is this a true story? Maybe, maybe not but it makes the point that actions rather than words are inspirational to others.

Abraham Lincoln is often regarded as a leader's leader. He was President of the United States during one of its most difficult times and yet he was successful in ensuring that the nation remained united. He led by spending time with his subordinates and listening to them. By his own admission, he stated that 75% of his time as President was spent interacting with people and the majority of that time was spent listening. He felt that leaders often majored in speaking and minored in listening whereas he believed that it was better to reverse that trend.

Is the art of leadership becoming less important?

Leadership is core to our society. There are numerous leadership schools being developed at any one time, although it is questionable as to whether real leadership can be taught.

Leadership will always be important to every business and society as it is core. But the question remains – what makes a leader?

Leadership in the modern era

As has already been noted, many believe that leadership will change with the advance of the new age of social media. This is natural and nothing new. It is an old standing debate as to whether one of America's greatest Presidents –Franklin D. Roosevelt – would have been elected in the television age as he was in a wheelchair? Or whether JFK would have become the icon he did if he had looked like Richard Nixon?

Whether it is correct or not, leadership has to change and adapt with the communications tools of today. The actual fundamentals may not be different but change is still inevitable.

The conversation between leaders and their audiences is changing and there are questions as to how it will impact. The reality is that old problems will be tackled in new ways with new tools. One of the questions that this will raise is whether we are witnessing a period of social change that will reflect the scale of the 1960s. Leadership will not change dramatically but it will adapt.

One of the factors in today's society is that there appears to be a loss of confidence and trust in traditional institutions. There is a clear decline of trust in politicians. It can be argued that this has been a gradual erosion over many years but there is also a decline in confidence in banks and other key bodies to a level that is unprecedented. In such periods, often new ideas and innovations come to the fore in all areas – ranging from the environment to human rights to financial institutions to education, and health. The leaders of today that really set a mark will be those that enable change. As the world becomes smaller with inventions such as Facebook, then people become more global and focus more on broader issues. The world today is becoming increasingly international and this will set challenging objectives for the future.

It would be interesting to ask today's leaders – especially political leaders – as to whether they believe they are in control of events. Leaders are seen to be in charge and in control and yet today, most leaders appear to be reacting to events. At the time of writing, the best example is how the current UK Prime Minister David Cameron is reacting to both Libya and the state of the economy. When Libya was first bombed, few understood the reasons as to why the UK, France and the USA had taken such action. Most people were just bemused by the unfolding of events. It just does not come across as being clear and considered. Events and communication are moving faster than organisations are able.

This is not a political point … the issue is less about Cameron but more about how large organisations work and the question is how can a leader in today's world influence and enable effective change and success.

Events are moving at great speed. Few suspected Libya would be a trouble zone even a few weeks prior to the commencement of the unrest. World events in at the time of writing this book in early 2011 are offering real challenges, whether economically or via social disturbance or natural disasters. Running a government is very difficult as it is such a complex system which is multidimensional where decisions taken at different levels can all have a direct affect on how Cameron is viewed. If events move at pace and the system is complex then it will appear that the leader is unclear and lacking clear vision or objectives. Once events lead the politicians, then it is very hard to regain the initiative. And, of course, in the modern era this is all heightened with the immediacy of international communication.

The leaders we all admire will generally dance to their own tunes. In good times this is easy. In challenging days such as 2011, this is far harder. It is important to bring people – in teams, organisation and nations – together in a united fashion and the successful leaders of today and tomorrow will learn how to use the new tools that are emerging to their benefit. They will set new agendas that capture the imagination and support.

New tools will mean new rules and it is not going to be an easy process and there will be many that will struggle and fail to work within the new rules that emerge.

Why is this important?

One of the key traits in leadership is vision and understanding the moment. The great leaders that emerge will have a real understanding of exactly what is taking place and how to use these tools. Cameron will be judged to a great extent on how he and his government adapt. Tony Blair was viewed as the master of spin but at his peak the Blair–Alasdair Campbell axis did not just understand the moment, they were able to use it to their benefit and enable change. History may not be kind towards Blair but between 1997 and 2001, he broke new boundaries and did enable change. Blair was a leader as he broke mental barriers – the first Prime Minister to use his first name so strongly – and he challenged old rules and brought in new ones.

Who will that be today and tomorrow?

The answer lies in what we can learn from those that are proven leaders; not so much in their stories – these can be misinterpreted – but in their own thoughts and the lessons they have drawn.

Leaders profiles and interviews

The following section is a mix of profiles written for this book and a series of articles that have been previously published in *EP Business in Hospitality* magazine. These are the thoughts and case studies of proven leaders in the industry and the questions that we need to consider is what lessons can be learnt and what is real leadership?

Hotels – UK

Peter Lederer CBE

Chairman of Gleneagles

Peter Lederer has been a driving force at Gleneagles over the last two decades. It is hard to imagine the hotel without Peter's input, even from afar. Gleneagles has always been one of the great hotels but under Peter's stewardship it has become far more – one of the premier resort hotels in the world with a turnover in excess of £40 million.

He joined Gleneagles in 1984 as General Manager and was appointed Managing Director in 1987. He became Chairman in November 2007. Previously, Peter had held operational and senior management positions in Canada; for ten years with the Four Seasons hotel group in Toronto, Ottawa and Montreal, and with Plaza Hotels in Toronto.

Peter's contribution to Gleneagles is well documented and proven by the hotel's standing but this achievement has been matched by his contribution to the industry as a whole. He is President of the Institute of Hospitality (formerly the HCIMA), a Patron of the Hospitality Industry Trust Scotland, a Trustee of the Springboard Educational Trust and Chairman of the One & All Foundation. He was awarded an Honorary Doctorate of Business Administration by Queen Margaret University, Edinburgh and is a Doctor of the University of Stirling. In addition, Peter is a Master Innholder and Freeman of the City of London, as well as a Liveryman of the Worshipful Company of Innholders.

Peter was Chairman of VisitScotland from 2001 to 2010 and is a board member of the Leading Hotels of the World and Hamilton & Inches. In 1993 he won the Tourism 'Catey' award and in 1997 was honoured as Hotelier of the Year. In the 1994 Birthday Honours List, he was appointed an OBE for his services to the industry. This was followed by a CBE in 2005.

This all tells part of the story but does not touch the character.

Peter is one of those rare people who will often leave one thinking about a point well after an encounter. It is rarely a singular comment but something that strikes a chord. He will often listen and say little but when he does speak, often cuts straight to the core of a problem.

Peter is always asking the question: How can we improve? He will often be heard asking 'What does success look like?', meaning that it is vital to be able to visualise what success looks like before embarking on a project or venture. This is an important feature in Peter's outlook for he will visualise the destination that he is working towards. He will take setbacks in his stride for he does take his eye off the goal, but simply adjusts the route.

To many, Peter does stand apart. To explain why, a good place to start is with three short stories.

The first real time I ever really had a conversation with Peter was at a black tie dinner in a grand dining room at Cliveden. We had been placed next to each other. It did not take Peter long to test me. By the time the starter had been served, he casually let me know that he thought my business would be 'out of date' within five years. He did not say this to be rude or discouraging but more out of curiosity, slight mischief and I assume out of interest to see how I would react. To place the story into context, the comment was said at a time when the Internet was taking off and was becoming a challenge to conventional methods. The heart of his approach goes back to whether I understood where my destination lay. The answer, of course, was 'no' as no-one understood where the Internet would lead us but that was the thought process that Pater was challenging. It was a fair question and has stayed with me ever since – not because I took offence – but because the challenge provoked me, was sadly spot on and made me smile. I felt like a young apprentice and in truth, I would normally have tried to stand my ground but Peter's way is never confrontational or threatening; he gently teases. As I have come to know Peter over the years, I have seen him many times almost guide someone's thoughts through to a conclusion. He mentors rather than directs. He lets you come to your own conclusion and agree the way forward. It is no surprise, therefore, that so much great talent has emerged from Gleneagles under his tenure. The two do go hand in hand.

The second is the time I took Peter to lunch to ask him to become directly involved in The One and All Foundation (a charitable foundation focused on diversity in the hospitality industry). I was hesitant as I knew that many organisations wanted Peter's involvement and One and All covered a subject which was, at best, controversial. Diversity is not everyone's 'cup of tea' and could alienate some. I remember being almost shocked as he not only agreed but said 'Of course, it is a leader's role and duty to ensure that we leave things better than when we took over.'

I was shocked because so few talk in that way anymore; although we would like more people to do so.

Peter has strong values and ideals but is at heart a pragmatist – one can see this from Gleneagles achievements over the years. Their performance and growth has been a role model for many other businesses. He has delivered where it counts and to Gleneagles owners – Diageo – but also built a culture which lives empowerment and a belief in the importance of people. One will often find Peter discussing the importance of development programmes and investment in training.

The final story is about the high regard that Peter is held in Scotland, even though he was born in London in 1950 and then lived in Canada. I remember sitting in a meeting with a stereotypical, passionate Scot who when we began to discuss Peter turned and called him 'The Boss'….. probably as high a compliment that any Scot can bestow on someone from outside. I was half surprised and half not. This accolade is probably bestowed for four reasons:

- His commitment to Scotland is total. When he did not feel that Scotland was getting a fair commitment from one industry charity, he simply set up a charity, HIT Scotland, that has unified the Scottish industry and really contributed. The Scots are passionate and committed to those that support Scotland.
- His achievements speak for themselves.
- Peter would never promote himself.

- Peter believes in giving back as much as he has been given by the industry. He believes that it is his duty to do as much to support the greater good as is possible whilst he is in positions of influence.

Peter is a rare man but what helped create him?

Peter is dyslexic and clearly found his school years a struggle. There are two leading dyslexics in the sector – Peter and William Baxter and both share three common traits:

- Their verbal communication is very good.
- They possess an empathy and understanding of others' weaknesses. It would be a very rare occurrence to hear either be critical of someone else.
- They are proactive and positive thinkers.

Peter's dyslexia was an important contributing factor to the makeup of the man. He is a quietly determined figure who found his own way and his own style to achieve success.

But it is Peter's values and idealism that make him stand apart. He is trusted by his peers and competitors because his achievements stand the test and because he is happy to help others. He always makes time for others and I have often stood in awe at just how much he does take on. In fact, I have often felt slightly guilty as he has always made time to offer advice or a helping hand even though I have offered nothing in return. This is the mark of the man – he stands for more than just the average or acceptable.

So what can be learnt from Peter's story?

- Gleneagles has gained from a long period of stable leadership and consistency.
- Peter has a strong sense of values and a belief in people that has been a cornerstone to his career.
- He will stand for what he believes is right and take risks.
- He challenges the norm.
- Peter does understand others' weaknesses and is compassionate.

Hotels – UK

Charles Prew

Chief Executive, Von Essen Hotels

(Former Chief Executive, Barcelo Hotels)

Charles is an experienced hotelier who readily admits his leadership style has changed over years to reflect developments in the operating environment, notably in the style of interaction with his team. By his own admission Charles has gone from being a 'tough old nut' to more of a coach and mentor. This may have been a tough call for some, but Charles is an immediately likeable character who embodies the traits of leadership which are to listen and empathise with others, acutely sensitive to the complexity with which hotel managers of the present day have to operate in comparison to the past. Charles was appointed as the Chief Executive of Von Essen Hotels in March 2011; this interview was conducted whilst he was in the same role at Barcelo Hotels.

We are paid to outperform our competition

It has often been said that there are two economies at play in the UK – London and the provinces. The latter is seen to be a far more difficult market in which to operate. Charles Prew, Chief Executive of Barceló Hotels, discusses the challenge of operating in this market and how this recession compares to others

As the discussions over how each segment of the industry has and will perform during the recession have raged on, many have predicted that the great old country house provincial hotels will struggle to maintain their status and even, in some cases, survive. If true, Barceló Hotels would certainly be directly in the firing line as they boast many great operations within their portfolio – hotels such as the Lygon Arms, Billesley Manor, Combe Grove, the Imperial Hotel in Torquay and Buxton Palace, among others. How are such hotels holding up in these choppy waters?

Barceló's Chief Executive, Charles Prew, is one of the UK's most experienced hotel operators, having held senior leadership positions over the past 20 years with Ladbrokes, Hilton, Jarvis and presently with Barceló Hotels. His views and thoughts are, therefore, very relevant in a market that is arguably as vulnerable as any that has existed in many decades. Interestingly, Charles does not appear to be daunted by the prospect of further difficult days ahead but just sees the recession as a challenge which his team has to face.

'The market does vary right around the country. Every hotel is different. Without question, conference business has been weak but conference bookings for the first quarter of 2011 are looking very good.

'We have a simple theory in our organisation – we are not paid to perform according to the market. We are paid to add value and to outperform our competitors. That is our focus and I expect us to work each and every day to outperform our competition.

'We can all complain about the market but the truth is that there are enough people wanting to stay in our hotels and it is up to us to make sure that we capture this audience. It is not just about rate. It is about managing our sales processes as well and effectively as possible. We must understand the needs of our guests – if we fulfil those, rate is secondary.

'If we do not outperform our competition, then we are in the wrong and we need to learn.'

As one would expect of such an experienced operator, he does not appear fazed by the issues of the market and talks with enthusiasm about Barceló, the hotels and the future.

'We have many stand-out hotels and some fabulous people.'

How does, I asked, this recession compare with previous ones?

'It is very different to the last major recession. In the early nineties we came off a higher level and it was a steeper fall. It happened very quickly. This time, the conference business plateaued a couple of years before the crisis hit. The problem is that it is the larger conferences that have been cancelled and, of course, this will impact on any company's performance.

'However, overall we have performed well. We do have some outstanding properties and they have held their own in this market. Last year, we performed really well as Revpar was down by 6.25% and revenue was down by only by 8.9%. I think that considering what was going on in the market this is pretty good going.

'The highlight this year is that our beauty revenue – spa treatments, etc. – are up by 54%. Membership of our leisure clubs has held up well too as we have 14,000 members today as opposed to 15,000 when we entered the downturn.

'It is an exciting time for the hotel business as a whole. It is becoming increasingly aware of the market fluctuations and sophisticated in its approach. Revenue management has changed so much and every hotel and company is constantly aware of the market and changing rates. It is all about revenue generation. If I could add £1 to the average room rate across the board this would equate to an extra £1 million to the bottom line. It is a fine line and a very competitive market.

'The managers today are the real unsung heroes. Their jobs are tough; far tougher than in the old days. It is about HR management, cost control, occupancy, rate, service levels and cleanliness – they are responsible for so much.'

I noted that this approach appeared to be one of the patriarchal.

'It is all about our people. We employ 2400 and they are all important in contributing to our performance. In my experience, people who are mistreated do not perform as well and don't give their best. We want better for our people. After all, we are all the same. We work for our families. I want to be approachable and make sure that I am supporting my directors to be the best that they can be.'

Has he changed over the years?

'Yes, I have. When I ran Ladbrokes, I was a tough old nut. Those days were different and we had to be seen to be tough. Maybe it was just impatience.

'That style doesn't work anymore. I don't tell any of my senior people what to do. I coach and mentor. It has all changed.'

Charles had grown up in the hotel industry starting at the age of 13 as a kitchen porter, and the passion for the industry is still evident. He talks very fondly about the hotels in the group and how he still plays an active role. He recounted how when one particular guest stays at the Lygon Arms, he will often come and cook crêpes Suzette in the restaurant.

'It is a great business. We are working twice as hard in this market just to get some half reasonable results. I have never worked so hard and with the ever increasing changes in technology we seem to get less time to think. It is my job to think for the key players in our company and help support them. My job is to think and plan.'

After such a long fulfilling career, what is his objective now?

'We have 20 hotels around the UK. I would like hotels in London too. I want to double our hotels and go to the key cities. I want the number of customers that come back to our properties to increase as this means that we are getting the job done in the right way. It is about customer experience and this is the ultimate benchmark.

'I want the team to grow and develop. I want us – as a team – to have fun. If we have smiles on our faces, then the customer will feel it; it will impact on them and on our business. As I said earlier, this is a great industry as every day is different and we have some stunning properties and people.'

Charles is an interesting character as in some ways he is very old school and yet in others very modern and in touch. Maybe the mix of his passion for the hotels in his portfolio and his experience of three or four recessions is exactly the right blend for this time. True or not, his positive approach is certainly refreshing in a time when many feel daunted.

(January 2011)

Hotels – UK

Kiaran McDonald

General Manager, The Savoy

This book would not be complete without the story of The Savoy's redevelopment under the leadership of Kiaran McDonald. Few people can truly understand what project of this scale involves. The Savoy represents so many memories to people all over the world so to say that the new hotel would be open to scrutiny and criticism is an understatement as to the risks and consequences involved. Yet, Kiaran's enthusiasm, eye for detail and sense of perspective shape this unique project and is a case study in leadership. He plays what is in front of him and is not fazed by challenge.

Preparing the ground

The Savoy stands apart. Nearly everyone possesses a particular memory of the hotel that holds a very special place in their hearts. Maybe it was a ball, a dinner dance or simply afternoon tea or champagne in the American bar.

When the hotel re-opens in early 2010, the re-opening team will carry a weight of expectation that it needs to meet – a weight that very few can truly appreciate. It is not too dramatic to say that reputations and careers will either be made or broken by the reaction to the reopening.

Kiaran MacDonald, The Savoy's General Manager, discusses the challenges and pressures involved, as well the plans for The Savoy.

'When guests walk into The Savoy, they will see a lot of change but the overall feel that they encounter must be the same,' commented Kiaran as we met at Simpson's-in-the-Strand, their temporary location. 'It is important that once they are in the hotel they know that they are back in The Savoy. It will not just be the physicality that determines this, but the overall style and service.'

I comment that people generally find change difficult to accept and adjust to. With a hotel such as The Savoy, the challenge in being able to keep clients and guests comfortable and onside with change is heightened. Kiaran nodded but noted:

'The hotel was in need of change and our guests voiced this to us. There was work that needed to be done and our responsibility has been to undertake the refurbishment in the most considered and sensitive fashion. There is over £100 million being invested. This is a significant project. It is a restoration and we have tried to stay true to that principle.'

In the global credit crunch, all investments are under scrutiny. With the delay in the re-opening, how are the owners reacting?

'They are being absolutely excellent. They understand that we all need to stay the course and that we need to get it right. There is pressure on them, just as there is pressure on us, but we are all committed to the project.

'With a project such as this one, of course, the pressure is that much stronger. That is just part of what it is to be involved with such a great hotel. As you said, people do not like change. With the high expectations as well, it will naturally lead some to be critical and I suspect that it will be a challenging time as people adjust to the new Savoy. But we are passionate about our work and believe that we are covering every angle and taking every care, so I expect the overall reaction to be extremely positive.'

Fairmont Hotels & Resorts are one of the world's leading hotel operators but perhaps have not had fair credit as yet for their involvement. In some ways, Fairmont's own reputation in the UK market seems to be interwoven with The Savoy's re-opening.

'Fairmont has been superb in their support. The London market can be very mistrusting, and would be of any large company that took on The Savoy. We have done a lot of work in this area and they have understood that this is an important part of the project. The hotel is almost an exception to the normal rules. We have looked at and studied the best way forward and I think that this will in time be appreciated and that Fairmont will both win over the doubters and also gain some real kudos after the re-opening and re-positioning of the hotel.'

A couple of years ago, EP interviewed the UK Managing Director of DNC at the new Wembley Stadium – another British icon that had changed. He stated at the time that there was quite a bit of pressure resting on his shoulders on the day of opening, commenting, 'In some dark moments, it would be unnatural to say that I didn't know that my career was on the line. Of course it was, but isn't that the type of situation that we all want as it is in those moments when we prove ourselves?'

Can you identify with this and was it any different for you, Kiaran?

'Sure. It is certainly a very humbling experience and I expect that I will approach the re-opening with a mix of excitement and trepidation.

'It would be fair to ask if I was the best candidate for this job. I had never done an opening. I hadn't been a General Manager in London. Yes, there were others who could have been considered. But I did know Fairmont and was comfortable with the challenge at The Savoy. Others will judge it, but I have surrounded myself with strength – people who in their own discipline are better than me. We have a team that is totally committed, passionate and motivated, and I believe in their ability. One of our key responsibilities is to build a team that can represent The Savoy.'

What has been the hardest part of the project so far?

'Getting our arms around the project. It is not as simple as it may seem. There is so much history and heritage to be taken into consideration. We needed to really understand the building and the emotion involved. I spoke to a whole variety of people in London that really knew and loved The Savoy so that I could completely understand the essence of what it meant.

'I needed to find the DNA for the future. It took time. I was captivated by it all and understood that it wasn't just the physicality but the overall feel and environment. I needed to take that emotion and combine it with a very pragmatic approach.

'Restoration is not easy in terms of what it means. People forget that the hotel has changed a lot already in its history. In the 1930s, an

Art Deco style was introduced. At the time, the hotel was established as one of the world's great hotels and there must have been people who were concerned at the new introductions but it soon settled down. Restoration, with the history in mind, has to be our guide and Pierre-Yves Rochon has completely understood this in his design approach.

'We believe that we have found the right balance and that guests will react well to the changes.'

The service culture is clearly going to be a key factor for the hotel. How is this being approached?

'Absolutely true – it is so very important. We are building the service culture around two words – charm and spontaneity. Charm because it will be reflective of the Edwardian era and spontaneity because it reflects the Art Deco period plus the theatrical roots. The key elements will be etiquette, discretion and style. Words are easy and it will be the personality of the team that will determine our success.

'We have reintroduced The Savoy training academy because, as we re-launch, we want to re-communicate our commitment to the learning and development of people to deliver the highest standards.'

Will the team be ready for the opening?

'There are no excuses. We have time to prepare and we know what we need to do. The team has been excellent in working as one to take a hotel that will have closed down for over two years by the time of re-opening, and restored it so that it will still be one of the great icons of the industry.'

'It is certainly a very humbling experience and I expect that I will approach the re-opening with a mix of excitement and trepidation.'

(*August 2009*)

The changing face of hotel general management

Hoteliers feature heavily in this book, and the collection of individual stories demonstrates the unique qualities required to succeed in this particular market. Undoubtedly hotel management is both an art and a skill, and successful hoteliers retain a strong relationship with their customers and staff. However, have the pressures of modern hotel management seen the hotel keeping become less of an art and more of an exercise in process? Most hoteliers will talk about the ways in which they like to keep close to their customers, so arguably this has principle changed little. But as reflected here, the emphasis on commerciality and hotel ownership has necessitated a more complex array of skills and knowledge on offer.

Have hotel managers changed?

It is often said that today's hoteliers 'walk the floor' and interact with their customers far less than in the past. However, is this true? David Levin, the Capital Hotel, Harry Murray, Lucknam Park Hotel & Spa, Nick Halliday, aBode Hotels and Andrew Mckenzie, The Vineyard at Stockcross joined a round-table discussion to debate the major issues.

Many believe that today's General Managers are more behind-the-scenes business managers. Is less time spent with the customer today than in the past?

Harry: David and I have been managing hotels for over five decades. The fifties and sixties were a very practical period, the seventies became the accountancy period, the eighties was the decade of sales and marketing, the nineties became the property period and the noughties have been the technological age, where people run their business from an office.

There has to be a balance of all those things, but the more time spent with customers, the fewer problems. The power of observation is crucial.

Andrew: You cannot replicate people and I think the luxury end remains very pro-service. At the mid-market and budget end, buying a hotel room has become like buying a commodity and there is no premium for a 'present' manager – it can be a bit indulgent to be in front of the customer too much.

Nick: Customer focus is interlinked with managing your business. You have to understand them and interact with them to know who you are marketing to. However, I am not sure much has changed – you cannot ignore your customer in order to know how you can market to them and, in doing so, drive the top line. The advent of the budget hotel sector means that they offer a more sanitised and automated product, so customer interaction is not required as much.

David: In the fifties, hotels didn't understand profit and weren't there to make one. British Transport Hotels, which had around 50 hotels in the UK, didn't understand profit – they were there to generate money. This was ridiculous. In contrast, the sublime scenario is that today, everything is motivated by profit. So we are dealing with two completely different sets of circumstances. Managers in the fifties were around customers, but they wore carnations and had the best table in the restaurant! How has the customer changed?

Harry: At the luxury end of the market, the perception of what the customer wants has changed and everything we do is focused on them. They are looking for excitement, quality and value for money. We undertake a lot of research looking for 'wow' factors to make people want to come back. The budget sector has persuaded a lot of people to use hotels and there is a market there – you know the price and what you will get.

David: Guests have much greater expectations because the standard in their homes has risen in the past 40 years. Middle England parents expect their own bathroom and so do their children. Fifty years ago it was an experience to go to a hotel to have your own bathroom and crisp linen sheets.

Andrew: Affordable mid-market hotels have upped the ante of the physical product so service is the differentiator. Today customers are far more promiscuous. Part of the unwritten contract used to be that if they liked you, they would come back. But this is not the case today and regular customers are far fewer; it is as though they are looking to tick off a list of experiences instead.

Nick: As long as you understand your values, stay true to them and deliver consistently, guests are not necessarily looking for more. There is always a desire to have added 'wow', but customers are savvy to understand the values of the brand, so guest recognition and loyalty becomes very important. Comparison websites drive a lot of decisions.

Harry: I believe the media has helped enormously – it is far better to be open with feedback than the old British way of sending a letter. Feedback from guests is vital.

How has the management of people changed?

David: The impact of immigration has been significant, as it is now so challenging to recruit British staff. However, this is not a new issue. When I was working for BTH, the majority of staff were European, as it was perceived that French chefs were the best, and so on.

Nick: I think this might be a London issue, as it is less of a challenge in the regions. In my view, perception of the industry has changed for the better; there are a far greater number of British role models. Many people do want a career and not only senior roles.

Harry: Teamwork and leadership have become more important – in the old days you were called by your surname and did not speak unless you were spoken to. Today we have to cuddle staff, praise them and provide constructive feedback. The more investment, the happier they are – and it pays.

Nick: I have seen managers becoming far more business aware in their own departments and accountable in a larger operation, purely through good practice. They want this for their own development. Equally, communication has improved and there is the sense that it is one message, one team.

Andrew: As an industry, I think we are living a bit of a lie. There are a significant number of people who work very hard, including a lot of unpaid overtime at a very low rate of pay. Yet there are too many others taking profit out of the industry – investors, property, private equity – and in order to service that, we have got to pay lower wages. How has the development of revenue management changed hotel operations?

David: One of the most important points is that room rates have not risen, so we have had to become more efficient. In my view airlines have had an impact on our ethos with its huge emphasis on yield management, and the hotel industry has fallen into a lot of unpleasant practices. Frankly, I resist reducing my rates when we are not so busy then doubling up when we are really busy.

Nick: It is a question of integrity and it depends on your values. Our commitment is to not increase rate when there is increased demand, but we will track supply and demand and reduce rates to fill the hotel.

Andrew: People will buy on price. You have to be careful what you wish for, as we have the access to market through price comparison websites, but it can be hard to stand out and not play the game. As an independent, is it worth holding out for a rate?

Nick: There will be a backlash against independent sites. There are sectors outside hospitality that are now not subscribing to these sites. There will come a point where there is some kind of rebellion; it is commission-heavy whereas you have the flexibility with your own website to up-sell. Asset management has become increasingly important. What are your views on this?

David: We could have sold The Capital and had a management contract, but chose not to. It's very tempting but the problem with management companies is that they operate on a percentage of turnover, regardless of profit or loss. There is a huge clash between giving ROI and justifying investment in the hotel. It's unhealthy and I wonder where it will take us as an industry.

Andrew: In effect you can have two bosses, the manager and the owners. Owners used to be faceless but they have become much more active in making their assets work for them. Traditional owners looked for a reasonable return. In contrast, there are some leveraged deals in existence which, in order for it to work, want an unreasonable IRR for their business. Asset management is one of the big issues for the industry.

Harry: Property companies are taking the heart and soul out of hotels. When they buy and sell hotels, customers and staff are not taken into account. This issue has changed the industry and not for the better.

In conclusion…

Harry: I started my hotel career more than 50 years ago and wish I was 50 years younger today. I'm just as passionate as when I started, and believe that there have never been more opportunities and challenges.

Nick: Hotel-keeping has changed for the better. It is a vibrant industry and I am quite confident as we look to the future. We have become more efficient, but the customer gets a better deal. People are far more career-minded, driven by nature, and wanting to engage with the customer.

Andrew: For all the changes, the hotel industry it is still about looking after people, so not much has changed since Bethlehem really. Hoteliers are businesses but it's a bit like a Premiership football club; one which is about good players and good content.

David: People still say that this is an antisocial industry and it frustrates me. I think this is the greatest industry. It is not one that will spoon-feed you, you have got to want to succeed. While this is not easy to do, it gives great personal satisfaction. I never allow people to tell me 'well, it was alright for you'. There is always something in your way, some obstacle. But with dedication, the career gives so much back.

(July 2010)

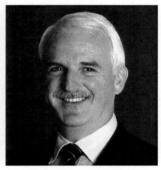

Hotels – International

Gerald Lawless
Executive Chairman, Jumeirah Group

Gerald is a consummate professional and has a high degree of morality and integrity. He is straight-talking, a major attribute of successful leaders. As (he is now) Executive Chairman of Jumeirah Group, he is responsible for what was once a fledgling hotel brand but is now rapidly expanding into an international operation based out of its Dubai headquarters. Thus Jumeirah, along with Emirates Airlines, is today seen as a jewel in Dubai's crown. This article explores Gerald's early vision for Jumeirah, and the values which underpin the brand.

Believing is making it happen

The development of Jumeirah over the past 15 years has caught the imagination of many industry observers. Most people know the story of Jumeirah Group but few know the man that lies behind this success. Gerald

Lawless, Executive Chairman of Jumeirah Group, began his love affair with Dubai in the late 1970s when he undertook his first appointment in Dubai with Forte Hotels. He experienced firsthand the potential that this destination could offer and from then onwards, he continued to remain focused on returning to Dubai. At that time, he was just in the infancy of his management career and it would be over 10 years later that he would finally return once again to the Middle East but the impact of this initial experience of the region had left its impression. Gerald Lawless is a man who is driven by success. He has a deep need to succeed. This drive and passion has been instrumental in both his long career with Forte Hotels and latterly for Jumeirah Group. His career had been destined towards hotels from an early stage.

As a graduate from Shannon College of Hotel Management, he launched his career with Forte Hotels with two key objectives. The first was his drive to work overseas and the second was to become a General Manager by the time he was 30 years old.

'If you can believe it, then it will happen. I wanted to be a General Manager by the time I was 30. By the time I was 29 I was in South Africa in my first General Management appointment. When I was first offered a role in Dubai, I said yes without a moment's hesitation. I accepted first and then asked where Dubai was later!'

An international career

Gerald's career with Forte Hotels spanned 23 years. For over two decades, his career was shaped with Gerald's appointments taking him to Glasgow, Dubai, Durban, London, Bahrain, Dublin and the Caribbean. Yet with his focus still on returning to Dubai, Gerald's penultimate role with Forte was the Regional Manager for their properties in Dubai and the Caribbean.

'I was "based" from Slough and travelled frequently between Dubai and the Caribbean. I found myself stopping off at home to change suitcases and briefly see my family. But I was still driven by my ultimate goal of securing a permanent role in Dubai.'

After 23 years successful years with Forte Hotels, he parted company to join Jumeirah Group as Managing Director. At the time of the move, it was seen as a risk for it meant taking a step back to have the opportunity to develop a whole new hotel business. However, he believed in the opportunity and in the fact that he was well prepared. Gerald was greatly influenced by his career with Forte Hotels and reflects on his time with the company with respect and affection towards Lord Forte and Rocco Forte. For Gerald, Forte Hotels excelled at training and development and their strong support for his international career truly shaped him as a manager and leader. For Gerald, if things had turned out differently, then by now he may be running his own hotel business. But there is still time yet! As he recollects, Colonel Sanders launched Kentucky Fried Chicken at the tender age of 65. However, in some respects he feels that he has achieved the same degree of satisfaction by having the privilege to work so closely with Sheikh Mohammed Al Maktoum, the ruler of Dubai. The autonomy to take key decisions and to be the driving force in the development of Jumeirah 'Group's plethora of hospitality businesses has been the key for him.

Training a culture

In reflecting on his experiences with Forte Hotels, he feels strongly about their approach in training and developing a culture across a diverse geographical portfolio. With their varied portfolio of hotels and global expansion, they were successful in formulating a strong corporate culture. For many past managers of the Forte era, this strong belief in establishing and maintaining a company culture still emanates today. This has been synonymous with Gerald's approach to establishing the culture in Jumeirah Group which has been trained and developed in tandem with the company's dynamic growth. With the rapid expansion of Jumeirah Group in less than eight14 years, he has been determined that, like Forte Hotels, the culture is driven from the top and disseminated at all levels throughout the international estate and replicated throughout all businesses. He professes that Jumeirah Group prides itself on their approach whereby all staff must know who the senior management are, as it is from the senior management that the culture will emanate. Part of the development of the Group has been to develop its key Hallmarks which everyone in the organisation works by.

1. Every time you see a guest, smile and greet the guest before they greet you.

2. Your first response to a guest's request should never be 'no'.

3. Treat all colleagues with respect, as you would want to be treated.

Other initiatives that may often be taken for granted have proved successful for Gerald. Alongside the Executive Team, he will meet all new staff at their induction and insists that every new joiner, no matter how senior they are, must attend this induction. They must exude the company culture right from the start.

Today's emerging talent

Gerald is not only inspired by the past, but also by the future. He is stimulated by an emerging talent that offers the potential to take the hospitality industry to another level.

When Jumeirah Group launched the Emirates Academy of Hospitality Management in 2001, Gerald was keen for students to be given the tools to reach their full potential. For him this is not an academy that will solely feed the need for graduates to join Jumeirah Group, but develop to give the students an avenue to launch their career with both hospitality and non-hospitality businesses alike. He feels that we are now experiencing a generation of graduates and younger managers that exude a fear of not trying, which is evident in American society.

Passionate about this younger generation, he feels that many companies in the hospitality industry do not reap the rewards of developing this group. As a generation of students that have paid for, and value, their education, he feels that they should not be put through the mill again when they graduate, but should command the roles that they are qualified to do. The need to succeed truly is driven by success itself. Tantamount to these successes are those who continue to influence Gerald, whether from the past or the new talent of the future. If you can believe it, then it will happen.

(June 2005)

Hotels – International

Richard Hartman

Chief Executive, Millennium and Copthorne Hotels

Richard Hartman is a veteran of the hotel industry whose knowledge and experience is second to none. His strategic vision and knowledge of the commerciality of hotel management is insightful, and what makes Richard stand out is his vision for the way in which the hotel business model has to change. His style is to inspire through respect and foresight, and he is intellectually a force to be reckoned with.

The story has to change

Richard Hartman was appointed as chief executive of Millennium and Copthorne Hotels with the remit of bringing stability and strategic direction to the business. Is he achieving his objective, and what has been his experience to date?

'If you are completely brand-focused then the story is one of growth, that's all it can be: new brands and new destinations. However, out of the top five hotel companies, four have almost 4000 hotels. The story has got to change sooner or later; it is not possible to keep adding and adding.'

Millennium and Copthorne Hotels (M&C) operates 102 hotels in five major markets: Asia, New Zealand the USA, Europe and the Middle East, with 16 hotels in the pipeline. The company's chairman is Singapore billionaire Kwek Leng Beng, who has a controlling stake of 53% in the business. Prior to Richard's arrival in April last year, the most recent CEO had had a tenure of six months, and some were surprised by Richard's appointment, assuming that he had retired after leaving Intercontinental Hotels Group (IHG) in 2007. With more than 40 years' experience, he is regarded as an industry veteran and M&C has perhaps been fortunate to have Richard's foresight at the helm just at the moment the worst economic crisis in living memory began.

'The questions I am most often asked are: have you ever seen this before? And how long will it last? The answer is: no, and I don't know. When you are confronted by a crisis it is very difficult to understand whether it is structural or cyclical, and it is very possible to make the wrong decision. If it is cyclical then it will work through, if it is structural then a whole new world will emerge, and there will be change.'

Richard has a wealth of knowledge and as we talk in more depth, it is clear that he is someone who takes nothing for granted and does not shy away from difficult situations. He questions and challenges assumptions regularly throughout our interview. It is evident that his motivation to join M&C was partly a desire to get back into the kind of hotel business that he prefers, namely one that owns property. Unlike the 'big five' hotel companies – Accor, Marriott, Starwood, IHG and Hilton – M&C is positioned as a destination-led business, not a fee-based business that is part of a franchise or management contract. In Richard's view a hotel business, at its heart, should be an integrated one – some owned, some managed and some leased.

'M&C will never compete by ubiquity. Our success will not be measured by the size of our pipeline. The difference is that we own 80 of our hotels, rather than just booking a management fee or franchise fee, so we book the whole profit and loss of those properties we own. The big five are distribution driven and it is possible to put hotels in marginal locations. M&C has to be in the right place, in the right town and the right city.

'I am not against disposing of properties or strategic acquisitions; we came fairly close to selling Korea last year and in 2004 we sold the Plaza Hotel, which at that time was probably the biggest transaction in New York. We will buy and sell opportunistically when the price is right, and would like to overlay our portfolio with some key locations such as Tokyo, San Francisco or Sydney, but we will not sacrifice yield.'

I ask Richard what he sees as M&C's competitive differentials.

'There are very few differentials in this business when you think about it. Anything that is different becomes a qualifier in a matter of months if it is successful. There are some differentiated brands – W, for example, has a small distribution but punches way above its weight in terms of its reputation. Four Seasons is another, as are Malmaison and Hotel du Vin here in the UK. These chains are limited by their differentiation; you cannot put a Hotel du Vin just anywhere.'

Noting that he has retired several times, and would possibly do so again in the future, Richard explains that he had also known Kwek for more than 20 years, having lived and worked in Singapore prior to taking up the M&C role. More importantly he states that he felt comfortable he knew what he was getting into. With the business having recently announced a 50% drop in first-quarter profit, M&C has suffered during what it has called a 'predictably challenging' trading environment, and Richard is under no illusions.

'We are paying particular attention to market share and pay very close attention to recovery rates. If we are going to drop a pound of revenue, we are looking at how much can be saved at the profit line. The reality is that it is about learning to do business at a lower price. There is still business out there, but the pricing has been recalibrated.

'There is less company spending and more discretionary spending, which is one of the reasons that pricing has changed. That is true of almost every market. Take a simple statistic like double occupancy; traditionally that is 1.3 guests per occupied room, and recently it has gone up to 1.6 in our business. This indicates that there is a different kind of person travelling.

'A lot of fixed costs have been built into a hotel because business has been good for so long. What would have been variable costs, such as labour, have slowly become fixed costs because business got predictable and fixed costs on an hourly basis are cheaper than variable costs. So, if a hotel is always 90% occupied the argument is that you are better off with fixed costs – and the whole world got like that.'

Leveraging the most potential from M&C's existing properties is central to Richard's strategy for the business, partly driven by looking at existing fixed costs but also, as he put it, just looking at what we do in business. He confirms that in New York and London, two of M&C's key markets, he has taken the decision to remove the hotel restaurant from day-to-day operations, and use it for functions.

'In these cities the hotel restaurant is most often full when it is raining or snowing. Unless it is a real destination restaurant, and the hotel is willing to put quite a considerable effort in for relatively little return, you are better off not trying to compete. I have had no complaints since we started doing this last year.'

For the moment Richard is focused on leading his business through the current market challenges. Having retired for the first time at 52 and found that he was not satisfied with just doing sudoku, it's clear that he sees himself working in the industry in one form or another for some time to come and is philosophical about what the future holds.

'It is possible to get stuck in a modus operandi and think it's the right thing to do, just because it has been done that way for 20 years. But things change.'

(June 2009) Hotels – UK

Hotels – International

Brian Williams

Managing Director, Swire Hotels

Originally from the UK, Brian has developed an international hotel career working at Mandarin Oriental amongst others prior to joining the predominantly Asian-based Swire Group, to set up Swire Hotels. With a love for his craft, Brian's has created two high-end, innovative hotel concepts in the Chinese market which he hopes will be a testament to the business and the rapidly expanding luxury market in this region. What comes through in Brian's leadership style is that, despite his depth of experience, he is able to step back and listen to his team in order to create the right culture which will make the hotel concepts work. As a result it is clear that he is greatly inspired by working with Chinese people and its culture.

Adding value to the mix

Listed on the Hong Kong Stock Exchange, Swire is an international company which employs 125,000 people. A major investor in mixed-used properties in Hong Kong and China, it is also the major shareholder in Cathay Pacific. Will its experience and diversified business model support the evolution of Swire Hotels in a challenging climate?

A 2005 survey of hotel executives found that 73% of respondents believed that mixed-use developments would be the predominant model for growth in the sector. Luxury hotels add a wow factor to such projects, although budget brands such as Travelodge have signalled their interest in opportunities for retail partnerships and new opportunities, particularly as an increasing supply of commercial property becomes available. In an economic climate which has been defined this year by the depth of recession and ensuing knock-on to the property market, it appears that the relatively recent decision by Swire to progress with the formation of its own hotel group is one of calculated risk. Will it succeed?

Its highly varied portfolio of business interests, which includes aviation and marine services, provides one clue. Despite being founded in 19th-century Liverpool, England, the business has established a long history of trade with China dating back to 1861. In 2006 its ownership of Cathay Pacific gained further strength when it became the parent company for Dragonair and established a cross-shareholding agreement with Air China. So whilst Swire is a comparative unknown quantity in the hotel playing field, their experience does, to a degree, precede them. Swire Hotels is a subsidiary of Swire Properties, established to create products which complement their portfolio of investments and capitalise on new opportunities for market share. The cornerstone of this evolution to date has been in the launch of House Collection, namely the Opposite House in Beijing, China and the Upper House, recently opened in Hong

Kong. Alongside these niche creations, Swire operate EAST, upper mid-scale hotels which service tenants in office space with around 350 rooms and are also preparing to launch a new brand of regional boutique hotels in the UK. So why make the move into a more risky playing field now? Brian comments:

'The business likes to adapt to new opportunities as they arise. Swire Properties were big investors into hotels already with brands such as Mandarin Oriental, Conrad, Marriott, Shangri-La and Novotel used in their portfolio. We employ a number of brands in these developments, depending on the market. But within our mixed use developments in China the business saw new opportunities. It seemed to make sense that, if we had a long-term view, we could create our own niche brand for mixed use developments.

'Creating brands for Swire Hotels enables the business to maximise real estate use and the inclusion of a luxury hotel creates a certain shine which flows on to the rest of the mixed development. We are unusual because we are developer, owner, significant investor and operator; however, we are not a management company, so there is no immediate pressure from shareholders to grow the business through management agreements.'

'A lot has changed in 20 years and now a key target market for House and EAST is inter-regional traffic into Asia which accounts for 65% of business, although long-haul remains important.'

Although Brian believes that there may be other cities which could support such a luxury product, the focus on this brand at present is on stabilisation and reputation. The second element to Swire Hotel's portfolio is EAST, an upper four-star brand attached to its office locations. It is the neighbourhood hotel brand of the business according to Brian.

'EAST is predominantly a bedroom product servicing our corporate clients. We are not including multiple F&B or large-scale catering and conventions, as there is normally a plethora of that product already available. The beauty of this product is that, from an investment perspective, you can maximise your real estate and focus on profits in accommodation. The House Collection is the innovative, creative portal of the business which focused on up-scale, individualised properties within mixed use developments in Asia. The first of these to open was the 98-room Opposite House in Beijing in October 2008, whilst the 117-room Upper House in Hong Kong opened in October this year. In addition to highly modernised, urban design, the brand assumes that guests will be independent in thought and deed and looking for a break from the 'predictable'.

Brian believes that Asia, particularly China, is evolving into a market in which this positioning appeals.

'Our guests in the Opposite House are amazingly sophisticated, fashion conscious, quality driven, interesting people. Many are entrepreneurs and are developing brands themselves.

'At the time that I first started to look at this idea, smaller-scale luxury end hotels had not yet taken off in Asia, so it was a very good niche and I believe that Beijing lends itself to a really interesting brand – something edgy but not faddish. It's difficult to create a new product in this market with 35 new luxury hotels opening each year, so we wanted to create something which had a certain style and sense of place.

'Clearly you need a market where the level of demand can sustain this sort of product. There have not traditionally been that many areas in China where this would be the case, but it is growing, namely in Beijing and Shanghai. I think Guangzhou – the third largest city in China – is massively over-supplied, so we would not look to put a House Collection property there yet. Instead we have used an established brand, Mandarin Oriental in the mixed use development there; I was involved in this decision and this is where the flexibility in our business model helps.'

The final element of Swire Hotels is an as-yet unnamed brand of boutique, regional hotels to be launched in the UK in October next year. The business has three properties in the UK previously trading under the Alias Hotel brand, and these are being redeveloped with a launch planned for the first site in Cheltenham. It is an intriguing step for the business, and I am keen to learn why the UK was chosen?

'The Group is always looking to find new businesses that are not necessarily of a massive scale. In Swire terms it is a small scale investment but it is a business that we believe has good potential. We will only know when the full circle of business implementation has been completed, and that will be around one year after Cheltenham is opened.'

Brian has been Managing Director of Swire Hotels since its launch, having joined Swire Properties in 2006. During his career he has spent 17 years with the Mandarin Oriental Hotel Group, during which time the company grew from five to 25 properties and he comments that the potential to repeat this experience held appeal. Immediately prior to joining Swire he had been chief executive of the Scotsman Hotel Group. Brian gives the impression of one who keeps his eye on all elements of a hotel's operations – he loves to read the daily arrivals list for its tactical information – but could happily debate hotel strategy. In Asia he is building a very young team which is clearly an inspiration.

'You are really building for the future with these people – we are trying to build a service style which is appropriate for today. Guests are looking for a little more confidence in people when they are being served a little less subservience and more individualism – they are happy for people to have personalities.'

Whilst Brian concedes that the last two years have been incredibly challenging, he notes that the Asian market bounces back time and time again. The bounce has not been at the same speed of other downturns, but he believes the long-term vision of Swire, largely unfettered by shareholder pressure, makes the business possibly better placed to weather the storm. Within this context, Brian's view is that mixed-use developments are a major opportunity for the hotel market.

'It is an opportunity for the sector, and does not have to be simply a luxury opportunity. If you can evolve hotels into residential, retail and office space, then it will be very interesting to see how the service style adapts.'

(*December 2009*)

Hotels – International

Jean-Gabriel Peres

President and Chief Executive, Movenpick Hotels and Resorts

Jean-Gabriel is a leader who seeks to inspire others with his enthusiasm and passion. His style is to engage and develop people in order to deliver core brand values. Equally, Jean-Gabriel possesses a sharp, analytical mind and has a clear vision of where he would to drive Movenpick Hotels and Resorts, which undoubtedly serves to help the business maximises opportunities.

'The key word is trust'

The current economic crisis was recently summed up as a 'once in a century credit tsunami' by Alan Greenspan, former Chairman of the US Federal Reserve, whilst Charlie Bean, the Bank of England Deputy Governor, has called it the 'largest financial crisis of its kind in history'. In this regular international feature we speak with Jean-Gabriel Peres, President and Chief Executive of Mövenpick Hotels and Resorts to gain a global perspective on what he sees as the opportunities and challenges facing the industry at this time.

'To me, I think that one of the challenges for companies who react to a crisis by cutting labour, is that it sends a very wrong signal. The hospitality industry always needs people and we operate in long cycles. Companies have values and vision; it is important to stick to these, and panic will be very damaging. At the moment as CEO of Mövenpick, I am investing a significant amount of my time with my team in developing our strategy to attract and retain talent in the business. It is a top priority.'

In January next year (2009) the UK is bracing itself for Office of National Statistics figures for economic performance, widely predicted to show a second quarter of shrinking economic output; the technical definition of a recession. An obvious question is how long and how deep it will last? The UK hospitality industry has already seen a 1.7% reduction in output, and there has been talk of a 'services recession'. Yet, the predicament is fundamentally a global challenge. Jean-Gabriel has been at the helm of Mövenpick Hotels and Resorts since 1999, with an international career in building upscale retail and hotel businesses of more than 25 years. We asked his views on this challenge.

'It is an acid test for the hospitality industry. Lots of people were looking for short-term returns. The current crisis shows that some of the financial instruments, such as Real Estate Investment Trusts (REITs), were flawed. REIT performance in the UK has been 30–40% down on where it was expected. Some trading results, when compared with the regional stock exchange, show that certain hospitality businesses focused too much on the financial return, reliant upon unrealistic valuations. I believe that we will see the restoration of the achievement capacity of leaders' performance – this is what drives business. Market considerations have been purely financial. Leadership quality will be what drives value in coming years.

'The key word is trust. We are working hard to ensure we build this with guests, trade partners and employees more than ever. The current world crisis is really a crisis of trust. In our case, Mövenpick has no debt, we are not listed, we have two solid shareholders and cash for acquisitions so we are in an interesting position. The danger is that we move too early and the world is far from stabilised.'

Mövenpick has doubled in size under Jean-Gabriel's tenure, and the business is about to sign up their one hundredth hotel, ensuring that the goal of realising this number of sites either built or under construction by 2010 is realised. The business will be increasing its current workforce of 12,000 by an additional 9000 globally over the next two to three years.

'The hospitality model is certainly being challenged right now, however I believe this will result in a more sensible market. I think we all know that there were ratios used to value businesses which did not make sense, such as the huge multiples of EBITDA. Our Executive Meetings do not start with the bottom line. We spend time talking about talent. Our EBIT has increased regularly by 50% year on year over the past five years. It shows that if you get the right things together with talented people, you can achieve significant bottom line growth.'

Resilience has become one of the buzzwords throughout the industry, with companies looking to attain competitive advantage through a variety of tools, including targeted expansion and utilising different methods of production. In Jean-Gabriel's view, locally focused marketing methods are one of the major questions:

'Mövenpick Hotels and Resorts is focused on driving the top line. Where some businesses may cut their revenue management units, we take a contrary position. Revenue management is a key sales strategy. It is about engaging sales executives at a different level. They work on a site-by-site basis to advise General Managers of potential missed opportunities. It is about looking at partner marketing and other marketing initiatives.'

Globally, Mövenpick Hotels and Resorts operates in 26 countries throughout Europe, the Middle East, Africa and Asia. Jean-Gabriel states that:

'We will see further growth in Africa and Asia, including China and possibly India. Our business is very well represented in the Gulf and the Middle East.'

What are his views on the performance of Mövenpick at the moment?

'The hospitality industry is affected. We are seeing clients booking seminars for shorter time periods and with fewer people. However, as an upscale hotel business, I strongly believe our market positioning is more favourable than the luxury hotel segment, and other market segments.

'We are anticipating a slowdown and delay in our openings in the Gulf area. Some of our sites are highly dependent on corporate US business, and they have seen a bit of a downfall. It is by no means a collapse. People are travelling less frequently, for a shorter time. Some global companies have started to implement travel freezes, so we are taking that into consideration.'

One industry leader recently commented that the debate about how to retain staff during a recession was one often ignored, and yet it was one of vital importance. Talent management is one of the central areas of focus for Mövenpick, where we are working hard to become an industry reference, and Jean-Gabriel believes it is a major strength of the developing business:

> 'Our vision is to be the preferred and most enjoyable upscale hotel management company of Swiss origin for guests, employees, hotel owners and shareholders. This vision will be delivered and over the next three years we are concentrating further on the quality of our welcome, the quality of our farewell and the quality of the culinary experience. I do not see the current crisis having any impact to change this course.
>
> 'We have an extremely personable approach, strong relationships between us and our hotel owners. The selection of the right General Managers is key to this success, as they represent the brand in the local markets around the world.'

As organisations continue to wait for a degree of stabilisation of the world markets, many will be questioning how to position their business in coming years. As Mövenpick Hotels and Resorts continues with its expansion, Jean-Gabriel believes that the situation will have a positive benefit on the business in the long term.

> 'These kinds of crises force organisations to look at processes, innovation and drive opportunities, and I don't think you should ever lose sight of how important this is. I think it will be the land of opportunity for Mövenpick Hotels and Resorts. With the strong support and partnership from our long-term owners, an upscale positioning and our approach to talent, I am confident for the future.'

(December 2008)

Hotels – International

Duncan O'Rourke

Chief Operating Officer, Kempinski Hotels

Kempinski is one of the most highly regarded, luxury hotel companies in the world, having been founded in Germany in 1897. Duncan took up the COO in 2008 and went on to lead a significant organisational development project which sought to redefine and shape the business culture. His objective was to emphasise the European heritage of the Kempinski brand, whilst also ensuring that the management team were consulted and involved in the process. The concept of 'luxury' and the creation of brand differentials in a competitive market are intrinsically linked to service and people. Duncan is a positive, enthusiastic hotelier who seeks to inspire others through a simple vision and ensure that consultative measures enable leadership development.

Regarded as innovative for their approach to hotel development and standards, Kempinski have a great deal of potential to develop further in the luxury hotel market.

'Luxury is still exclusive'

Kempinski Hotels has spent 12 months revitalising its business culture. Had one of the world's oldest luxury hotel companies lost some of its soul?

Kempinski has experienced the most rapid period of growth in its history over the past 12 years, growing from 26 to 60 properties with a further 44 in the pipeline. They have built up a reputation for the quality of their new developments and established a benchmark for the luxury hotel market, by blending local tradition with modern technology to great effect. Throughout their history the company strap line – A Collection of Individuals – has been a hallmark of Kempinski's strategy, as the business has sought to celebrate the distinctiveness of their properties and location.

So the launch of a new range of European Lifestyle concepts designed to boost consistency and integration of the brand is an interesting step. While the business adamantly refutes the idea of using a cookie-cutter approach in hotel development, it is clear that this process of internal review has been underpinned by an objective of greater employee engagement.

Duncan has been responsible for driving the initiative, the construct of which is simple: general managers create new brand values which are consultatively approved by their peers, providing an increased level of unity within the business. But what brought about the need for this change? And will the approach prove to be effective?

Founded in Germany in 1897, Kempinski has since expanded into Europe, the Middle East, Africa and Asia. The business operates as a management company and works with a number of hotel owners, which brings about a range of differing local demands and sensitivities. This clearly plays into Kempinski's focus on innovation and uniqueness. However, it would appear that the business has reached a stage in its evolution where it believes that there is a need to embed an internal commonality in order to strengthen identity.

Duncan is an extremely open and enthusiastic character, who has previously worked with Rosewood Hotels, Marco Polo and Mövenpick. Appointed COO in June 2008, he explains that the decision to undertake a period of 'soul-searching' was initiated by the company's President, Reto Wittwer – one of the most highly regarded leaders in the hotel industry:

> 'He felt that our hotels were good but not the best and that it was time to consolidate the culture and brand. Kempinski needed new ideas and had to raise the bar.

> 'We really wanted to establish what it was our customers were looking for and what we stood for. It became clear that, as we are a European company, our heritage needed to be there for everyone to see.'

A group of 10 hotel general managers were tasked with leading project teams to develop new ideas that they believed reflected Kempinski's brand values and could form a common thread to each hotel's service provision. The groups covered all main areas of the hotel's operations and after a period of development, ideas were put forward to the whole general management team for consideration. An 85% acceptance rate was required in order for a concept to be rolled out and in December last year a set of European Lifestyle brands were launched. The basis for the brand's new look and feel revolves around four themes:

- Beauty – The Kempinski Spa.
- Culture – the Kempinski Ball.
- Savoir Vivre – the Lady in Red, a mix of concierge and guest service agent
- Gourmet – new food and beverage concepts supported by training from European bakers, chocolatiers and baristas.

The goal is to create recognition for Kempinski as a brand throughout all of its properties, without sacrificing the ethos of ensuring local traditions and individuality of destination. Any organisational change programme brings with it a degree of scepticism, and there are some who might question the true level of engagement throughout the business and whether the reality is more superficial. However, it is clear to Duncan that the results reflect Kempinski's heritage and that there is a subtlety to the process:

'Europe is not really united if you think about it. It is a collection of individual nations. It is elements like food that are really the common denominator.

'Nevertheless, the process was challenging given that it was not something we had ever done before and I actually believe that the second stage will be more challenging, as the ideas need to be pertinent, and must reinforce luxury.'

Privately owned, Kempinski has a very clear vision for its hotel properties and how it seeks to work with owners. The core of this ethos is embedding distinctiveness into all of its operations and design. This measure of control is extended to plans for long term growth, and its objective is to never have more hotels in its portfolio than the number of years it is old. Kempinski does not want to be over-represented as a brand in any one market. Duncan explains:

'Luxury is exclusive, so it is limited by definition. If you are a luxury product there are certain expectations and guests expect a mix of tradition and innovation at the same time.'

As the recession of the past two years has taken its grip, luxury hotel companies have been placed under the microscope and been forced to restate their values as a measure of their commitment to their product and status in the market. While Kempinski's admirable approach may have provided a platform to continue growing and strengthen their brand, the real question now is how it will boost its external perception, both as an operator and as a culture. As Duncan concludes:

'Brand equity is a long-term consideration. We have supportive shareholders and some very exciting new developments in the pipeline. Kempinski is growing into a major player.

'We wanted to characterise our heritage and underwrite what we believe, but we have had to take a hard look and stay true to our legacy as an exclusive five-star operation.'

(February 2010)

Food Service

Hamish Cook

Chief Executive International Services, Spotless

Hamish came to the UK in the summer of 2010 to oversee the development of Spotless' development in the UK, USA and Middle East. Spotless is the market leader in Australasia in the provision of facility services and Hamish is now a central player in their growth internationally.

Hamish is a thoughtful, measured character. He is one of those men that prefer to be judged by deed rather than through his words. When one meets Hamish, it is clear from an early stage that this is a character who is naturally driven. He appears almost unassuming but very comfortable in his own skin – he is a very able and competitive sportsman and also at ease in the business suit. He enjoys a challenge in whichever way it presents itself. He likes to test himself against high challenges and even if he struggles, he will learn the lessons and find positives from the experience.

One of the key components to Hamish is the fact that he has been able to translate his competitive spirit from one arena to another with seeming ease for the simple reason that he is very self disciplined. He works hard, is focused, thinks deeply and is passionate about his work and family. As one speaks to Hamish, it becomes clear that he believes that leadership is about how one behaves.

'I enjoy the topic of leadership and have thought hard about the subject. There are many factors that come into play but if we keep it simple, success is about how we approach life; how we work and think. If a company is going to be successful, it is – in our business – about people. It is important that we build teams that want to work together to deliver objectives.

'I have enjoyed working and representing Spotless because my personal values and those of the company are very much aligned. I believe in what we stand for as a company and am more than happy to take that forward. As an organisation, we believe that our behavioural traits are very important in achieving success. This is the foundation stone to everything. We need to act in the right way in the interests of all our stakeholders. This includes our clients, customers, staff and suppliers as much as our investors. If we act in the right way, I don't believe that we will need to compromise on what we believe in or on our strategy.

'I believe in long-term relationships. To achieve this, both sides need to have trust and respect in the other. It is no different than from a personal relationship. If a friend doesn't respect you, then that friendship will soon suffer. In the professional arena, we make sure that we deliver on our promises and bring new value to our clients allowing us both to share in the upside of any growth; then trust and respect will follow.

'Look, it is not always easy and it requires discipline and character. Sometimes, it is easy to compromise and take a short cut but it rarely proves to be a successful strategy.

'I am not saying that I have got it right throughout my career or that I have all the answers. I have made my fair share of mistakes but I have learnt my lessons. One of the great opportunities that this role has presented to me is to allow me to bring a new dimension to the way that I approach work. I have had my rough edges and these have been polished over the years. It is a long journey and at times there can be dark periods … but I am a naturally positive character and I have a strong sense of belief in myself – not in an arrogant way I hope but because I just back my own abilities.'

'Any new role enables one to reinvent oneself and to grow. This is a really good opportunity to achieve this. As Spotless grows in the UK, I am sure I will continue to develop my skills and approach to management in a global market.'

It is interesting to note Hamish's response to whether he can transfer his success in Australia to the UK.

'We have clearly defined objectives but I am not sure they are worth talking about as we have to prove ourselves over a period of time and then we will see business grow. I have no desire to sound arrogant. We do believe that we can bring new ideas and concepts to the market. We feel that we have some tried and tested concepts that have worked for us in Australia and New Zealand that we can implement in the UK market. But it is important to get the perspective right. There is also much we can learn and gain from the UK. There is an opportunity for the best of both the UK and Australia to be used and swapped. We can transfer lessons back to our Australian operations and vice versa.

'Will we be successful? Yes, I believe so but first we need to get those that are working with us to believe in what we stand for and what we are trying to achieve. It takes teams to be successful and there needs to be belief in our objectives and values. It is my role to set the tone and the benchmark. I am accountable and that is fine but I need to also ensure that we all understand our responsibilities to each other. I am comfortable being accountable if we are judged on how we act and work with our clients as I know we will deliver and be good partners.

'Success is about adding value to our existing relationships and growing in our preferred markets over an extended period. We also want to grow a strong management team. This will take time and investment. I am sure we will have our setbacks but we are prepared for that and we have belief that success will come from how we act and behave with both our clients and our people.'

So what have been the key ingredients that have led to Hamish becoming CEO?

It is interesting to note that the basis of his character lies is his approach to how he views even failure. One suspects that he absolutely hates failure but would reflect and learn from the experience. It is often said that people need to be positive and how important to take a positive approach but this is not as easy as it sounds for it requires a specific mindset that many do not possess. It does require a level of self-belief that one can be successful and this, in turn, comes from success in whatever form is important to an individual. One cannot just be positive. It is a long process of proving one's own abilities to oneself and Hamish is such an example. His self-belief and approach will have come from the challenges that he has set himself in both his professional work and also when he has competed in the sporting arena. Over a long period of time, he has built and developed his character.

This is one dimension; another is the strong value set that Hamish holds close to him. He is a trusted individual as he too treats people with respect and trust – and sets a benchmark for what he believes is the standard of behaviour to ensure success. His approach is almost old-fashioned. He will roll his sleeves up. He will lead by example and if he makes mistakes, he will hold his hand up. In a world that can be very cynical, the honest approach can be remarkably effective. Hamish is also passionate about giving back to the wider community and has worked with a range of 'not for profit' organisations and community groups over the last 10 years to share his business and commercial knowledge.

'In many instances we are fortunate to have exposure to such a wide cross-section of business and experience that other community organisations can benefit from, I think it is important that as a business leader you share this experience so that the community as a whole improves, you may also learn something new yourself in the process.'

Food Service

Tim West
Chairman, Lexington Catering

Tim is the Chairman of Lexington Catering and was previously the Chief Executive of Elior UK (1993–2004). He is regarded as one of the 'statesmen' of the contract catering sector.

Tim's career is an interesting study of a consistent leadership approach that always seemed to manage to raise Tim above the minutiae. Few will have seen him ever be different to the polite, thoughtful, calm character that is. He has faced his dark days just as everyone does and still his character did not waver. It is this quality that has been the foundation for his achievements as a leader.

Tim's story is one of how calm, patient consistent leadership combined with strong values, good behaviour (professional conduct) and a belief in people led to success with different organisations.

Tim graduated from what is now Oxford Brookes University in 1977 and initially joined the Health Service, then after a successful five years moved on to join the Compass Group for a further five-year spell. He joined High Table, then a private company, in 1987 as an Operations Director, and became Managing Director in 1990 by which time it was owned by Elior, the French contract and concession giant. Over the next 15 years, Tim led Elior's growth in the UK, which saw the acquisition of five companies and growth into new markets and repositioning with the launch of the Avenance name into the sector. This may sound like a normal story of growth but the acquisition and the merging of the three largest companies was completed almost simultaneously.

The years 1994 to 2000 were highly successful ones for Tim. Firstly, High Table grew from being a predominant London player into having a UK presence with regional offices in Leeds, Bristol and Manchester. It was a steady, organic evolution that was a mark of the company. High Table was seen to be a role model company which was respected by competitors. In 1998, Tim was rightly awarded the Food Service Catey.

In 2000, Elior increased their presence with the acquisition of Catering & Allied, Nelson Hind and Brian Smith. Tim brought all three companies together as one with High Table and rebranded all with the Avenance name, the same brand name as Elior utilised. At the same time Elior UK entered the concessions market.

It was a brave move as all four companies had strong local reputations and support in their own right. Catering and Allied and High Table markets were leading names in London; Nelson Hind and Brian Smith in the Midlands. In contrast, the name Avenance needed to become established. It is one of those strange contradictions that the British are often seen to be a very reserved people and yet on the contrary, they are often emotional buyers. The companies that often do well in the contracting sector are those that have open and accessible leadership with a clear understanding of the service offer. The British are also conservative and do not always react well to unnecessary change.

As the four companies came together, it is fair to note that many questioned the strategy and it was Tim's leadership which carried the strain as he was the face of the new Avenance. He was open and accessible and a very popular figure – these factors alone helped to cover many cracks as the market watched and judged. Major factors for Tim in this strategy was the assimilation of the operating companies, the creation of career opportunities for all throughout and the ability to bid for national contracts.

Any experienced observer will note that it is very difficult to successfully acquire one company let alone three and merge them together under a new name. It is fraught with problems. Whether the strategy was a success or not can be argued from both angles but it is to Tim's credit that:

- the market gave the company the benefit of the doubt
- the company had the 'goodwill' factor. People wanted it to be successful.

However, there is no doubt that it has taken Elior a long time to ensure the Avenance name carried real 'punch' in the market. Arguably it is just beginning to have a clear meaning in 2011 – a decade after the mergers.

Tim moved into a Chairman's role in late 2004 and left the company in 2005. It must have been a very difficult time for him as he had helped build the new entity and had guided it through some turbulent early stages. It is often said that when a CEO leaves a role for a major company it is like bereavement. Tim had worked with the French parent company for 15 years and recognised his job was complete and that he needed to pass the baton on, and he never once acted or behaved in any way other than he had always done.

It can be argued that if Tim stayed at the helm of Elior it would have been achieved greater success far more quickly. There is no other case study which has shown that the strategy followed by the company has been successful. In fact, there is much evidence to show the opposite. There are many who believe that Avenance has underachieved since 2005. Yes it has grown but has often been seen as ineffective and underperforming.

One of Tim's greatest strengths is that he has always been able to see the bigger picture and also been a trusted leader and colleague. As the new Avenance came together, there were a number of high profile resignations from senior roles in the company – Mike Sunley, Clare Prowse, and Andrew Wilson amongst others. Each one slightly weakened Tim's position as each set up in competition but Tim never viewed it in such a light and would probably disagree even today that it had any impact.

In retrospect, it was natural that Tim would join Lexington Catering which was being led by his old colleague, Mike Sunley. Gossip is notoriously inaccurate, as between 2002 and 2005 it had been assumed that the relationship between Mike and Tim was strained. It was a fair assumption as theirs had previously been a close working relationship, and many would be placed under pressure when one resigns from the board to set up in competition. It says much for both that it had no such effect. Perhaps this should have been no surprise as they had worked together since 1984 in both Compass and High Table/Avenance before Lexington.

However, Tim joining Lexington was still a major story. He had been the face of both High Table and, later, Avenance since the early 1990s. He was one of the industry's leading figures and many wondered what he would do after his departure. Where would Tim go now? Would he leave centre stage? He certainly considered it.

When Tim and Mike joined forces in January 2006, Lexington was small, loss-making and needed reinvigorating. The relationship between Tim and Mike was proven – but would it work as well in new circumstances?

In 2010, EP interviewed the two and they discussed just what their relationship worked but it also gave an insight into what makes Tim a successful leader.

Tim: 'I was at a stage in my life where I felt I had enjoyed a successful career, but also that I had one more good fight left in me. When Mike approached me, I was interested as I knew we could work together and shared similar values.'

Mike: 'I think that business relationships are often formed for the wrong reasons. Sometimes you start with an agreement of what you are moving away from rather than what you are trying to build for the future. It is so important to get these relationships right. Tim and I had a good relationship before and we knew that this firm foundation would be essential to future success.'

It is this relationship that has attracted confidence and comments in the media, and also attracted a very strong team to work with them. So what is it that makes their relationship work?

Tim: 'A major factor of our success over many years has been that we have been able to pick good people and grow with them. In Lexington I think that we have brought an excellent team together that really wants to work as one.'

Mike: 'We think along similar lines and there are no moments of high drama. We adjust to each other and get on with things.'

Tim: 'Mike is a no-fuss operator and this helps. We have no egos – no need to be in the limelight. We just want to build Lexington. We believe in each other and in what we promise.'

Mike: 'I think that is right. We do not over-promise. We believe in what we do and we can sell it.'

Tim: 'Partly because we have worked together for so long and partly because of our approach, we just let each other get on with our roles and trust one another. Mike is excellent at building teams. Running our own business has revitalised him and the team has so much positive energy that we all want to drive things forward.'

Mike: 'Tim adds balance and perspective. He is very calm in his approach and he understands the bigger picture.'

Tim: 'Clients like to see drive, delivery and vision. If we deliver on what we say we are going to do, they will talk about us and recommend us to others. We are caterers and have been working in this market for more than 20 years and believe that it takes time to understand this sector and to build up appropriate knowledge.'

So what are the key stories one can take from analysing Tim's career:

- Tim enjoyed early career success with strong interpersonal and commercial skills and rose quickly in the management ranks of the health service.

- This trend continued in Compass, in a completely different sector he became recognised as the leading executive in the City region.

- Tim led High Table to become a market leading organisation through a calm, consistent strategy that was developed in a steady fashion over a number of years. He took on the philosophy of the founders and gradually refined and evolved it.

- If one goes back to 1998, High Table was not just a strong and consistent company, it had a proven, closely-knit team that had been built by Tim over five years. One of Tim's great qualities is his patience and he never seemed to expect immediate success and impact from any senior players joining the organisation. He understood that it took time for senior players to adapt and settle in a new culture.

- The founding of Avenance could have been a potential disaster. The fact that it was not is very much down to Tim's influence and leadership. He allowed the company to find its new legs and built almost a new team. The proven High Table team broke up with the mergers and he lost some of the key influencers in the acquired companies. This must have been painful at times for Tim but he brought together a team that did take Avenance forward – maybe not as he would have hoped but still far better than could have been the case.

- However, his greatest legacy was the fact that the company maintained the 'goodwill' factor from clients, competitors and employees. This factor should never be underestimated as it is can act a basis of a company's culture and confidence.

- The fact that Tim is trusted allowed him to help the team at Lexington to turn their fortunes around to the point where today it is growing very successfully and is now one of the strongest forces in the London market.

Food Service

Sir Garry Hawkes CBE
Former Chief Executive and Chairman – Gardner Merchant

Sir Garry Hawkes is one of great leadership figures in the hospitality industry from the last 30 years. The man built Gardner Merchant to become a global force and market leader, led a management buy-out from Forte (1993) and saw the company sold to another global giant in Sodexo (1995) becoming the Director General of the combined company. He has since been a standard bearer for the importance of vocational education and training, creating the Edge Foundation in 2004, with capital of £75 million from the sale of Edxcel, the awarding body.

For many years, Sir Garry was the face and champion of the foodservice sector. He was a formidable character but as with many of those profiled, the base story only tells part of the truth. In an article that appeared in the *Daily Telegraph* (2006), Garry described his own road and what influenced him in his early days:

The words 'contract catering' have to be among the least romantic in the English language. But, as Garry Hawkes, now President of the Edge Foundation would testify, romance is relative.

Hawkes, born at the beginning of World War II, grew up in Sheffield during some of that city's toughest economic times. For this culinary Billy Elliott, catering was an exciting form of escape from an unexciting northern heartland:

'As a kid, I went to the railway station and checked the times of the trains to Paris. I wanted to be an actor or an artist. But having no talent decided to become a chef which sounded exotic, eccentric even, for Sheffield in 1955,' he says.

No trail had been blazed by Jamie Oliver or Gordon Ramsay, but the young Hawkes' ambition received a sympathetic hearing from his school, and he enrolled in a catering management course at Huddersfield Technical College.

'I was taught by people who were real pros, people who'd been chefs on the *Queen Mary*. They offered me a great combination of skills and knowledge,' smiles, the now avuncular, 67-year-old. It was at college that Hawkes picked up his love of training, a theme that has run through his career.

He started out his career not thinking of catering as a big business: 'It was peripatetic, sales-oriented and offered lots of opportunities. I enjoyed it.' In 1963, he joined Peter Merchant, the forerunner of Gardner Merchant, part of the Trust House Forte group, and Hawkes had an even better time: 'I spent the years from 23 to 60 there, and in that time I did everything from run a single catering unit to running the whole business'. He grew the business from a turnover of £100 million in three countries to £1.5 billion with 60,000 employees in 30 countries.

In 1993, he led a £402 million management buyout from Forte, involving in share ownership for some 1000 personnel who benefited from the distribution of £70 million on the subsequent sale of Gardener Merchant to French rival Sodexo for £760 million two years later.

How did he achieve such success as a manager? By using two strategies that were learned during his seminal experiences in Holland and Germany between 1975 and 1977, which have also served him well as he moved more into the public sector in the late 1990s.

The first was to use consensus as a form of leadership. 'I'm a consensus-driven manager, definitely. It might not be fashionable, but it worked for me,' he says. As he built up his business, he realised consensus was a tool to get people to buy into the company ethic. 'I managed by devolution and empowerment, which at the time created a company ethic of fairness and opportunity' he says.

'I tried to create small structures near the customer where the focus of everyone was on sales, a focus that permeated the organisation. People are good at dishing out responsibilities, but not the power that should go with it. Once we had established psychological ownership of the business, we moved forward collectively.'

The second principle was training as investment in the workforce.

'I recognised that our only resource was our people. There was no plant, no brand other than our name and our reputation. Therefore, it was necessary to treat people well and invest in them for the long term. So we promoted from within and gave people reasonable rights in the workplace.'

It is interesting to read how Sir Garry analysed his success in leading Gardner Merchant was down to his consensus-led management style and the company's focus upon training. Without question at its peak, Gardner Merchant was renowned for its training and development programmes. It was the envy of every competitor. With his then Human Resources Director, Sir Garry acquired a mansion located in Kenley, Surrey, which was turned into the company training centre and head office. The acquisition of the house cost £1 million but it returned far more over time for the grand building became almost a symbol for the soul of the company. Those employed within Gardner Merchant were proud of the organisation's commitment to training and how their CEO championed its importance. Any client or supplier that visited the centre saw the resource behind the service and the importance of the co-location of training with the head office.

By placing his people at the centre of the core management philosophy, the company was illustrating its desire to ensure that employees were trained and cared for. It is an arguable case that the company made a major mistake with the sale of the training centre in 2001. The sale marked the end of the company's commitment to training and it has to be asked as to whether the company's subsequent difficulties in the UK were heightened by this action for it subliminally stated that people development was no longer core.

It is about cultural and psychological belief in an organisation. The focus upon training with its grand centre made people feel important and valued professionals and they responded in return. There was trust in the organisation by its people who would then generate success.

The other key component of the company's success was that Sir Garry had a board of very experienced and able professionals. Sir Garry is a charismatic, dominant character and yet his fellow board members were no shrinking violets. They were often vocal, strong passionate characters and over the years, I have smiled as I imagined them together as they would have been lively meetings. From afar, one would imagine Sir Garry to be the dominant force but the truth was that he built a very capable board that was strong and empowered. He clearly enjoyed the challenge and they probably pushed him to be better in return.

So what is Sir Garry's legacy? Sir Garry stepped down as CEO back in 1996 and yet, 15 years later, he is still talked about and can attract an audience. Many still fondly discuss Gardner Merchant's culture and highlight the Kenley Training Centre. Even today, so many key figures have emerged from that culture.

Far from retired he has continued to champion vocational education and training, through his chairmanship of Edxcel, the Basic Skills Agency, NTO National Council and others. 2012 will see the opening of the Edge Hotel School at Wivenhoe House, a long-held passion and aspiration that will move management training away from just the classroom and textbook and back to the professional traditional roots, Sir Garry believes in so much.

Food Service

Aidan Connolly
Chief Executive, Sodexo UK and Ireland

Ian Sarson
Group Managing Director, Compass
Group UK and Ireland

Ian and Aidan head up the UK's two largest foodservice companies, Compass and Sodexo.

Ian is a classic caterer who has grown up in the industry, and was appointed to the UK Managing Director role from his previous role in Compass as Managing Director of government, defence, education and healthcare. He possesses a style of leadership which seeks to inspire through action, and has a depth of hands-on experience which others respect.

In contrast, Aidan was originally Sodexo UK and Ireland's Finance Director prior to his appointment as Chief Executive. He is a strategic, analytical thinker whose approach to change in the business has focused on the business model, its clarity for customers and commercial measures of success.

Both Ian and Aidan have distinct leadership styles, and it will be interesting to observe how their journey unfolds as both companies are making the transition into the integrated facilities management market.

Time will tell

Sodexo has been a market leader for many years and has now developed a new strategy. Can the business successfully reposition itself?

Despite a tough 2009, Sodexo has demonstrated its resilience and operating profit for the first half of 2010 was €24 million, up by 32%. The recent reorganisation of Sodexo has generated much discussion yet Aidan Connolly, as its architect, has been a less-visible figure. In meeting him, it is evident that strategy is core to Aidan's mindset, along with a good dose of commercial shrewdness. Humble and incisive, he is also a realist.

Aidan acknowledges throughout our interview that the business's presence in the UK and Ireland market has faced challenges for a number of years. In talking about the change required to address this, it is clear that his goal has been to both reinstall a strong sense of identity, and capitalise on the company's strengths in building long-term relationships. Of course, no such process is ever straightforward and, in one moment, Aidan tells me wryly that he starts each day with the reminder to 'communicate, communicate, communicate'.

With 43,000 staff, it's not hard to empathise, particularly when undertaking a major reorganisation against the backdrop of global recession. So can the business reinforce its strength and position?

Having joined the business as Finance Director in 2007, Aidan explains that he had been looking at the way in which Sodexo operated and how it might do better from the outset. Prior to his initial appointment, he was the FD of MyTravel UK and had formerly held CEO roles in luxury brands group company Walker Greenbank plc and a number of private companies in the UK, Europe and the USA. Aidan argues that the main driver for change in Sodexo was the need to become more client-focused, ensuring that the business offered a wide range of services that met expectations on a number of levels.

> 'I undertook the reorganisation partly because the business was getting a bit large to manage as one, but also because it genuinely needed to be more outward looking.'

The process saw the UK and Ireland business separated into three streams:

- Prestige – top-end catering and the former Prestige business, which includes its leisure, hospitality and events contracts, as well as its business in Scotland and Ireland.

- Corporate Services IFM – created to provide on-site service solutions to clients requiring a full range of soft and hard services including food. (This division includes land technology and technical services.)

- Corporate – delivering food and soft services consistently with excellent service.

One of the interesting developments was the amalgamation of high-end catering services in both events and corporate services under one banner. This has never been done before and is potentially an area for debate, given the operational requirements and differences in mindset required. However, while Aidan acknowledges that this is the case at one level, it is a different matter for customers:

'In the execution they are separate, but from the client side they are quite similar. In both cases it is about delivery on the plate with no failure rates. A five-star Open Golf Championship is different to corporate dining in the City, but clients want the same thing.

'In the long-term my vision for Prestige is to remind people why Sodexo has been so successful. It was well known in the past for excellence, and Prestige allows us to focus on that. The frustration of most chief executives is consistency and we have looked at ways of improving this so the gap between good and bad service narrows. So by changing the focus, there is a closer range of service excellence. On the flip side we have the ability to cross-fertilise techniques and there are areas that do this very nicely. For example, chefs at the top end are on the same team; food delivery comes together and that attracts more internal investment.'

Aidan believes that companies are emerging from the recession with a desire to look at things in a new way, and that clients are more nervous in general about the appropriateness of their offer. The message that he wants to deliver is that client needs can be addressed from every angle. While Aidan believes the provision of Michelin starred in-house dining has been scaled back, he is confident that Sodexo's range of service offerings allows the business to compete over a broader spectrum. At one level, Sodexo's global hospitality contract with the Rugby World Cup is one significant area of development, as is its work with LOCOG for the 2012 Olympics. With the split of Sodexo's UK and Ireland core business around half in government, including numerous PFI contracts, and half in the commercial sector, Aidan believes that growth opportunities will also be driven by the business' established success in developing long-term partnerships. Specifically, while outsourcing has been a major area of focus for the public sector, he sees real potential in increasing demand from the commercial sector.

'Commercial companies will see people look at their business through the lens of having survived the recession and are looking for a better-value solution. Food is a long-term, mature outsourced service, but there will be a lot of opportunities in the less-mature FM outsourced market, so the next decade will be a period of tremendous opportunity for Sodexo.

'We can cross-pollinate ideas from public into private in terms of the breadth of offer and in driving the supplier base. It has been rare to see clients in the private sector embrace outsourcing to the degree of a PFI initiative in one go, but we will see more of this. Recession forces people to look at all ends of their business, and the more forward think-ing ones will be looking at core and non-core skills – it is now almost mandatory to think in this way. What we will see is volume growth in big service lines – catering, cleaning, maintenance, reception.'

With the political environment in a state of change, Aidan believes there will be a hiatus of new business as the coalition implements its emergency budget provision. What does he think of the impact on public-sector contracts?

'It would be electoral suicide to withdraw services. Commercial enterprises will be in new partnerships with governments simply because they cannot walk away from commitments that people have got used to. So there will be growth in public work.'

Sodexo UK and Ireland is the third largest trading division within a major global enterprise. The reorganisation process has been viewed positively within the extended company and Aidan notes that some of the changes he has overseen are already being copied elsewhere.

'There was a period of time, at the turn of the century, when the UK and Ireland business was in tough times. It has steadily recovered, particularly since Philip Jansen came on board in 2004, and there has been intense interest in what we are doing in the rest of the company. In particular, we really understand the value of long-term partnership in a way that others do not.'

While Aidan recognises the challenges of repositioning the business, particularly in a market that has been badly impacted by the recession, his vision for the future is one of optimism.

'Other than the impact of taxation I think the UK is an exciting market to be in and has a lot of opportunities. I would like to see Sodexo providing high-quality, integrated facilities management solutions across the board, across a much wider range of services with more depth of self-delivery. The extent to which we achieve that will determine our level of success.'

(*July 2010*)

An interesting adversary

In April this year, Ian Sarson took the helm of the UK's largest catering company, as Group Managing Director of Compass Group UK and Ireland. What were his views on the market and Compass's opportunities?

In EP's recent catering market survey, opinions were split regarding the direction of catering and the balance between clients seeking individual operators seen as 'best in class' or the increasingly popular integrated services model. With Ian's background in the Health and Education sectors, two areas with heavy involvement with the integrated services model, many feel that his appointment may lead to a change in direction for Compass and a tendency towards the more integrated approach of its largest rival Sodexo.

Is this the case? Where does Ian see the future lying and what does he see as the key priorities for clients at present? We quickly moved to the integrated services debate. He says:

'For 20 of my 30 years in the industry I've been an integrated service provider. Compass has about £250 million worth of business in the UK today that has nothing to do with food so it's not a new development for us. The dilemma comes in how quickly you resource and build up that area of the business and ensure that it is not at the cost of our food service heritage, we are very clear on this. For instance, we have no desire to contest stand-alone cleaning – yet we will certainly offer cleaning as a part of integrated services for our client. We come at it service first, as opposed to contract. The integrated approach is driven by the hospitality aspect of our business. It is funny that people see integrated services as a departure from catering and hospitality, I would actually throw the debate back the other way. After all, isn't integrated facilities management just what a hotelier does every day? They take care of the cleaning, the maintenance, the gardening as well as the restaurants and room service.

'There are obvious synergies through integration. However I think creating a 'service team' is the important aspect of this, simply delivering one invoice isn't really helping anybody. You've got to underpin it with a cultural shift and that team service mentality. When integration is just about removing administrative burden it will only ever liberate limited value.'

Value is a word thrown around a lot at the moment. There is pressure on spending which inevitably leads to a tightening of the collective belt; costs and value for money will continue to be important areas of focus.

'We have to focus on controlling costs. We know that we have to be the lowest sensible price provider for our clients because, if we're not, why wouldn't they go somewhere else? This means ruthlessly reviewing our business resource and build up that area of the business and ensure that it is not at the cost of our food service heritage, we are very clear on this. For instance, we have no desire to contest stand-alone cleaning – yet we will certainly offer cleaning as a part of integrated services for our client. We come at it service first, as opposed to contract. The integrated approach is driven by the hospitality aspect of our business. It is funny that people see integrated services as a departure from catering and hospitality, I would actually throw the debate back the other way. After all, isn't integrated facilities management just what an hotelier does every day? They take care of the cleaning, the maintenance, the gardening as well as the restaurants and room service.

'There are obvious synergies through integration. However I think creating a 'service team' is the important aspect of this – simply delivering one invoice isn't really helping anybody. You've got to underpin it with a cultural shift and that team service mentality. When integration is in place, we concentrate on making sure we eliminate all those processes or interventions that do not add value. At the same time we are in a position where much can be achieved through leveraging our scale.

'Value will always be a key driver and we must ensure that we can still evidence value to our consumers and clients. However there are other equally important factors – quality, informed choice, variety, convenience and agility are all important too. Local sourcing and provenance remain key issues. Customers want variety and to be able to make an informed choice, so we introduced our Balanced Choices programme and provide nutritional information on our Core Concepts range of signature dishes. We vary meal choices according to consumers' different mood states throughout the week. People are still, more than ever, becoming cash richer and time-poorer so ensuring that queues are short is also vital.'

Much of this is about the needs and desires of the consumer. What is it that Ian believes clients really want in this market?

'It may sound a little clichéd, but we want to delight people with what we do – not just deliver a contract. What is great about the hospitality industry is that every day we get three million chances to make people's days a bit better and that's enormously satisfying. We really want to bring that focus to it, rather than saying, 'we will come and deliver this contract'. Ultimately this is what clients want too.

'Taking this further, our overall ethos has switched and we now look at our relationship with clients differently. In the past our role could be viewed as the outsourcing of problems; now we see it as insourcing expertise. It's a very important change of language. We've lost a huge amount of value by using that word 'outsourcing' because it creates a sense of no longer belonging. We recognise that we need to be an integral part of an organisation in order to maximise the value that we can realise.

'This mindset is relevant in procurement processes as well. For UK plc to be really successful, clients and the public sector have got to move from this adversarial procurement model where their success is our failure and vice versa. We've got to move to a place where we sit around the same table, judged by the same things and try to unlock value collectively.

'To have a rigorous procurement process is really important, but to have an objective that has mutual success in mind, will be more beneficial than this 'I win, you lose, approach' that can sometimes be the case from historic models.

'We've had to tear up the rulebook and had to ask: How can we do this better?'

The past 18 months have certainly set the scene for change and many companies are looking at how they can do what they do better or more efficiently. With a marked downturn in the economy and the prospect of public sector cuts and private sector jitters on the horizon for the foreseeable future, where does Ian see Compass' key opportunities?

'We have got to be prepared and ready with offers that will unlock greater value for our clients whether they are public or private sector and we must be prepared to fight harder for our share – it doesn't come as a right. I do think we are ready.

'We are looking to grow our business in all of our sectors. In the public sector for example, the majority of business in healthcare and education are in-house supplied so we see this as potentially a significant growth opportunity. At the same time it would be wrong to ignore the fact that there are cost pressures and risks across the business at the moment and so we must use our scale, our ingenuity, experience and insight to make sure we are leading the way in evolving our offers quickly to take advantage of these opportunities and grow our client base.

'There is no doubt that we are in uncertain times, but from our perspective, the opportunities outweigh the risks. We are facing an unprecedented review of the public sector, that we welcome and we stand ready and able to assist. Then there is the Business and Industry market. It is our heritage, it is where we started but it is a highly penetrated market. Yet we believe that there are still areas where we can develop. It will remain a very key part of what we do.

'Across the business, we have a common sales language and process. We spent the last three years really re-engineering our sales function putting science and insight into these areas. We wanted to underpin sales with fact rather than just opinion and anecdote. We have also sharpened up our back of house which supports our sales team and we now have really good development and design processes in place and people with great expertise to create the right offers and proposals.

'However, ultimately, I don't believe you can sell anything you don't believe in. So for the last few years we've made sure we do believe in what we are doing, and this can only be achieved by showing everyone just what we can do.'

(October 2010)

Food Service

Andrew Main

Chief Executive, ARAMARK UK

Andrew is a consultative and approachable character who is probably more comfortable on the 'shop floor' than in an office. As a result he sits in between the role of leader and manager. Andrew has a high degree of empathy in his leadership style, is an intelligent thinker and has a clear vision of how he wants to transform the ARAMARK UK business. The question is whether he will be able to blend his hands-on approach with a more strategic perspective. Undoubtedly ARAMARK's return to private ownership, coupled with Andrew's experience in the USA, will create numerous possibilities.

'The art of the potential'

The traditional business model for foodservice has to change. Retail appears to be the way forward.

The economic climate is far from easy and 2011 has already proven to be a challenging period. Consumer confidence is being hit harder than it has been since the onset of recession and for foodservice operators, in constant competition with the high street and under greater client scrutiny, questions over their business model pervade discussion. With pressure on margins having been a significant issue for many years, discussion is now moving to price points as the impact of inflation takes hold.

ARAMARK is a global operator with an annual turnover of more than US$12 billion, with the UK division generating more than £400 million turnover for the year ending 2009. In 2010, ARAMARK was named as one of the World's Most Ethical Companies by the Ethisphere Institute. Andrew has been with the business since 1994, having joined initially as divisional director of Scotland and Offshore Operations. He spent three years in the USA working for the parent company as president of the Business Services division prior to returning to the UK to take up his appointment as Chief Executive in 2005.

Change was on Andrew's agenda as he returned to the UK, both in terms of leadership and business strategy. Robbie Wheeler, the UK's Human Resources Director, joined Andrew for our interview; she was appointed to ARAMARK in 2005 and has presided over some key changes to the people strategy. Prior to our interview I was struck by Andrew's comment made in 2007 stating that he wanted to shift from being a purchasing-led business to a consumer-led business. What did he mean by this?

'In the US the P&L model underpins the hospitality offer; subsidies were already a thing of the past. On my return to the UK, my view was that purchasing departments held significant influence, whereas in the US it was consumer taste. So I felt there was a significant opportunity for change. Our strategy has been in three parts. Firstly, we invested in talent creation through the establishment of the retail development team, which is the real engine of innovation in the organisation. The second area has been customer service and increasing our engagement with customers. Finally, we have looked at how to make the 'third space' a destination, breaking away from the idea that foodservice is about lunchtime and filling a need.

'Customers are grazing more and foodservice operations are in multiple day parts, so unless we created an informal environment where people want to meet up then there was going to be a missed opportunity. Historically, the industry has tended to invest in the servery up until the cash register but moving forward, I wanted to ensure more investment in the third space to create destination environments.'

I met Andrew and Robbie at their extremely impressive Pricewaterhouse-Coopers site where the company's flagship for its business and industry (B&I) concept, the Original Food Company, was launched. Led by an enthusiastic head chef and manager, and with creatively presented food, it is easy to see the potential. The concept has been rolled out to 40 B&I sites to date and Andrew is looking to replicate it throughout the division. However, the broader focus has been to develop individual offers within each of their five core sectors; B&I; offshore; and government, including defence, healthcare and education. In a challenging market, how is Andrew hoping to capitalise on the innovations in the respective offers?

'Each of the sectors has a very specific defined proposition that is appropriate and designed to meet needs of customers in their environments. The economy caused us to look at things in a different way and a major point was to ensure the right focus of resources, to create value for clients, customers, people and stakeholders. The focus on these five markets has been very well thought through and all of the major businesses are in the US, so we are looking to leverage global best practice.

'Retail is leading the way in ARAMARK, but we have also been creating a greater partnership with our purchasing suppliers to ensure we can meet demands for local products and provenance, which is what the consumer wants. The business has been able to create greater efficiencies through the consolidation, with one main supplier meeting our client needs, while allowing hundreds of suppliers to provide their goods.

'Ultimately, we want to exceed expectations in both service and environment and ensure that the whole value piece is at a higher point than the high street.'

With inflation at 4% and rising, the VAT increase and additional competition, the trading environment has never been more challenging. What are Andrew's views on the foodservice model?

'The pressure on operating margin is twofold; what is the tariff and the impact on the cost of doing business in the UK? If we look back over the past two years at the levels of client subsidies before and after the recession, there has been a further step change in the erosion of client funding underpinning the provision of staff dining, so we are at the point of getting close to the US model.

'The pricing model is driven by value creation for the consumer, which is the combination of great fresh food, great service and great environments. Because we are working to a retail model, margin compression can be significant so there is a lot of focus getting these three parts right. The real question is ensuring we get more flow through to the bottom line and Robbie, along with our head of Retail Development, Morag McCay, have been great partners in sourcing and developing the appropriate skills in our teams to create real added value for our customers and clients.'

RW: 'Different competencies and skills sets were required over and above the challenges of recession. We felt there was a real opportunity and that we could capitalise by refocusing skills and rebuilding early enough in areas where we knew we could have a positive impact. The management team is now finely balanced with the P&L model to ensure a retail approach. We restructured our senior team, particularly in operations, and invested heavily in developing our senior and middle management.

'The level of engagement with employees is critical during a recession. Without this, everything falls flat so we worked closely with Gallup as part of our activity and challenged the way we do things. Our frontline managers are the critical people in our business, so we had to change the way we think. A very simple example of this was the outsourcing of the HR provision to offer a 24/7, 365-day service which meets the needs of the operational managers and helps to pre-empt issues. Some people were quite uncomfortable initially; the feedback now is excellent.'

Changing perceptions of ARAMARK has been one of the major elements of the transformation process. Interestingly, the business relocated from its central London base in Millbank Tower to Farnborough late last year. What is the significance of this?

AM: 'It is partly to do with matching best practice amongst our client organisations that were open-plan, but it is also about cultural change. Millbank is an office in London. Was it appropriate for us? In reality no. We wanted to co-house with our operations team, not a head office. The experience has been incredibly liberating so far and I think it has been an accelerant for better interactivity, decision making and teamwork.'

Looking ahead what does Andrew see as the key opportunities for developing ARAMARK UK?

AM: 'I think for the private sector it is engaging potential clients to see the art of the potential by bringing them to sites already converted. Similarly in education. On the government side there will be a broadening of services underpinning growth, particularly people-provided services such as reception, cleaning and helpdesk. We made a small acquisition last year, Veris in Ireland, and acquired some great competencies, which helps drive multiple service provision.

'Delivering profitable growth is about having a really focused value proposition for each sector; it's not ARAMARK UK, it's ARAMARK Healthcare, ARAMARK Defence, ARAMARK Offshore, ARAMARK Education and OFC. The rigour underpinning OFC is phenomenal and I am keen to see this replicated consistently going forward.'

RW: 'Importantly we want to ensure that our propositions have depth. We do not want employees to think of it is a brand, but something that has real substance to convey to clients. It has to have a level of integrity.'

It is undoubtedly a tough environment, so where does Andrew see the business now?

AM: 'We are on a continuum. I think we are at a great juncture with excellent propositions for taking to individual markets that are resonating with clients, both new and existing, because the value piece has come together well. The executive team has a real diversity of talent which is truly exciting, and our investment in the frontline teams is about bringing the value propositions to life.

'I would like our business to be the partner of choice for clients in the provision of employee services, because they recognise ARAMARK truly understands what their employees, our customers, are seeking in their particular environments and that we are generating tremendous value for them.'

(April 2011)

Restaurants

Des McDonald
Chief Executive, Caprice Holdings

Heading up a selection of high profile portfolio of restaurants which includes The Ivy and The Caprice might prove to be a daunting balancing act for some, but Des is an impressive character who possesses a clear vision for the business which is rooted in a set of simple values. He is highly adaptable and has actively sought to make the transition from hands on operator into strategic leadership role. Yet, Des maintains a deep passion for the business, and has a clear understanding of his customers needs. This is the bedrock of the various brands within Caprice Holdings, and something which has allowed a whole range of concepts to be successfully managed together, under one roof.

Staying humble

Caprice Holdings has seen a lot of change in recent years since being acquired by Richard Caring (2005), and then expansion with the purchase of Soho House Group; new openings in the form of Rivington and the Mount Street Deli and an agreement with Jumeirah, giving the latter rights to roll out Caprice Holdings in the Middle East. Des discusses his approach to managing acquisitions and how he views the future.

Des McDonald is in many ways almost an old-fashioned CEO; a man who has worked his way up from the factory floor to lead one of the industry's most glamorous companies. Over the years there have been many stories such as Des's but what makes his slightly different is the way in which the man has reinvented himself as the company has expanded. Acquiring and merging companies into a cohesive structure is a testing challenge for even the most experienced of chief executives. There are arguably four or five expert exponents of this skill within the industry and maybe Des is becoming another? These include strong creative talents – such as Nick Jones, founder of Soho House Group – who are hardly known for taking a backward step to anyone. To make the story that much more interesting, it has grown in terms of turnover by 15% to £40 million in the year 2008–09 and by 20% to £8.4 million in net contribution. The last 18 months have seen spin followed by more spin as companies tell of their good performance in a difficult climate. However, the figures stand up and the feel is that Caprice Holdings is actually delivering real value. So what has the approach been?

> 'Our approach to business is humble. We want our customers' loyalty and for that, we have to deliver consistently and be seen to add value. It has not been an easy couple of years but we have really focused on quality and back to basics.'

It is, I noted, quite a difficult task to keep creative spirits such as Nick Jones content within a company structure.

> 'Sure but Nick has adapted really well. We have a strong platform. We have worked very hard at ensuring that our back of house has come together to give each business the best level of support. This allows our Creative Directors to be exactly that…creative. My role is to provide that foundation and bedrock for them to do what they do best. Part of that task is to ensure that everyone understands each brand and ensure that the identity is not thwarted. We don't mix the brands together. We keep them very separate.'

One suspects that Des's calm, no-nonsense and clear-cut approach is instrumental in keeping the creative talents online.

> 'I used to be very hands-on in approach. Over time, I have become far more strategic. I used to be a 'touch and feel' player…instinctive… but now I am much more into the details and facts. It helps being in a business I know so well. I understand the brands. I provide the support mechanism around the brands to operate in.'

It is worth just pausing for a moment and detailing Des's career with Caprice Holdings as it gives a feel for the step change that he has needed to make as the company has grown.

- 1993 Des joined Caprice Holdings

- 1998 Promoted to Managing Director
- 1999 Oversaw merger with Signature Restaurants
- 2005 Purchase of group by Richard Caring
- 2009 Purchase of Soho House Group
- 2010 Deal with Jumeirah Group.

The above indicates a character that is able to grow, change and adapt. However, when one meets Des he appears to be a very straightforward, honest character but clearly he also thinks deeply and carefully about the business. One simply does not survive leading such a business for 12 years unless one possesses these traits; let alone increase profits from £2.8 million in 2007 to £8.4 million in 2009.

'I am lucky to have a good senior management team,' he remarks modestly. 'Beyond that, I make sure that we are brutally honest to ourselves and that we are aware of the facts. It is easy to get into trouble if one is not completely on the ball. We do a lot of strategic planning. We are risk averse but we do like good opportunities.'

Des has had a steep learning curve – who have been his mentors?

'I have been lucky to work with some great talents and Chairmen – Richard, Luke Johnson, Chris Corbin and Jeremy King. One learns from each. But also my old sports master who taught me true grit…to never give up or take no for an answer.'

I noted that growing a business internationally has been the cause of much pain for many and yet Soho House has opened successfully in Los Angeles, Miami and New York. It was not that many years ago that it was said British companies could not successfully enter the US market.

'Soho House has opened very successfully in the US because we moulded the offer to the local market. We are not arrogant. We go out and understand what is different in each locality and meet those needs. For example, in Miami, we needed to understand what the local South American clientele wanted and we worked to deliver to them.'

Why, I asked, the deal with Jumeirah?

'Opportunity. We looked at the region. We looked at the opportunities in Abu Dhabi, Muscat and Dubai and we felt that Jumeirah were a good partner who understood our brands.'

How does he view the market, 2011 and 2012?

'There are some challenges as VAT will impact in 2011; interest rates will probably go up. To a degree, we are being held up by the Eurozone as we had a major influx of tourists. As a result, we are trading well. I suspect quarters one and two will be tough but the UK is resilient and we create opportunity. We are not quite in the trenches but we need some good old British spirit. 2012 should see a lift with the Olympics.'

After 12 years leading the business was he still as hungry? Des smiles slightly wryly.

'I am 45-years-old and I am enjoying the challenge. I am enjoying what we are achieving. These brands are my babies. It is a great business.'

It will be interesting to observe the next steps as the company develop further breadth. Undoubtedly, there are tough times ahead but one does suspect that the 'brutally honest', customer-focused approach which lies at the heart of Des's approach will hold the company and allow it to continue to expand safely.

(January 2011)

Concession

Simon Dobson

Managing Director, Delaware North UK

Simon is one of the youngest leaders featured in this work. It is interesting that he does embrace the fact that he is still learning and developing as the leader of Delaware North Companies (DNC) in the UK. In fact, it is a feature that he relishes as he knows that he has to constantly prove himself as a leader. As he will note: 'Surely we are all learning and developing and that is a challenge for everyone?'

Delaware North is an American-owned company with an annual turnover in the region of US$2 billion. The company has been established for close to 100 years and operates in a number of core markets: sports and entertainment venues; travel hubs – airports and stations; resorts and parks; gaming destinations. Over 55,000 are employed by the company in the USA, Australia, New Zealand and in the UK. In the UK, DNC operate Wembley Stadium, Emirates Stadium, Derby County's Pride Park as well as airport operations in Edinburgh, Glasgow, Gatwick and Heathrow. The UK turnover is an estimated £45 million after entering the market in 2004.

For a company as large as Delaware North, it is interesting that it is still exclusively owned by one family, the Jacobs family, and logic would say that theirs should be the story to focus upon but Simon's journey brings an in teresting point into focus for he is almost a half-way house between being a corporate leader and an entrepreneur.

Simon joined Delaware North in 2004 from Sodexo where he had been the Deputy Managing Director for the Prestige Division. The initial task was to build a team to open the newly rebuilt Wembley Stadium which, at the time had been a controversial project. Wembley Stadium had, over the years since its opening in 1936, become a national monument. It had certainly become dated but, as is normal, many do not like change and the critics were ready – pencils and pens sharpened – to criticise anything to do with the new Wembley. The pressure was immense and failure was simply not an option. It may seem strange to write this now for the rebuilding of Wembley is now seen to have been a great success story but in 2004, the views of the press were hostile. This hostility became worse as the building was delayed for a further two years through dispute with the construction company and normal delays. With each delay, the pressure just grew until the day of opening.

I recall talking to Simon about that day which brings a wry smile to his face.

'Yes, it was slightly pressurised scenario and if it had gone wrong, I guess I would have been clearing my desk. I certainly wouldn't have been staying around for very long. But, if we are being honest, I reckon I am one of only four or five people within the industry who could have managed that day: stood at the front doors as they opened and made sure that we carried it off as well as we did. I do not mean this arrogantly in any way – it is about possessing the experience this level of quality on such a scale.

'Of course, there those that criticised some of the service but overall it was a good day's work and we have kicked on from there. I think Wembley is today seen to be a very good operation and a benchmark for others to compare against. That makes me feel very proud but yes, sometimes I will look back at the first day and wonder what would have happened if it had all gone wrong.'

In some ways, this quotation cuts to the heart of Simon. He is leading a corporate organisation and yet he will, by instinct, lead from the front. There was simply no option to Simon not being on the floor and with his team on the day of opening. Simon is, at heart, an operator's operator with very high expectations of both himself and his team. Over the last seven years, he has taught himself to grow and develop his thinking and leadership style through trial and error. He will often be his own worst critic and he will listen and drive himself on to the next challenge. He was exactly the right man to set up Delaware North in the UK.

'I do smile when I think how large a company we are, for on day one, I was the person responsible for organising an office, setting up bank accounts, organising a mobile phone. And that was fine. In fact, I quite enjoyed it but we built it from scratch.

'I really am not being critical. In fact the opposite is true for I was happy to be given a blank piece of paper and told just to get on with it. I was essentially given a licence to develop a business with someone else's investment and a new contract as large and exciting as Wembley. Really – how can I complain about that? It was very exciting and it was a challenge that I embraced.

'Of course, there were days that were very daunting. And there were days which were really quite dark. I remember how we had recruited so many of the management team for Wembley and then had the call about the delay for a year. That is quite a cost to be carrying and it is pretty hard to keep operators happy when it is all about planning.

Operators like action. They like to be out there delivering a service, dealing with problems and handling the pressures that come along with it. So, I was sitting at my desk wondering what on earth I was going to do when the phone rang and Arsenal Football Club were on the line wanting to talk about the new Emirates Stadium.

'It is funny how life works out sometimes. In retrospect, I think it all worked well and the work we did with the Emirates Stadium prepared and polished us for the launch of Wembley.

'It was a demanding period of time. I do expect a high level of performance from my team and I do think that I should as we are operating some of the best stadiums and most high profile airports in the world.

'We should be aspiring to a high level, but I have learnt that I need to lead the organisation in a different way to maybe how I sometimes did previously. In the past, I expected to lead by example and my actions and words. But this can only achieve so much. We have built a structure and a team around some very clear core values. We ensure that all the managers understand the core values and buy into them for it these values that provide us with the bedrock to perform.

'I have learnt so much over the past seven years. I am not sure that I have changed that much but we have built a £45 million business almost from scratch and possess market leading contracts that we are proud to operate. I am sure that at times I have been too tough and hard on people but rest assured I am far harder on myself. It is just how I am. I am driven to achieve but I have learnt that not everyone sees things as I do and there are other ways to bring the best out of them. If everyone was like me on the team, we would be pretty one dimensional and we would probably have failed. Good teams have different qualities and different approaches and I believe that the team we possess today is multi-skilled and able on a number of levels.

'I really do believe that it is important that we develop people, trust them and empower them. We want a culture that will embrace new challenges and not be afraid to break new ground.

'I think that this is best illustrated by the way that we have moved into new markets. There were quite a few people who thought that I would not be able to adjust to another market and to be successful. I guess I can understand this as so many people struggle to make the transition from one sector to sector as each culture is different. But we have a wealth of experience within the company in the USA and in Australia and we have used this as well as made sure that we all learnt the key lessons ourselves. Have we got everything right? For sure, not at all. But we have learnt from any error that we have made and come back the next day. We have built good working relationships and we have grown successfully. I am now looking forward to the future as we have set the foundation stones and the focus is now on growing our presence. We have great potential to be a major player in the UK and we must act like one and play a role as leaders in the community, so the next step is to ensure that we are competing head to head with the market leaders in all the markets in which we wish to grow. In stadia, we are already key market leaders but we will grow in travel and also look to enter other sectors where we have been successful elsewhere in the world. We are not chasing market share. We have a strategy that seeks only profitable growth for the right reasons. It is an exciting prospect.'

Simon's comments are very candid and it is clear that he has acted just like an entrepreneur in a corporate environment. This is very rare to find and see and sets Simon a step apart from others. Simon's achievements over the last seven years are clearly there for all to view but it is interesting to listen to how Simon talks of his journey in that time. He is clearly learning and adapting; enjoying the challenge of building a company from scratch to compete with all.

Concession

Adam Elliott
Chief Executive, The Lindley Group

Adam was on the board of Elior UK before taking over as CEO of the Lindley Group in September 2010, so his role is still very new at the time of writing. The Lindley Group are experts in retail catering operations within stadia.

It was not an easy role to accept for it was stepping into the shoes of a much-loved CEO – Alex McCrindle – who had sadly passed away in late 2009 following a heart attack. This left quite a difficult leadership challenge.

It was difficult for a number of core reasons. Lindley is a venture-capital-backed catering business with a leadership team who were also shareholders and friends of the former CEO. The period prior between Alex's death and Adam's formal joining – never a short period of time with any CEO appointment – was an unavoidable period of limbo. Adam would, of course, bring a new ambition and vision for the company which could cause friction for the existing team.

The natural consequence was that Adam has had little honeymoon period. He needed to hit the ground running as both clients and employees sought to discover what the future of the Lindley Group would look like. The company was well placed with a £45 million turnover but there was still much work to be done.

'I think that taking on any leadership position has its own issues and baggage that one needs to manage. It is rarely straightforward. You just have to manage what is placed in front of you', remarked Adam. 'Nothing is ever easy in life and especially in an economy that has been less than stable. You just have to play what is in front of you and get on with it. There is just no point complaining about this or that.

It is what it is and people expect – quite rightly – that I would bring a new energy and vitality that would help them grow. They didn't want a new CEO to come in and say this is wrong and that is wrong. Pointless. We have to show a path ahead and help bring them along that path with us. That is what leaders have to do.

However, to place the picture into context, it is worth noting that Adam was not standing alone in one corner whilst everyone else was standing and watching. He was fortunate to be supported by an experienced Chairman in the form of Ian Daly – formerly a Director of SSP and presently also Executive Director of Ping Pong, USA – as well as three experienced Lindley Board Directors, Paul Heathcote (of Heathcote's fame), Paul Biffen and David Hulme. However, it is still no easy task and yet the opportunity is great, as the market does appear to be favourable towards independent operators that are able to show innovation and flair.

Lindley's great strength over the years has been founded on its expertise in serving high volumes within stadia environments. This is a very specialised skill set and is not an easy discipline to master, as time is so limited in which to capture as many customers as possible. It is one of those thought provoking statistics that 80% of retail sales in a stadium are made in the 15-minute period over half-time.

It is logical that if Lindley can excel in such a difficult environment that it would look to enter new markets, which also would provide substantial new growth opportunities as well as broadening the base of the business mix.

After the last 12 months, how does the Company stand today?

'We have a very good business,' noted Adam as we started to talk about the company he has inherited. Adam had been with Elior for six years and had developed to board level relatively quickly.

'Elior is a great business and I still have friends in the company. I will always think fondly of my time there but how could I turn down the opportunity to lead a company that does really have so much potential? Elior is an established player. Leading an independent is a very different proposition. It gives me a chance to be captain of my own ship and build on some very good foundations.'

Adam is a considered character who is very upfront in his approach. There appear to be no hidden angles with Adam – a man who can be taken at face value. As he talks, it is clear that he is excited by the challenge ahead.

'We have a strong business base. Our aim is to grow the company to the £100 million level. We are certainly bullish about the future. We have a good team and some excellent knowledge and experience but also we have the backing of Sovereign Capital that has been very supportive to this business. They bring another dimension to the board as they look at the market with fresh eyes and bring a different business. It is a great asset for us to have around.'

In difficult times, is increased growth practical?

'The market is very knowledgeable today. One does not just turn up and win new business. It has to be about substance, expertise and good working relationships. Over the past decade, the whole industry has raised the bar – service standards are better, food quality has improved beyond measure and pricing is very competitive. So for Lindley to be able to be successful we need to ensure that we have good people who understand the market and can move the whole agenda forward. We do have a great business that does generate profit but we too need to develop a mentality and culture that is constantly seeking to raise the bar and exceed our customer's expectations. One cannot underestimate how important the team factor is. One person cannot run a business like ours – it is a team effort. There needs to be a number of capable decision makers in all parts of the business. Good people are essential, as is knowledge.'

So, was it difficult to hit the ground running?

'Alex's death was terribly sad for everyone. He was Lindley and the company was left in shock. It has taken time for everyone to adjust which is natural but again the good news is that he left a very good business from which to grow. I think it is important to possess a positive psychology in any team and of course, this takes time to come back after such a shock. It has been a long 12 months for everyone but now we all need to all look forward and focus on what we can achieve. Of course it is very hard to take over as CEO with such a background but the other side of the story is that it also gives almost a blank canvass on which to plan ahead.'

So what are the plans for the future?

'We are experts in our area … in our discipline and we have real credibility. We can take our skills and move them into new markets. Why can't we enter new markets? We can certainly do the retail operations very well indeed.'

But surely it is asking a lot to enter a new market at this time?

'I accept that we have work to do to establish ourselves as potential players in this market. We are working in the background on this – both by bringing new expertise as well as looking at possible key strategic alliances that can really capture the imagination of clients and make them feel comfortable in the proposals that we send forward. I think that this could be a very exciting period for the company. At the same time, there are great synergies for the heritage market with what Heathcotes already deliver and to an extent, Green's St James [a restaurant owned by the business]. We already have the tools in our kit bag. We just need to communicate this to that market.'

Maybe the market has not known enough about the Lindley Group in the past?

'I am sure that this is true. It is up to us to get the message out. How many people know that we own Green's Events? Or about our association with Paul Heathcote? There is no doubt that we put forward a very strong case for consideration today but this will, over time, get better and stronger. We have a jewel that just needs polishing. I think some people haven't realised just how good it is and the judgement of how successful I am in the role will be based on how I can educate and tell the market about Lindley. If I can do this well, then we will win new business as we do have such a good story to tell. I accept that this will all take time. Change does not happen overnight. I really cannot complain. I have a fabulous opportunity. I suspect there are many CEOs who would like to have a similar opportunity – a company that has a good bedrock, makes profit, and has real clear market opportunities on which to focus. So yes, it may not be easy to take over in such circumstances but it could also be a far worse picture.'

The art and leadership of event management

The event industry is sometimes overlooked as an entity, but is a rapidly maturing sector of the hospitality industry. With this in mind, the skills and abilities required of leaders within the industry are changing as the operating environment becomes increasingly risky and complex. In the next few pages we explore the contrast between leaders of earlier generations with leaders of today, and the issues around building a qualification in the event management discipline.

A golden generation or natural evolution?[1]

Hospitality service at sporting arenas, large events and social parties has improved immeasurably over the last 20 years. Some believe this has been led by a generation of exceptional operators such as Johnny Roxburgh, Frank McCartney, Richard Tear and Chris Robinson. Some believe it has been natural evolution. What is the truth?

In bygone days, people would go to a major event and not possess too many high expectations of the hospitality. It was expected to be good but the event was the main attraction. Today, this has changed. The food and catering provision is almost as important as the event itself and expectations have risen accordingly. It has been a gradual evolution. This progression has happened across nearly all sectors – not only confined to the event catering market. The individuals who emerged during the 1980s seem to have led an era of quite dramatic improvements in hospitality provision. The underlying question is why? Or has it just been a coincidence? Undoubtedly the people involved have been larger-than-life characters. They have played hard and enjoyed themselves along the way. They really have lived and breathed the industry and inspired many others. But was this just the way it was? Is it different today? What do their successors believe to be the legacy of this generation?

---

1   First published, *EP Magazine*, August 2008

It would not be an exaggeration to say that these leaders have helped the industry to become world class in its own right. Hype? There are few to match Johnny Roxburgh and Rolline Frewin at Admirable Crichton; or what Frank McCartney has achieved at Wimbledon; or Richard Tear during his career with J. Lyons and Searcy's. Simon Dobson has opened Wembley to increasing acclaim. Just consider the cast list of other names that sit or have sat on this stage: Alan Payne, Martin Joyce, Bob Reeves, Chris Proserpi, Charles Boyd, Chris Robinson, Steve McManus, Sean Valentine, Nick Moorhouse, Russell Morgan, Alex McCrindle, David Cheeseman, Adrian and Ian Willson, Alan Duff, Glyn Woodin and Damian Clarkson. Quite a list, and not complete. To try and answer the questions posed, EP spoke to a number of the people mentioned above. There are such contrasting viewpoints and they raise some interesting questions.

Chris Robinson, Chairman, Heritage Portfolio

'In the late 70s and early 80s we were probably the generation that pioneered the development of corporate hospitality into sporting venues and outside catering. The market evolved from working in small venues, often providing buffets, into special venues and special event catering of a high calibre. We also pioneered fixed contracts and persuaded venues to work with caterers exclusively. I think we created our own set of rules and had to figure out ways of feeding 1000–2000 people in outside space or unusual venues. You had to be very resourceful; for example we snapped up six ovens from a Glasgow school, as they were ideal for what we needed, but no one else had a clue what they could be used for! We had some fantastic adventures where you may have had a greenfield site requiring quite sophisticated facilities for six months and then you knock it down. These were fun and exciting times. I think it is different today as corporate hospitality at big venues is seen as much more sophisticated and is more high risk. The supply chain has evolved, and the infrastructure that is available can often be better quality than a top hotel. I stand back in awe at the successors, the next generation, as they have taken it to a whole new level. They are transforming the service into a 'wow' factor which we could never have achieved.'

Richard Tear, Chairman, Searcy's

'What was different was that things were a great deal simpler. In my early days during the 60s you were mostly focused on getting the food on a plate and served. I think it was fairly straightforward; the menus were longer but the dishes were much more simply cooked, so it was fairly easy to deliver. We were more regimented; everyone knew their role and got on with it. It wasn't until the 70s and early 80s where the expectations went up. We were able to 'deliver well in a field' and provide restaurant quality food; this was a major change. Some of those that I looked up to were Alan Payne and Richard Byford, both of whom no longer work in the industry, but they were the 'over the top together' variety.

'Today it is becoming more complex. People are expecting a holistic experience including entertainment: where people once wanted a small orchestra, they now expect Madonna. This has been a quantum leap. Whereas our generation felt we were at the frontier, young people today are more likely to look at their watch and wonder why they are not in bed by midnight. For us there was a sense of comradeship. You forgot the bad times of having no plates an hour before lunch at Highgrove, that didn't matter. You only remembered the good times. We also understood that you were only part of a team. We bonded better, there was a sense that you fought as a team. Those bonds last forever.'

Bob Reeves, Director, Compass Leisure

'I am not sure that it was a golden generation, but what success we had was probably underpinned by the foundation of our catering education. I think it was stronger and more work-based rather than academic. You had the likes of Allied Lyons and Forte, both of who were very committed to training. There was much more involvement at the sharp end. Over the past 30 years catering has become an industry in itself and its growth has been quite spectacular. Opportunities for our successors are still there and the application of the individual is very important. The approach is becoming more sophisticated.'

Chris Proserpi, consultant to the leisure and event industry

'I learnt from some great managers – great team leaders – Richard Tear gave me my first break and I worked for Peter Byford, who was old school, Joe Lyons who taught me how to act with a professional pride and integrity – he also taught me proper standards including how to lay a table cloth properly!! There wasn't the close budgetary accountability that there is now, it is more commercially driven. We learnt, and were influenced by, the old school of management who taught standards, principles and behaviour. This has influenced all of us – and we are rather an old-fashioned kind of manager. It is neither good nor bad, just a different style, which I think, was influenced by the 60s.We had a love for food, everyone was very driven by food standards and by precise standards for which there was no compromise. A lot of people at university were seconded to work on events at one point and they either loved it or hated it. It actually acted as a kind of benchmark for entry into the catering world – once you worked at Chelsea Flower Show from 6:00am–11:00pm… you just knew. It seems to enthuse them for a life in the catering industry – or kills them off!'

Simon Dobson, Managing Director, DNC (UK) Ltd

'I think the legacy of the previous generation is that they raised the expectations at events by doing a terrific job through good relationship management and positioning catering as a partner to events. They were not just people who nodded their cap and then went in through the back door. Catering is now such an important part of the profile and income of these events. The position of the catering leadership now means that there is most often a seat at the table for the caterer and this gives opportunities to influence outcomes for the whole event, adding significant value to all the stakeholders. We have the leaders included in this list to thank for that.'

David Cheeseman, Managing Director, Graysons Hospitality

'I had the privilege of working with Frank McCartney until last year. I think that what sets him apart is his absolute focus on quality in a setting which is traditionally price driven. He understands the power of service. If you cook great food and then throw it at people, they will never come back, but great food beautifully served brings people back time after time. His starting point is always 'what does the customer want to eat?' He then purchases the best ingredients, rather than sourcing 20,000 lamb shanks because they would deliver a great margin, and then serving it at every single event of the summer season. Fundamentally, these people understand that this is a people business. Lots of people say this and most of them spend their lives behaving in a way that illustrates that they don't actually believe it to be true. These leaders are sensitive to people's needs at both client level and with all of their teams.'

Sean Valentine, Managing Director, Aspire

'I worked with Bob Reeves when I was Sales Director at Ascot so he is a particular person that stands out for me. He has spent 35 years in the industry working events at major racecourses and has done so consistently well. Bob's ability to motivate and lead the team, against some pretty heavy odds, is to be commended. Richard Tear is someone who has headed up a niche operation at Searcy's, competing with the larger players. He too has consistently grown and headed up the business, most recently getting it ready for sale to AHG. I think that the ability to be consistent in this particular market is what makes you stand out. They have walked the talk and led by example, over many years which I believe makes successful leaders.'

(June 2009)

Does the industry want or need an event management qualification?

The job title 'Event Manager' is the hardest to quantify when assessing a candidate's specific skill set. Do they manage, co-ordinate or sell? The differences can be vast, with the best event managers possessing a combination in their 'locker'. Some event managers however, only seem able to co-ordinate, and don't have the necessary experience to fulfil a number of roles. However, in this market, it is apparent that there has been a cut in events and a lack of corporate activity. Competition for event managers has been raised and the need to stand out has become critical, with unique skills providing particular value.

The challenge is that there is no specific route into events, and talent can be difficult to recognise. Following debate with various parties, it has been decided that there is a market to create a specific event management course, focusing on a practical route to qualification. Since events cover such a vast section within our industry, this qualification may have the potential for candidates to branch down different avenues. EP posed this argument to a number of the industry's leading figures.

Alex McCrindle, Chief Executive, Lindley Catering

'The industry has grown over the years and there has been an ensuing growth in the event manager role. To be honest, it does not matter whether you are organising an event for 10,000 or 20 people, there are certain skills required: organisational skills, sales and marketing and financial skills, for example. Given that there are a lot of event managers, some of whom already possess a strong operational background and effectively learn to add in management skills as they make the transition into the role, I think it is an excellent idea to create a qualification. The European Venue Management Institute has been focused on doing something like this for people working in stadium management, which looks at health and safety, financial knowledge, marketing and strategic planning. It is important to highlight that it can be easy to underestimate how many people are involved in the organisation of one single event. There is real accountability, as event managers are entrusted to ensure the health and safety of people in a whole variety of settings. If a qualification was available it would be a good way to help to develop and identify talent by having a benchmark for what are fairly critical roles.'

Philippe Rossiter, Chief Executive, Institute of Hospitality

'The events industry has certainly changed over the past 10 years and therefore we need to adapt. Running an event in a hotel has a certain structure in that most of the skills are transferable from a staffing point of view, where it seems more of a day-to-day activity. Event management really comes into its own when it is off-site or at a venue and there is a vast amount of logistic skills to take into consideration. It's a much more complex activity.

The demand for successful events has certainly risen and there is, therefore, a market for a more specialised qualification from more of a practical angle. A great example of this is in the leisure gaming industry. This has become a mainstream activity where in the past it was expected that potential croupiers could learn basic training on the job. Now there are professional levels of qualifications in place and it is seen as a skilled sector for many individuals. This is the same with events; we need to provide a pathway for people who have taken an interest in this subject to develop and become the best event managers.'

Damian Clarkson, Managing Director, Red Snapper Events

'I think a specialised event management qualification would benefit young people looking for a structured entry into the industry. However, you can never underestimate the importance and benefit of first-hand experience; any official qualification should definitely involve a placement period so that students can see exactly how the industry works. Every year we employ at least one student on a placement basis; they always exceed expectations in their knowledge and passion for events.'

Richard Tear, Chairman, Searcy's

'In 1967, when I was the most junior manager for Lyons at a garden party, I realised that there was a complete world of catering in event organisation. Thirty years of event and outdoor catering with Town and County and Searcy's with luminaries like Freddie Meynell have convinced me that the industry is not only more complex but far more demanding than it was when I started. Anyone who thinks that delivering food is enough is sadly mistaken. When I started booking, the Joe Loss Band was enough, now Madonna is an expectation and all that goes with it. Single marquees have given way to multi-storey tented structures, numbers have increased from hundreds to tens of thousands, three-course menus in a field have improved to Michelin-star banquets. No catering occasion is more complex or more difficult.

We must have specific training and specific qualifications for this the most demanding part of our industry.'

Nick Gratwick, Senior Operations Manager, Keith Prowse

'At the end of the day, university qualifications just aren't working. Lecture rooms and dissertations are too different from the actualities of running an event. While we often employ applicants with university degrees, we are also looking for experience and 'can do' competency. We have had many people with unrivalled qualifications apply for roles within Keith Prowse but in some cases the applicants have lacked the personality and flair expected of the service industry. In many cases they have graduated as business managers competent at costing and return on investment, but they may be devoid of the personality expected from our sector. Conversely, we have had students with degrees in event management who have been trained as highly-skilled service staff but they have very little idea of the greater picture. From my point of view this is due to the scope of the term 'event' being too wide; it can range from a venue-finding agency to a production company, from a caterer to organisations like ourselves. This is reflected in the events management degrees where there is little commonality and standardisation of skills and learning. I certainly believe that some kind of 'on the job' certification would give everyone in the events sector both confidence in who they are employing and the peace of mind that potential employees will possess the willingness to work hard.'

June 2009

Leisure

Neil Goulden
Former Chairman, Gala Coral

Neil possesses a combination of humanity and experience that makes him an inspirational leader in the hospitality and leisure industry. He likes to lead from the front and remains hands on, although his most recent role in the largest privately-owned company in the UK, Gala Coral, has necessarily meant that Neil's style of leadership has adapted to become more of a coach and mentor to his broader management team. Opportunities and challenge in the gaming industry are in equal measure and Neil has a clear vision for how his business can succeed. This article represents only a fraction of a live event during which Neil discussed his career; he made a comment during the event that he likes nothing more than walking around a casino at 3 a.m. – which was poignant and insightful as to his vision and dedication.

'It's vital with gambling you act responsibly...'

A summary of EP's Interactive Discussion event with Neil Goulden, Gala Coral Group, hosted on 25 April 2007

Neil Goulden is one of the most experienced and well respected figures within the leisure industry. He has been Chief Executive of the Gala Coral Group since 2004 (becoming Chairman in 2009). Employing in excess of 17,000 people, Gala Coral operates 144 bingo clubs, 27 casino venues and nearly 1600 licensed betting offices. In June 2006 the company was ranked as number one on the *Sunday Times* Top Track 100 companies, recognising it as then the largest private company in Britain. Neil was also Chairman of Business in Sport and Leisure – a group which represents sports and leisure industry interests to government for over 100 private sector companies, and he is also Chairman of the South Central Ambulance Service and a member of the Low Pay Commission.

On Wednesday, 25 April 2007, *En Passant* hosted an Interactive Discussion with Neil, where he offered some fascinating insight, particularly into the current picture within the gaming market. Some of the key points are highlighted below:

'The government is currently trying to sell the Tote (Britain's state owned bookmaker) and was originally intending to sell it back to the racing industry via a consortium for the sum of £120 million. However, the European Union blocked the sale on the grounds it was significantly undervalued and thus state aid. A consortium of bidders have subsequently tabled a bid of £400 million, and this too has apparently been blocked by the Chancellor due to the presence of Lloyds TSB private equity arm because he does not believe the consortium is truly representative of racing. Gala Coral will be a bidder if the Tote is put up for auction.

'Having already faced the implications of the smoking ban in Scotland, it has been interesting to observe the impact in bingo halls. We prepared and researched the potential implications of the ban very thoroughly and believed that we would see a real and immediate impact in the loss of sales during intervals. This was a key issue for us, as the intervals in bingo halls are only half an hour in length but generate 60% of our revenue, so we ensured we had plans in place to reverse this trend. These ensured that there was a fairly limited impact initially. However, the real change occurred once winter settled in when people could not face going outside in the rain and cold for a cigarette, so the admission numbers really dramatically reduced from this point.'

'The government has implemented changes to taxation on betting, removing the taxation on winnings, and instead taxing profit generated by the company. This has resulted in a real win–win situation for both government and punters – the government gets a source of income and the punters receive their entire winnings. I believe that there is a similar win–win situation to be achieved for bingo, provided that it is administered correctly.'

'I am looking to establish a leadership group within Gala – normally the MD or CEO is like the centre of a wheel with spokes where all information comes into and out of, whereas my vision to develop a group of 110 people who all sit around the rim of a wheel and communicate rather than information having to always pass through me.'

'It's vital that with gaming you act responsibly; like the serving of alcohol, it's OK as long as you sell it in a responsible manner. I believe that the industry could do more to work with associations like Gamcare who work to support people with gambling problems. Gala Coral actively supports Gamcare and has been recognised by the association for our policies aimed at ensuring that we act in a socially responsible manner. I have found it difficult to get other gaming organisations to support this initiative – and the point is that we need to.'

(June 2007)

Uri Danor
CEO, El Al UK and Ireland

As CEO of El Al in the UK and Ireland, Uri can be described as a breath of fresh air in the travel market. He is not afraid to confront difficult issues head on and his enthusiasm is infectious. A young, dynamic leader, Uri's vision for the airline industry's business model is extremely interesting, as is his views on tourism in Israel. It is these kinds of individual characters that make exciting leaders in the hospitality industry as they seek to challenge tried and tested systems, and play the hand they are dealt in a matter-of-fact manner.

'Our business model has to change for a new age'

Uri Danor, CEO for El Al UK and Ireland, discusses the challenges of managing an airline in today's climate and also to discover why Israel is becoming an increasingly popular destination for business and tourism. In a very candid and open interview, a number of thought-provoking points emerged.

It was clear from our opening exchanges that this was an interview that was going to be different to most – there was no need for clever probing as Uri's style is one centred on straightforward dialogue. He is from the school of 'what you see is what you get' – a very approachable man who clearly enjoys discussing and debating ideas. As we sat down together, I asked whether business was going well.

'The words 'going well' for an airline is an impossible phrase,' he noted with a smile. 'For the last 20 years, the industry has struggled to make any real profit. Last year (2009) was awful. This year is much better – totally different.'

Why?

'I have a theory. A good year that follows a bad year is normally very good indeed. It is logical; in the bad year you take all the measures necessary in order to ensure that you remain competitive. So when the next year improves, it is natural that it is very good as you are not carrying any fat, plus the morale within the team improves as they see the tide turn. It builds a momentum.

'2010 has seen this for El Al with a 30% increase in revenue locally (UK and Ireland). globally, income is up around 15–20%.'

So why are the UK and Ireland figures better than the overall global figures?

'A number of factors. Firstly, last year was very bad indeed for the UK and this year has seen some recovery. Secondly, Israel didn't suffer from the economic crisis in the same way. When the financial crisis occurred it didn't hit the Israeli economy to the same extent that it did the major Western economies. Last year was good for the Israeli economy. Therefore it's hardly surprising that UK businesses would look for ways to build trade with an economy that was performing well.

'Thirdly, Israel has seen an increase in tourism from all over the world. Perceptions are changing and Israel is an attractive destination.'

So, I wondered, does Uri believe that El Al is a competitive unit after the troubles of 2009?

'Yes, of course. We still have areas where we can improve, but I believe we have an advantage in the UK market for a range of reasons that include our own efforts as well as the approach of our competitors. For example, we have improved service levels. We traditionally operated out of Heathrow but we have opened flights from Luton, which we have found to work well for business travellers. Although based North of London, it is easily accessible from the motorways and, I have to say, Luton Airport have worked very hard with us to ensure that the overall service is excellent. The result is that we have won back lost passengers as service levels and speed of access have improved. We have also attracted small and medium enterprises (SMEs) by creating an incentive package for them.

'We have been helped by our competition too. In principle, I like competition but in this instance we have been helped by British Midland's decision to step out of the market and British Airways too has suffered from threats and union problems.'

However, I was still intrigued by Uri's opening comment that it is nigh on impossible to make money from running an airline. If this has been a problem for the last 20 years, surely the model needs to change? Uri smiled.

'Absolutely and we are working on this. Making money from tickets alone is impossible but a ticket is just one ingredient in a passenger's holiday.

'We need to turn El Al into a one-stop shop so that you can buy your whole holiday with us. By offering the whole package, we can generate margin and profits. There is no reason why El Al can't become the number one player for the Israeli market. My role is to turn El Al locally into a tourism company.'

This is logical, but I noted it would require a radical change in mindset.

'Sure. It does take time but we can't stay as we are. It is a two-year process of change but we have already started the process. We have a subsidiary company – Superstar Holidays – which has operated for 25 years as a holiday agent.

'The challenge for us is that we need to change our philosophy and approach towards the customer and become more user friendly. Just as we need to educate the market that we offer far more than just flight tickets, we need to develop our internal processes and change our mindsets to be more customer focused than we have traditionally been. We need to attract customers to come directly to our website rather than via an agent.'

Surely this was already happening?

'It is beginning to change but you would be surprised – there are still many who like to use agents. It will take time. The real change will come as we develop our own product range – city breaks, wine tours, classical tours, cycling holidays, etc. There is a large potential market but historically people have been put off. We need to educate the market and make it more knowledgeable. And this is happening far quicker than most realise.'

I noted that I assumed many were still put off by the image of troubles in the Middle East.

'Yes, but this too is changing. Did you know that Tel Aviv is so popular that every hotel room is booked throughout the peak season? We now need to develop new 'seasons' in November and December. As Tel Aviv is becoming a more fashionable destination, we launched a £7 flight between Tel Aviv and Eilat in August. It was very well received, with every flight full.

'The image of Israel is changing. People are not as concerned about the troubles as terrorism is now global and can just as easily happen in New York, London or Paris.

'We are seeing a dramatic upward trend in tourism. We have only started to build our tourism packages but word of mouth is spreading and has helped to develop the trade. Also Tel Aviv is now a very popular destination for the 'Pink Pound'. The age demographics work well, the classical tours attract the over-45s. The city breaks are proving popular with the young generation.

'So the potential exists. We have to now work on developing it so that we move our business model forward, to be increasingly competitive for the future.'

As I departed, I was left wondering how the landscape would change for all airlines. It has been clear for some time that the traditional models would have to change, but how far and in which direction is still going to be interesting to observe. El Al is clearly comfortable in the direction in which they are heading, but much of this will also depend on how Israel develops, both as a business and a tourist destination.

(January 2011)

Industry Association

Anne Pierce MBE
CEO of Springboard

Anne occupies a unique brief in the world of hospitality leadership. As head of one of the UK's most high profile charities, she has had to build her business from scratch and in doing so faced a great deal of adversity. Anne has proven herself to be resilient and strong leader in such circumstances, and she has garnered a great deal of warmth and compassion as a result. This drives many to support her efforts at Springboard, they buy into her both as a person and as a leader. Whilst there are some who will continue to question Springboard's purpose and achievements, Anne has maintained her commitment and dedication which sets an example for her team and supporters.

Has Springboard created a lasting legacy?

Chris Sheppardson met with Anne Pierce, CEO of Springboard

There have been endless discussions about the need for industry bodies to come together and merge. Springboard has been central to this debate. For the past decade, it has been one of the industry's leading charities. It has many admirers, and its critics. Some believe that their work has made a real difference; others question this and wonder if it is involved in too much and spread too thinly. It is also asked whether the industry is perceived any differently today than it was 12 years ago. Has Springboard created a lasting legacy?

In the past 12 years, much has been invested in supporting Springboard's work. It was always going to be a tough assignment, as back in the mid-1990s the industry faced a severe skills shortage with little strategy and wanted an organisation to provide the solution.

Anne took over the reins at Springboard in November 1997 and has led them ever since – receiving great praise and an MBE for her services to industry. She has also had critics, who have questioned whether Springboard has made the necessary progress, improved the perception of the industry and built a legacy that will last.

So where does the truth lie and where do Anne's own thoughts stand on some of the key issues?

I said that some question whether the industry needs so many industry bodies and asked here whether it would be better if some came together?

'This is a question that has come up time and time again and there are arguments for doing so. However, in my experience, when organisations have merged, new ones are soon created to fill a gap in the market. Yes, some rationalisation may be good but the nature of the hospitality industry is very fragmented. I've worked in the sector for 25 years, and there are different agendas involved, which I do not believe would be served effectively by one single body. Whilst it would be ideal to have one over arching body, this is not realistic as I believe the main bodies all have different roles to play. As far as Springboard is concerned we are unique – no other organisation does what we do promoting the industry day-in, day-out and improving perceptions. At the end of the day, industry bodies, like companies, are subject to economic laws – the market is the ultimate judge. Industry associations that provide the most value will be the ones that survive because they will attract funding. Springboard will continue as long as our supporters and partners continue to see value.

There are those that question whether the industry is truly perceived in any better light than it was back in the nineties and whether money invested in the past decade has made any real impact.

'I believe perceptions of the industry have improved – especially with young people. The world has changed so much since 1997. Springboard's progress was perhaps slower in the early years because we did not have the benefit of the Internet! However, our Perceptions Research year on year has shown that young people's views of our industry have improved. The attitude of young people is far more open and positive towards the industry today than it was when we first launched Springboard. The numbers seeking advice and guidance and participating in our programmes have increased considerably. Springboard is a small charity, so we have limited resources. It is said that we punch above our weight, which is probably true as people think we are bigger than we are. In reality our work is not about waving a magic wand. There are long-standing, deep-seated cultural issues related to service in the UK that will not disappear overnight. In my view it will take a couple of generations to change and, of course, we do not operate in a vacuum – events like the recession and 9/11 have an impact. Our job is to climb a mountain and we are probably 50% of the way up. There is still much to do but we have made good progress.

Certain critics argue that Springboard has been involved in too many things in the past.

'Looking back in retrospect, yes, I think that in the past we have been drawn into too many projects. But one has to remember that we were new and learning the ropes. We were not sure what would work and so we tried different things with mixed results, and there are some things that we would not do again. Our current business plan is focused on a number of things: ensuring that young people understand pathways into hospitality careers or a job by providing career information, and working with schools to provide educational resources that are focused on the industry. A major focus is improving the quality and facilitating work experience and work tasters, which are proven to be the most influential factors in making career choices. Ultimately, Springboard is part of a relay. Once we get people through the door, it is then over to industry to retain them – we 'get them in', then we pass the baton on.

From your perspective, what is the scale of the challenge ahead?

'Right now many companies are focused on survival, so investing in attracting talent for the future may not be top of the agenda. Yet, if we do so now, we will be ready when the upswing comes. But the biggest challenge here is with government funding. I suppose whoever wins the election, there will still be a real emphasis on reducing unemployment. The main change will be that rules governing funding allocation will be tightened, so we will be under more scrutiny in terms of what is delivered, and money will be harder to get. From Springboard's perspective, we have come quite a long way but we still have a way to go. Our challenge is to galvanise significant industry players and focus on the key sectors that need it. It's important to ensure that we 'influence the influencers', and they are not always easily identifiable or in one place; parents and teachers are not easy to reach. We also need a sustainable campaign for job centre staff, but this has been a group with high labour turnover, now facing public-sector cuts.

Where have the real successes been?

'Our Ambassadors programme has been a genuine achievement. It's a volunteer-based concept where people working in the industry attend a variety of external groups and promote the industry. They are doing this with the endorsement of their employers, so it's a really positive way of promoting an employer brand and the industry at the same time. To me, they work in the same way as football clubs' talent-scouting systems who have teams of scouts looking for talent. This programme is similar. Of course, FutureChef is a major success nationwide, helping more than 7000 12–16-year-olds learn how to cook, and to learn about careers first-hand – we are now seeing this as an important pipeline of talent into the industry.

Moving Springboard into a position where it is nationally recognised as an organisation. We are positioned very well in certain parts of the industry, including within schools. We reach more than a million people a year, facilitate 20,000 tasters and introduce thousands of people into careers or jobs each year.

What are your aspirations and hopes for Springboard?

'As I said earlier, I think we are half the way there. We have completed phase one. My vision for phase two is that we will continue to improve perceptions of the industry, attract more indigenous talent but put more focus into the areas that are needed. We want to positively impact on people's lives and get our industry to be able to change people's lives. Sometimes this job can be tough and stressful. There will be times when you wonder whether it is worth it, but at those moments I just think about those people where we have changed their lives or made a real difference, and that inspires me. Our job now is to inspire more and more people, and that is a great cause. So what were our thoughts as we finished? Springboard has built the foundation stones to create change, but there is no lasting legacy as yet. That will need to come from industry, and the question left hanging in our minds afterwards was whether industry is really expecting this one organisation to complete the task it has started. One organisation can only achieve so much and it does need others working alongside if a real legacy is going to be created.

(April 2010)

Political

Viscount Thurso

MP for Caithness, Sutherland and Easter Ross

John Sinclair, the third Viscount Thurso, is an entrepreneur turned leader and politician. The story of a hotelier who became both a Lord and an MP is unique. Viscount Thurso has strong views on leadership, namely the necessity for a clear vision and strong communication. This is perhaps what makes his political career stand out, as he possesses a real-world perspective and thus understands how his political influence can make a real difference. In addition, Viscount Thurso remains actively involved in the hospitality industry, and his experience prior to entering politics includes some of the most well-regarded hospitality organisations.

A man apart

With a career spanning over 35 years, Viscount Thurso's roles have included hotel operator, business leader and politician. Born into a politically active family, educated at Eton and trained with the Savoy Company, he has always been destined for leadership roles. Past positions include: MD of Champneys, the opening General Manager of Cliveden, Managing Director of the Lancaster Hotel in Paris, and Patron of the HCIMA amongst others. Yet, what has made him stand out is his sense of duty and genuine desire to make a difference to individual lives. The MP for Caithness, Sutherland and Easter Ross talks about his career and philosophy.

I first interviewed Viscount Thurso 20 years ago whilst researching a book on hotels. He was then the General Manager of the recently-opened Cliveden. I can still recall our meeting vividly, sitting in the library of the hotel. He was immaculately presented as one would expect. It was his thinking and language which created the lasting memory, as it was so markedly different to others that I had spoken to during my research. I had interviewed many senior industry players and they talked of the importance of people, but no one, other than John Sinclair as he was then known, spoke about the importance of building self-esteem within individuals. He put forward his 'theory of the equality of respect'. This revolved around a belief that people should be judged not by their status but by the quality of their work. John talked with enthusiasm on the subjects of leadership, business and a desire to see people prosper.

A lot has happened during the following 20 years. John Sinclair has developed from overseeing hotels to leading businesses in their own right and entered the House of Lords as Lord Thurso. In 1999 he left the House of Lords following the House of Lords Act, and became an MP. Meeting him again, I asked whether he believed progress has been made in how hospitality employees are perceived?

> 'Yes and no. Chefs are certainly recognised now and have become part of the aristocracy. But waiters and other service staff need and deserve greater recognition.'

It may have been 20 years since our last meeting and, although he is older, much is still the same. The focus has changed from leading a top hotel to the challenges of his constituency, but the desire to make a difference is still evident – especially when we discuss his remit in the north of Scotland.

'The planned closure of the Dounreay nuclear plant in Caithness has presented the community with a major issue as it employs 2000 people and played a huge part of the local economy over the past 50 years. The closure is over ten years away, so we have time to turn the situation around from one of gloom, to one of belief. I do not want to sound boastful but the community needed leadership and I believe that I have been able to make a difference with helping in the development of the Caithness Regeneration Programme. There is now hope in our future, and rightly so, because it is a fantastic place to live.'

I noted that it has seemed, from afar, that he had been born to leadership roles, but wondered whether this was as natural as it appeared?

'I remember an incident when I was about 11 years old. My father was away and I was left on the estate. One of the vehicles had got stuck on a riverbank and I felt as though it was my responsibility to take charge of organising a tractor and the guys to get the vehicle unstuck.

'What made me assume I should take charge? Partly, it was due to the ethos of the family. We have always sought to do well for the community – to lead and serve. As a family, we have a deep sense of duty.'

Viscount Thurso was the eldest son of the 2nd Viscount Thurso and the grandson of the 1st Viscount Thurso, better known as Sir Archibald Sinclair, the wartime Liberal leader and Secretary of State for Air.

'It has gone out of fashion to say that people are born to lead but I think that some people do have natural leadership tendencies. I have thought long and hard about leadership and I believe that anybody can lead. You can train people to lead.'

'To manage or lead?' I interjected.

'To lead. A leader needs to understand management but does not need to be the best manager. I believe that every leader needs to have three attributes. Firstly, a clear vision. It does not need to be their vision, it could be a collective vision – but it does need to be clear.

Secondly, and this is the absolutely critical skill, communication. A leader needs to be able to communicate effectively to colleagues, to employees and to stakeholders. And finally, a leader needs to ensure that the resources are in place. There is no point having a good vision without the resources to make it happen.

'I think that Caithness is a good example where we have created a vision that has been collectively agreed. We have worked hard to get buy-in and we made sure that we have communicated this vision to every household.

'Another example was from my time as Managing Director of Champneys. I recruited a team of top talents and built a strap line – 'Nowhere else makes you feel this good' – which worked as a communications tool for our employees, customers and stakeholders. All have different needs and the strap line gave each their own message. Investing in Champneys makes you feel good, working for Champneys makes you feel good and so on.'

Was leadership in politics different? Had it proven to be frustrating? Viscount Thurso smiled as he considered the question.

'Leadership in politics is different whether you are in government or in opposition. Look at Blair. He was excellent as an opposition leader and I can still recall the optimism we all felt back in 1997. It was a time of genuine belief that change could happen. This belief had been lost by 2002. It was a lost opportunity.'

Has it been frustrating?

'No. It is just different. I have been lucky in that I had a real life before politics. Politics is a slightly strange environment as many people have become MPs from being researchers and then assistants. They are career politicians. I have come from a different world.

'But it is rewarding, as I can get involved in some very real and live issues. I sit on the Treasury Select Committee, which meets every week and, in this climate, is very important. I have come to know Alastair Darling well and we have built a relationship of respect which means we can have a real discussion.'

Had he always been interested in politics?

'Yes, I think so. To what extent are we products of our background? My family have always been active in the Liberal Party and we spent many hours around the dinner table talking about the issues of the day.

'I also grew up in a fascinating period with JFK, Martin Luther King and the 60s. When I was a student at Eton, I remember trying to read *Das Kapital* but falling asleep. The late 60s was a period of student activism in a way that was very different to today. It was a time of belief in change. There was a mood of everything being new.

'At Eton, we wrote a pamphlet called 'Other people, other places' which profiled people from all kinds of backgrounds. The message was that there were other people out there that were different to us at Eton.'

Why enter the hotel sector?

'I didn't wake up and want to be a hotel manager. When I left school, I knew all the things I did not want to be. I didn't want to go into the military. I was fed up with education and didn't want to go to university. The City looked too traditional. I had spent summers working in hotels and applied for the Reeves-Smith Scholarship with The Savoy Company. Olive Barnett interviewed me and although I wasn't granted the scholarship, I came second and was offered an opportunity. Within a year, the bug had bitten me.

'My career just went from there and I have been very lucky – Claridges, the Lancaster in Paris, Cliveden, Champneys and more. It has been a fabulous time and I hope and believe that I have made a difference to those that I have led and worked with.'

(August 2008)

Historical Venue

Edward Griffiths

Deputy Master of the Royal Household, Buckingham Palace

One of the key traits that becomes clear is that leadership comes in many different styles and approaches. Good leadership is not just about moving an organisation forward but also how people and cultures are evolved. Leadership is about people and how they respond and react and given this, leadership does not need to be just about being the captain of a ship or senior player in a team but also about those who can bring real influence and change from within. It is a more subtle form of leadership but still very important. It often takes a very well developed skill to be able to visualise and implement change through persuasion.

One very good illustration of this lies within the Royal Household and the role played by Edward Griffiths since his appointment as Deputy Master of the Household in 2001. The Royal Household is, as one can imagine, an environment full of history and tradition. Change always generates resistance and friction, and yet there has been much change which has been thoroughly embraced by the teams within. It takes skill to modernise a traditional culture. The real success story though lies in the way that the whole team has embraced change and the clear enjoyment and belief that is evident at all levels.

Most people will have a perception of the Royal Household based on little first-hand information. It is certainly operating in an historic venue and this perception will be correct. What is likely to be wrong is the perception of those that work within, for the atmosphere is in fact forward-focused, warm and friendly. There is no little pressure placed upon those working within such an environment, as for almost every guest to Buckingham Palace, their visit will be one of the most important days in their lives. The teams are very aware of this factor and respond accordingly.

Of course, it takes experience to ensure that there is a sound balance and perspective in place as it does not take much imagination to see that things could go wrong and undoubtedly they do but Edward does provide a vast amount of knowledge and experience to provide guidance and leadership.

Edward had previously been the Managing Director of Roux Restaurants and Roux Fine Dining. As a character, Edward has always been very calm and thoughtful. He will often listen and observe before making comment – probably exactly the right skills to be able to bring change to such an environment as the Palace.

'I was brought into a newly created role as one of two Deputy Masters of the Household in order to bring together the three previously independent departments of food, service and housekeeping, which had all previously reported as separate departments,' noted Edward. 'The brief was to bring cohesion to the departments and to drive an evolution of change drawing on my previous experience in business. It is a common misconception that the Palace is old-fashioned, and yet when I came on board I was pleasantly surprised by the professional, forward-thinking organisation that I had joined. However, we needed to introduce further change and evolve continuously; this is not about changing five things then the job is done.'

'We started by bringing the departments together and focusing on cross-training and improving the skills of the team across all aspects of our work. I can most liken my position to that of a hotel managing director; we have most of the same departments across hospitality and domestic services but with a few key differences. Firstly, we have to be portable as we are predominantly based at Buckingham Palace but must move with The Queen to the other Royal residences as required. This is both interesting and exciting for the team, but it also presents certain challenges.

'Secondly, we are guardians of heritage buildings, traditions and priceless items. Our teams require certain skills and training that would never be necessary in a hotel environment. Our housekeeping staff and Palace attendants are responsible for the cleaning, upkeep and movement of antique furniture and incredibly delicate objects and must be specially trained in the treatment and conservation of these items. In a way this aspect is more like running a museum or art gallery than a hotel. Our footmen are handling china, glass, silver and gilt that are both very valuable and often old and delicate. We have no budget line in our P&L for breakage, it simply cannot happen! Can you imagine that in a hotel?

'And finally, we do not work in a hotel or a business, but in a private home, albeit one with both public and private spaces. This is where The Queen lives and our teams from the chefs to the housekeeping staff cater for everything in the Palace, from private 'family' dinners to state dinners and garden parties, always with a respect for the fact that this is The Queen's home.'

So what has changed in the nine years since Edward took the helm?

'One of the main areas for change has been the cross-training of our workforce. Previously there was a lot more hierarchy in the departments, for example there were footmen who would serve at dinners and receptions and under butlers who set up, laying tables and preparing the event.

'We have altered this; all footmen work across an event from beginning to end. We have also ensured that our footmen and our housekeeping staff are cross-trained. We used to rely a lot on a casual labour pool for larger events but this can be problematic both from a financial perspective and also from a security point of view. Our housekeeping team are now all trained in the food and beverage side of our work and will serve and be involved in larger front-of-house events, similarly, all footmen train in housekeeping.

'This has all been supported by the development of the new Butler's Diploma written by Nigel McEvoy, the Palace Steward, in conjunction with the Savoy Educational Trust, City and Guilds and Thames Valley University. Just like any organisation, we have had to adapt, modernise and become more efficient. Since the civil list funding was fixed ten years ago and The Queen's programme has become busier and busier we are effectively doing three times more 'business' than we were ten years ago on a decreasing budget. It is vital to drive efficiencies so that we can maintain and improve the standard and quality of the environment and service.

'Some of this efficiency is through the cross-skilling initiatives led by Stephen Gourmand, the Assistant Master responsible for service and housekeeping. However, we also make use of an in-house craft team based in Windsor to enable us to maintain and improve the fabric of the Palaces without incurring the costs associated with outsourcing. We have to prioritise and continue to work on the most important areas – it has been said that you never finish painting the Forth Bridge, as once you get to one end you start again from the other. It can feel a little like that!'

A decade on, how does Edward feel about the future?

'Motivation is high. We have a continued challenge ahead, and a lot to do. However, it is rewarding and we have an incredibly enthusiastic team with the same values. What is even more inspiring is that the team are actively contributing to the development of our collective values; we are living proof that good ideas feed in from all areas.'

2 Entrepreneurship

Entrepreneurship stands at the heart of British culture – 'a nation of shopkeepers' as Britain was once described. It has also been said that one can tell the strength of the economy by how entrepreneurship is performing but this is misleading for entrepreneurs will perform in any market as they are able to visualise opportunities that others cannot see. In every recession, new ideas and innovations come through and it is this that makes recessions actually quite exciting. As hard as they can be – and the downturn of 2008 to 2011 has been long and brutal – there are those that have been able to adapt and grow.

Entrepreneurs are exciting to observe as they possess the courage to stand up for what they believe and to put themselves on the line. Such people will naturally inspire others and it is no surprise that so many aspire to be entrepreneurs. Yet it is not as easy as just aspiring and having the desire to be an entrepreneur. Yes, anyone can start a business but entrepreneurship is a calling. A real entrepreneur has no choice but to follow this road.

So is this unique quality called entrepreneurship?

One of the key problems in describing it, is that the definition is simple but the word is used in a different context. Ask someone to describe an entrepreneur and they will describe not a small businessman but an innovator; a risk taker and a visionary. Of course the truth lies half way between the two.

It is well documented that President George W. Bush once commented that 'The problem with the French is that they don't have a word for entrepreneur'.

It will be a quotation that will be long remembered as one of the great Bushisms – although it is not apparently certain that he actually said it. Whether that is true or not, the term 'entrepreneur' is one that does cause much discussion as it means different qualities to different people. It is one of those terms that is very hard to define as it has changed and evolved over time. It can vary from meaning someone who has started up their own business to someone who is a visionary and who has broken barriers.

The key factor that was probably in Bush's mind when he made the comment was that it is seen to be a core factor to the success of any economy – especially a free economy as in the USA. It is believed that the strength of any economy is often determined by an environment, which is able to encourage entrepreneurs to prosper. They become an indicator of how an economy is performing – their success can be seen as a sign of an economy rising and their failure of an economy in decline. America has always been proud of its culture which encourages people to be individuals and free.

Definition

So how do we define the term?

Let's bring it back to ground level. The following are some observations from experienced professionals.

Jonathan Perrin, Director, Audit, Tax & Advisory, RSM Tenon

'The truth is that a lot of new businesses fail. An entrepreneur is someone who has really succeeded in business beyond normal expectation. It isn't just about setting up a business that is profitable; it is far more than that. They are people who have exceeded market expectations of both the business and often, themselves. Entrepreneurs possess a different set of skills to the average manager and that is what makes them so interesting.'

William Baxter, co-founder of BaxterStorey

'Entrepreneurs see opportunities. Do you need to invent something to be an entrepreneur? I am not so sure. It is about vision and seizing an opportunity.'

Malcolm Ross, chief executive

'Entrepreneurs do something that others can't. They just do not fit into normal structures and boxes that businesses are generally structured by.'

Alex Buchanan, journalist

'Very few people are going to change the world. Many may dream about it but it does not happen. Entrepreneurs see an opportunity that helps a business or industry to evolve. They believe they can make a difference – they possess an inner self belief that most people do not have.'

Robert Cook, Chief Executive, Malmaison and Hotel du Vin

'Entrepreneurs see an opportunity and have the courage to go for it. They possess both vision and the ability to see a gap in the marketplace.'

Is this how you view an entrepreneur? The following aim is to explore all these points in depth by talking to true, proven entrepreneurs to discover how they think and what they believe makes a difference.

It will be a fascinating journey as entrepreneurs do challenge us, inspire us and excite us. They do sit at the core of every economy – so yes, it is important to understand what it takes to create an entrepreneur.

One of the assumptions that lies behind this work is that a true entrepreneur displays traits that stand beyond the norm. This is true and will be displayed as we progress but the confusion of what an entrepreneur is starts with the true definition.

A key aim of the following is to analyse the views of proven entrepreneurs and not to become caught in management speak and theory. However, there is a need to start with a look at the various definitions of the word.

The English Dictionary Definition

–noun **1.** a person who organises and manages any enterprise, esp. a business, usually with considerable initiative and risk.

2. an employer of productive labour; contractor.

This is a straightforward definition that covers a very broad school – almost every business venture that has ever been founded.

Wikipedia

'An **entrepreneur** is a person who has possession of a new enterprise, venture or idea and assumes significant accountability for the inherent risks and the outcome. The term is originally a loanword from the French and was first defined by the Irish economist Richard Cantillon. Entrepreneur in English is a term applied to the type of personality who is willing to take upon himself a new venture or enterprise and accepts full responsibility for the outcome. Jean-Baptiste Say, a French economist is believed to have coined the word 'entrepreneur' first in about 1800. He said an entrepreneur is 'one who undertakes an enterprise, especially a contractor, acting as intermediary between capital and labour.'

So is this an entrepreneur? Clearly this is the true definition but it is not what is now understood as being a true entrepreneur.

Peter Lederer, Chairman of Gleneagles

'Scotland has 20,000 small businesses. Are they all entrepreneurs? Unlikely. There needs to be a clear definition between those that run small businesses and the true entrepreneur. Not every small business leader is an entrepreneur.'

As with most words, the definition of the words evolves and changes. Today when people talk about an entrepreneur, the immediate understanding is of someone who possesses a range of traits that run beyond the official definition.

Entrepreneur magazine

'Entrepreneurs occupy a central position in our market economy. They serve as the spark plug in our economy's engine, activating and stimulating all economic activity. The most dynamic societies in the world are the ones that have the most entrepreneurs, plus the economic and legal structure to encourage and motivate entrepreneurs to greater activities.

'Just what makes you such an integral part of a prosperous economy? It's entrepreneurial energy, creativity and motivation that trigger the production and sale of new products and services. It's the entrepreneur who seeks opportunities to profit by satisfying as yet unsatisfied needs. It's the entrepreneur who seeks disequilibrium – a gap between the wants and needs of the customers and the products and services that are currently available – and finds a way to fill that gap.

'Do you have what it takes to be a successful entrepreneur? You do if you fit the following description:

'Entrepreneurs are optimistic and future oriented; they believe that success is possible and are willing to risk their resources in the pursuit of profit. They are fast moving and flexible, willing to change quickly when they get new information. Entrepreneurs are persistent and determined to succeed, because their own money and ego are at risk.

'Entrepreneurs are skilled at selling against their competitors by creating perceptions of difference and uniqueness in their products and services. They continually seek ways to offer their products and services in such a way that they're more attractive than anything else available.

'Entrepreneurs are capable of dealing effectively with the legal and governmental requirements of business. They're creative and determined in satisfying regulations and acquiring the licences necessary to do business. They are excellent problem solvers and are continually seeking solutions to the obstacles that inevitably arise.

'Entrepreneurs are capable of setting up the internal business systems, processes, procedures and bookkeeping necessary for operating a successful business. They have a natural instinct for the financial condition of their businesses. And they're intensely focused on sales, cash flow and revenue at all times.

'Because entrepreneurs create all wealth, all jobs, all opportunities and all prosperity in the nation, they are the most important people in a market economy – and there are never enough of them'

('Are you cut out to be an entrepreneur?', *Entrepreneur*, 21 March 2005)

One has to accept that the above was written by Entrepreneur magazine but even so it does set out a definition that is far more refined to the original definition.

Now for the view of management theorists. The scholar Robert. B. Reich considers leadership, management ability, and team-building as essential qualities of an entrepreneur. This concept has its origins in the work of Richard Cantillon in his *Essai sur la Nature du Commerce en Général* (1755) and Jean-Baptiste Say (1803) in his *Treatise on Political Economy*.

Joseph Schumpeter saw the entrepreneur as innovators and popularised the uses of the phrase creative destruction to describe his view of the role of entrepreneurs in changing business norms. 'Creative destruction' is a great term that fit easily into our vocabulary and dealt with the changes entrepreneurial activity makes every time a new process, product or company enters the market. Schumpeter argues that the entrepreneur is an innovator, one that introduces new technologies into the workplace or market, increasing efficiency, productivity or generating new products or services.

Other academics say the entrepreneur is an organiser of factors of production acting as a catalyst for economic change (Deakins and Freel, 2009). Shackle argues that the entrepreneur is a highly creative individual who imagines new solutions providing new opportunities for reward (Deakins and Freel, 2009).

Most research focuses on the traits of the entrepreneur. Cope (2001) argues that although certain entrepreneurial traits are required, entrepreneurs' behaviour is dynamic and influenced by environmental factors.

Is this correct? Entrepreneurs just think in a different way and it is really all about psychology and this can be provoked by an environment.

Shane and VenKataraman (2000) argue the entrepreneur is solely concerned with opportunity recognition and exploitation; however, the opportunity that is recognised depends on the type of entrepreneur.

There is a growing body of work that shows that entrepreneurial behaviour is dependent on social and economic factors. The research into female entrepreneurs illustrates this quite clearly. 'Countries which have healthy and diversified labour markets or stronger safety nets show a more favourable ratio of opportunity to necessity-driven women entrepreneurs.'

(Minitti, 2010) What those factors are varies widely, based on local needs. Every country is different. India will see one type of entrepreneur emerge which will be different to that of the UK or USA. This is clearly true and environment/culture is clearly important but entrepreneurs emerge in any environment, economy or culture. Therefore, the key to finding the true answer is what is the psychology that lies within the entrepreneur and this is the journey that needs to be taken. If nothing else, the following should be to define what a true entrepreneur is.

Character traits

So what character traits should we see in an entrepreneur? Let's listen once again to the views of proven professionals.

Jonathan Perrin, Director, Audit, Tax and Advisory, RSM Tenon

'The entrepreneur rarely accepts defeat and would learn from failure – and maybe failure was the key to their eventual success.'

Gary Hall, entrepreneur

'Many entrepreneurs become entrepreneurs due to circumstance – often by having been made redundant. One of the real traits of the entrepreneur is how they react to adversity. They have a naturally positive mindset which drives them through difficult times.'

William Baxter, Co-founder, BaxterStorey

'They see the world differently and are therefore natural leaders…so they always come to the fore whatever the situation.'

David McHattie, Chief Executive, National Skills Academy for Hospitality

'Environment is important to creating the vision to be an entrepreneur. I think that many people are inspired by others to have a go or can just see something that they believe is wrong and want to do it right. I think that very often entrepreneurs are created by their value set. They see something that they just do not believe in and want to do it correctly or well. They are more driven than others because they believe in something that makes them want to excel.'

What makes entrepreneurs so admired?

> 'Entrepreneurs are risk takers, willing to roll the dice with their money or reputation on the line in support of an idea or enterprise. They willingly assume responsibility for the success or failure of a venture and are answerable for all its facets.' *Victor Kiam*

There are many corporate CEOs who wish they were entrepreneurial in nature or certainly have the freedom that entrepreneurs often appear to have. Ironically there are many entrepreneurs who wish they could be corporate CEOs but the truth is that they are very different animals with very different skills. Both find the environment of the other destabilising and frustrating. Both are kings of their own environments but should not cross the bridge to the other's realm.

I remember a discussion between an entrepreneur and a corporate CEO to discussed swapping roles for a month. The CEO commented:

> 'I would just love to have the freedom to make change that an entrepreneur is able to do. They can just do as they desire.'

A nice image but not as true as it may appear. Entrepreneurs too have to generate profit and stay true to normal business rules. They are not free spirits that just act on instinct. There is far more to it. Interestingly the entrepreneur involved in the discussion commented:

> 'It must be marvellous to have large departments waiting to be directed on command. I am lazy by nature and I think a structure would allow me to achieve far more.'

Again a simplistic image. People do not do just as they have directed. There was one CEO who often spoke of the 'car park syndrome' whereby a policy could be agreed at a board meeting, only for each member of the board to have subtly changed this policy to their own understanding by the time they reached their cars.

> The truth is that an entrepreneur will find corporate structure restraining and like a cage. A corporate player will find the lack of structure and freedom that entrepreneurs work from, frightening. I recall one observing quite correctly: 'The corporate need the entrepreneurs to generate new ideas and thinking and the entrepreneurs need the corporate so that they can stand out.'

Part of the problem is that it is easy to admire those that possess the courage of their convictions. Very few possess this quality but it is a quality that we place on a pedestal.

When we all look at those professionals that we respect, it is generally those that possess conviction, competence and a passion that goes beyond the norm. As we admire this quality, we aspire to it and it is a natural step to try and develop these qualities … but very few are able to do so.

Another good illustration is that one of the great ongoing debates is over leadership versus management. The debate is, of course, poisoned by the fact that everyone wants to be the former rather than the latter but very few fit this box. Leaders and entrepreneurs are seen to be the pinnacle of professional achievement and so the debate is close to the heart of many. But the debates become distorted and often silly as very few truly understand what is required to do either. Both leaders and entrepreneurs often achieve their position through the fact that they place others first and make sacrifices that the majority would never even contemplate making and this alone marks out a boundary.

There have many aspiring entrepreneurs who have presented their business plans to me and I always ask them to go and away and consider the following questions before we discuss their plans:

- How important is your personal life to you? Are you prepared to place it second in the immediate term?

- How committed are you to building something that truly represents you?

- Are you mentally able to take setbacks and rejection and still be standing in place the next day?

- Are you prepared to fail in order to succeed? I often tell people that cannot succeed until they have failed. It is failure that teaches us how to win through.

- Are you prepared to be feel lonely and vulnerable but still be committed?

- Can you handle stress and pressure?

- Will you represent your clients with more energy and desire than your competitors?

- Will go the extra mile for that client?

- Are you prepared to stay true to what you believe when everyone else tells you are wrong?

The first discussion with any entrepreneur is about their character and not their plan. Are they ready for what is required?

There is an old saying that states the 90% of people are frightened of life. They are frightened of taking risk? They are frightened of failure? We all fail and often. The question is whether the person can handle it?

Therefore, what is it that makes one stand apart from the norm.

It should be noted that the meaning of the word 'entrepreneur' has evolved and changed with time. The actual definition is very broad and covers almost every person that has started a business venture but when the word is used to describe an individual, a different meaning is applied – generally a person who has the vision, courage and ability to take risks, break barriers and create change.

> 'The important thing is not being afraid to take a chance.
> Remember, the greatest failure is to not try. Once you find something you love to do, be the best at doing it.'
> - Debbi Fields, founder of Mrs. Fields Cookies

Debbi Fields' comment is very apt as often entrepreneurs are exceptional in their ability. They are often some of the best in their fields. Of course, it takes courage to start any venture alone and this should not be underrated but the understanding of an entrepreneur has evolved beyond meaning just this.

So what questions are we seeking to explore here?

- What is the meaning of the term 'entrepreneur' in the modern sense?

- What does it take to be an entrepreneur?

- What factors create an entrepreneur?

So many people believe they are entrepreneurs when in fact they are simply good managers with high egos, a strong work ethic or both. These are not bad qualities and some will argue that these are important character traits to possess. There are no simple answers to the questions posed.

The assumption that lies behind the motivation for this work is that entrepreneurs think and act differently to the norm. These are people who are so exceptional that they are able to break barriers. They are creators, original thinkers and do not follow the crowd. To discover whether this assumption is true, a range of true entrepreneurs have been interviewed and their thoughts analysed.

Does it matter?

It is important to understand what we aspire to be and why. It raises so many questions and to understand what makes a difference, what we desire to be and what is the difference between an entrepreneur and a good business manager has value. I will provide some thoughts.

I have lost count of how many times I have listened to people tell me they are entrepreneurial when in truth they are simply good managers with some sound thinking and insight. They are being encouraged to take risks when in truth they are not prepared to do so and should be encouraged to be more comfortable with their own skill sets.

Some who believe that they are entrepreneurs try to break barriers and to follow a course of action, which is simply impossible. Entrepreneurs often understand their customer far better than most research departments or business analysts. They feel it and understand it. This is often termed as a 'gut feel' and for entrepreneurs it is natural but for others it is not and there are many business failures that have been founded on 'gut feels' but not enough substance. The natural entrepreneur really understands the customer – it is more than just gut feel.

As we so admire the qualities of an entrepreneur, we try and teach the qualities involved. There are few worse approaches. Just as one cannot teach courage or vision, so one cannot create an entrepreneur. Entrepreneurs can be created but by circumstance and environment, not by a person. So often advice can be misguided. One illustration is an article by Joseph Anthony that asserted that you would know if you were an entrepreneur if you displayed the following qualities:

- You are a lousy employee.
- You come from a line of people who cannot work for others

- You do not worry about job security
- You have gone as far as one can go
- You have done market research
- You have the support of your family.

Well, what is written is simply incorrect. Entrepreneurs will display many of the above traits but it this type of advice and thinking that is so far off line. Let's work through some of these points.

You are a lousy employee

Many are lousy employees for the simple reason they are lousy employees – selfish, and lacking in understanding. Entrepreneurs struggle in corporate environments because they naturally want to be in control, and feel frustrated at working within another's culture. They often take business more seriously than the the directors of the company and become unemployable because they want to take on more responsibility than their remit allows.

You come from a line of people who cannot work for others

Far too often, children of entrepreneurs believe they possess the same traits simply because they are their parents' offspring. It has been said that everyone wants to exceed the achievements of their parent. This is understandable but this not make one an entrepreneur. Entrepreneurs think differently and it does not follow that the child of an entrepreneur will possess the same qualities. In fact, it is often sad to watch a child trying to live up to this expectation.

You do not worry about job security

It is true that entrepreneurs are courageous but so too are those who know that they are experts in their field. Job security comes from knowing that one adds value and can make a difference – this does not make one an entrepreneur.

You have gone as far one can go

Again there may be a good reason for this to be the case. Lord Thurso talks of his 'theory of equality of respect' whereby it is important that society teaches people that it is acceptable not aspire high. We ask people to be high achievers when they simply do not possess the ability. They should instead take pride in their work, and this is something that not enough people do.

- **Your have done your market research**

A very good discipline but often true entrepreneurs break barriers for which there is no market research. Good business managers undertake market research. An entrepreneur understands their customer almost naturally and they trust their 'gut feel'. This is a quality not to be recommended as very few are accurate.

- **You have the support of your family**

A very important factor for anyone who wishes to take a risk, but again not an essential quality for an entrepreneur.

This was very poor advice and not even close to being helpful. Does it matter? Yes, because life is a harsh environment and poor advice can harm lives.

True entrepreneurs are as much inspirational figures as they are original. Their character traits are far more complex and deep. It is easy to aspire to such characters but they have travelled a path that very few would be able to do.

References

Anthony, Joseph (2008) *Seven Signs of an Entrepreneur*, MSN Business Report.

Cantillon, Richard (1755) *Essai sur la Nature du Commerce en Général*

Cope, J (2001), 'The entrepreneurial experience: towards a dynamic learning perspective of entrepreneurship', PhD thesis, Lancaster University. Lancaster.

Deakins, David and Freel, Mark (2009) *Entrepreneurship and Small Firms*, McGraw-Hill Higher Education

Minitti, Maria (2010) Female Entrepreneurship and Economic Activity, *European Journal of Development Research* **22**, 294–312

Reich, Robert B (1987) Entrepreneurship Reconsidered: The Team as Hero, *Harvard Business Review*, May-June

Say, Jean-Baptiste (1803/1834) *Treatise on Political Economy*

Schumpeter, J (1942) *Capitalism, Socialism, and Democracy*, Harper

Shane, S. and S. Venkataraman (2000), 'The promise of entrepreneurship as a field of research'. *The Academy of Management Review* 25, 217-226

Entrepreneurs profiles and interviews

The following section is a mix of profiles written for this book and a series of articles that have been previously published in EP Business in *Hospitality* magazine. These are the thoughts and case studies of entrepreneurs in the industry who all have individual stories. What are the common themes?

Classic entrepreneurs

Corporate entrepreneurs

Classic entrepreneurs

Hotels

Ken McCulloch

Ken McCulloch has been described as 'one of the few real hotel entrepreneurs'; an independent thinker who has a passion for making hotels with a difference. His unconventional approach has made him one of the key drivers in the industry over the past 20 years, having created One Devonshire Gardens, Malmaison, Columbus, Monaco; Dakota and many others.

His love affair with the hospitality business started as an apprentice with British Transport Hotels in 1964, a company which guaranteed good old fashioned, down-to-earth training and offered the opportunity to progress quickly if you had the appetite – which he did. However, Ken was always driven to manage his own business and it was not long before he began by opening Glasgow's first wine bar and then owning several restaurants in the city.

It was the launch of One Devonshire Gardens in 1986 that really brought him into the limelight – Scotland's first boutique hotel. Devonshire went on to achieve international acclaim and hosted many celebrities, diplomats and royalty.

During the early days, Ken faced many of the challenges common to entrepreneurs, however he always believed that with the right product and the right people success would follow.

'When you start out, it's only natural that you will go through some tough times and make mistakes. One Devonshire taught me early on that 'necessity is the mother of invention' and that the ability to be creative in your approach to business is essential to survive the inevitable ups and downs.'

The success of his first hotel encouraged Ken to do more, but it was the early 1990s and the hotel business was on the floor. However, ever the optimist, he believed that: 'For every person staying in One Devonshire, there were 50 who would love to, but didn't have the budget'. Clearly, there was a gap in the market, which he swiftly filled with the first new hotel brand in the UK for 30 years – Malmaison.

Malmaison became an amazing success story and subsequently synonymous with Ken McCulloch's name. It was a chic, cosmopolitan concept at a very reasonable price which hit the market at just the right time, when a recession was coming to an end and new ideas were much coveted. Above all, it captured people's imaginations as it challenged accepted industry norms, establishing a new trend which many have sought to replicate over the past 15 years. Malmaison, which was launched in 1994 with the backing of Robert Breare's Arcadian hotel business, was a phenomenal success. After just four years it was sold to US property group Patriot for €234 million (£157 million). McCulloch came away from the deal a considerably wealthier man.

In 1999, Ken moved to Monaco but could not stay away from the business – acquiring Monaco's Abela hotel in 2000 for £30 million. One of the investors in this venture was Formula One driver and fellow Monaco resident David Coulthard. Columbus followed Ken's proven philosophy of bringing excellence to the average person at a reasonable price. The rooms were €180 a night; considerably less expensive than most local alternatives and the hotel rapidly became the hip, stylish place to stay in the Principality. However, he found the politics in Monaco frustrating and so sold Columbus and returned to Scotland.

Ken is very much his own man. He will not compromise his values, is fiercely loyal towards his people, and has the ability to see his hotels through the eyes of the guest. The latter not only means that their experience always remains his top priority but also allows him to see opportunities others cannot, giving him a definite edge. In addition, he hates committees, the establishment, industry egos, yes-men and dishonesty. He will often recount the story of when he spoke at an industry lunch and one attendee stood up and asked him: 'Why should I come and stay in one of your hotels?'

Ken simply looked at him and replied 'You don't have to.'

To Ken, the product should speak for itself. He lives by the motto 'Success is the sum of many small things correctly done. Keep things simple, employ nice people and don't do style for style's sake'. His aim is to create a space where people feel good, where you get the impression that it couldn't be any other way. Hard to achieve, though with his track record, clearly not impossible.

It is no coincidence that Ken has returned to Scotland, he is and always has been an ambassador for Scotland and Scottish talent. True to form, his most recent venture in Scotland, Dakota, challenges conventional wisdom as these are located just outside city centres, close to business parks. Their stark, almost futuristic, masculine exterior betrays the inviting, warm, stylish interior within. As always his goal remains to offer excellent quality at an affordable price – apparent in the menu of the Dakota Grill, the attention to detail throughout the hotel and its staff. On this last point, another favourite expression of his is 'Good service isn't a mystery, employ nice people'.

When asked about what drives him, he replies:

'Being in a position to create places that people look forward to going to'. He believes that the major players in the industry have taken the romance and excitement out of the business. As he says, 'People used to dress up to travel, to go to hotels – it was seen as a real treat. Let's get back to that. We can do things the big boys can't do. That's our strength and it's the combination of great style, great food and great value that is at the heart of everything we do.'

Ken certainly believes in what he is trying to achieve but he is neither arrogant nor complacent.

'No matter how good your track record is, people will always ask – how do you know that it going to succeed? And the honest answer is I don't. I often have three or four ideas on the go at the same time and of course not all of them will become a reality. Yet, from instinct, I know what the guest wants, and if I develop the right product around this, I know I've got a success story… and who wouldn't want to be part of that?'

Hotels

Lord Charles Forte

The name Forte is synonymous with hospitality and Lord Charles Forte needs no introduction. His feat, to create a multi-service, global business operating in 40 countries from virtually nothing has not been replicated on any scale. Forte earned great respect for his approach to training and development, and his empire produced some of the most respected business leaders of the present day – all of whom share his core values.

Lord Forte – the last great entrepreneur?

Lord Forte sadly passed away in March. His story is well known – the tale of a man born into a small village in southern Italy; arriving in Scotland at the age of 5; opening a milk bar in Regent Street at 25 and building a global business with 800 hotels and 100,000 employees in over 40 countries. It is not an exaggeration to state that his record stands comparison with the industry's greatest names of any era including those of Conrad Hilton or César Ritz. Although the last 20 years have been full of successful entrepreneurs, few have challenged the achievements of Lord Forte in building a world-class business from scratch. Why is it then that the Forte story does stand so far apart from others? What made the difference?

We wanted to look beyond the simple story and ask: what has been the true legacy of a man who has arguably been the leading name in British hospitality?

At its height, Trusthouse Forte (THF) was a dominant force both in the UK market and abroad. The scope of the business ranged from hotels which included leading names such as Grosvenor House, the Waldorf and Hyde Park Hotel in London, to George V (Paris), The Ritz (Madrid), Eden (Rome), King Edward (Toronto) and Plaza of the Americas (Dallas), as well as Forte Village in Sardinia. The company operated not only within hotels but also in restaurants, contract catering, fixed site conference venues, outdoor event catering, motorway services and in airports.

It was an immense business that may have lost its way by the time of the Granada takeover but at its height was a popular and very successful household name. It was a company not without its critics and it had its battles – most famously with Lord Crowther and Sir Hugh Wontner – but it was one that did command respect. For many the story came to an end with the Granada takeover in 1996, which marked the end of the era. Much has been written about the takeover battle, and about Rocco Forte's subsequent rise again with RF Hotels (now the Rocco Forte Collection), but not so much has been written about the legacy, if any, that the Forte empire left behind, and also what really made his company so strong during its heyday. Was the story of Lord Forte really just about his leadership or was it about a business philosophy? How come so many of the industry's leading players of today – Gerald Lawless, Grant Hearn, Garry Hawkes, Peter Taylor, Guy Crawford, Peter Stephenson and Patrick Dempsey amongst others – came from the Forte stable?

To find out, EP spoke to a number of well-known senior players as to their views of Lord Forte, the company and its legacy.

The story

Lord Forte's story would have sat comfortably within the pages of a Jeffrey Archer novel. It is the tale of a boy born into a small, poor village in Italy with a population of only 400, where his ancestors had been minor landowners for 500 years. The boy was the eldest of four children. His father, Rocco, moved to Scotland to find a new life and at the tender age of 5 the young boy followed to this very alien land with the rest of his family. He rose to become a peer of the realm and the biggest name in UK hospitality, overseeing a global business which he had built from scratch. Not enough? Then add in a brief internment in 1940 at the start of the war, great battles with powerful business adversaries in Lord Crowther and Sir Hugh Wontner and large-scale takeovers such as the acquisition of the Imperial Group from Lord Hanson for £186 million. Finally, the boy who became a global businessman passes his empire to his son, Rocco.

Even his greatest critics, and there were many, would accept that his achievements were immense. But what made the man so successful? Why does the name Forte still have an aura about it?

Roy Tutty, Former Chief Operating Officer, Forte Hotels

'Lord Forte was an eminent captain of British industry. He operated some of the finest hotels and restaurants in the world and it was an empire which, at one point, employed over 100,000 people within 40 countries. There was truly no continent in the world where Forte didn't touch. He developed one of the earliest global businesses, which was ahead of its time and British-based, unusual at that time for not being based in the USA or Asia.

'The Forte business was built by the man himself, with the right support programme and grew via a steady rate of acquisitions over a 50-year period. It was, by the time Granada bought it, a truly outstanding business, from hotels to leisure markets. My earliest memory of Lord Forte (at the age of 19 years and still at hotel school) was when I was offered the opportunity to join Forte as a Graduate. We had been invited to a 'fashion parade' at the Café Royal. I was a pretty fresh young lad and we had an all-day interview process, which combined both individual and group tasks. As part of the process we were all individually seen by Lord Forte. As a young lad just starting out in my career and deciding what I wanted to do upon leaving college I remember that he just made a real impression on me. I think that this speaks volumes about Lord Forte's character and his way of finessing of every detail that was so important to him. After this experience the only company in the world where I wanted to be was Trust House Forte. It is a time that I look back upon with fondness, and I stayed with the company for 25 years. Lord Forte's approach was to develop the business through his training and development programme. He wanted people to evolve to the limit of their potential and use this as a point of leverage in the market. He always used to say that if you look after your people they would look after the customer.

'I don't think that you will get a similar example to the Forte business happening again. One could build up a successful business in a specific area but Forte was a true entrepreneurial conglomerate. It was the largest business operator in every sector – contract catering, restaurants, hotels, leisure, golf, airport and in-flight catering. The essence of the entrepreneurial strategy was to integrate people into a business and allow them to realise and find their own level. It was less of a takeover and that's not what today's business model is necessarily about.'

Gerald Lawless, Executive Chairman, Jumeirah Group

'I joined Trust House Forte in June of 1974 from the Shannon College of Hotel Management. This was shortly after the merger of Forte and Trust Houses. It was very exciting to be a part of such a dynamically growing company under the visionary leadership of Sir Charles Forte, as he was then known. Lord Forte was a great inspiration to all of us and it is interesting to still meet so many people who are in the hotel industry who have had their basic training within Forte Hotels and associated businesses. Lord Forte managed to establish an amazing culture throughout all of the businesses.

'This was a culture of high ethical standards, dedication to our profession and hard work. My fondest memory of meeting Lord Forte was at an event that was held for Queen Aliya of Jordan in Grosvenor House in 1990. As the Middle East representative I was also invited. Many of us had not met Lord Forte formally in the past and we were then introduced to him. Shortly afterwards Lord Forte returned to the room to introduce his executives to Her Majesty. He immediately took her along the line and introduced each of us effortlessly. He remembered our names and did not once hesitate during the introduction process. A true professional. He also had a great sense of humour and at the same luncheon we were served ice cream deserts in the shape of the Pyramids. In his subsequent speech he praised his chefs at Grosvenor House with regards to the culinary standard of the meal and then said: 'Though I cannot say the same for their knowledge in geography!'

'Lord Forte instilled in all of us the values of loyalty and honesty and it was a true privilege to have worked for his company.'

Guy Crawford, Chief Executive Officer, Jumeirah Group

'I have three very strong memories of Lord Forte, all from the 1980s and my memories and recollections of my time as a deputy manager of the Beach Plaza Monte Carlo.

- **Humility**: Lord Forte and his family were regular visitors of the hotel and I always remember him as paying his bills, not asking for discounts, or special service. This was so very different to the numerous personalities residing on the Côte d'Azur.

- **Ratios**: I remember being asked what a particular cost ratio was for the hotel during a period of difficult trading and not having the answer immediately to hand. Not something I repeated.

- **Customers**: We were decorating our fine dining restaurant, one lunch time, for a very high profile private diner later that evening, but the noise from the banging, etc. was quite loud in the adjacent all-day dining area. I was called to explain to Lord Forte's table, who was having lunch and explain what the noise was . His 'suggestion' that I focus on my current customers and not too much on the future ones remains something I still try to do and balance with future objectives – most days.

'Lord Forte – a great gentleman and Forte an incredible company that gave me every possible opportunity to succeed and grow personally and professionally. I consider myself privileged to have had a very small part in its history.'

Peter Taylor OBE, Chairman, Town House Hotels

'Like many in the industry, I worked and had great respect for Charles Forte. His determination, his talent at deal-making, his commitment marked him out as one of the hospitality industry's most determined and most successful operators and through his knighthood and peerage, he gave the industry class and status. Always impeccably dressed and mannered, always defending his employees, he was the softly spoken man with a pretty iron will. He must indeed be the greatest example of entrepreneurship in our industry.'

Maybe the last words should lie with his son…

Sir Rocco Forte, Chairman, The Rocco Forte Collection

'From a personal perspective my father was a great influence on my life, I learnt a lot from him and he was an inspirational role model to me. In speaking for his legacy I think that, despite his huge achievements, my father always retained a sense of humility and found time for everyone. As a communicator he was equally able at talking with heads of states and sovereigns and the most humblest of people, and I think that this gave him a rather special quality. My father earned his fame and fortune within the industry and he always gave a lot back – I believe that this explains part of the admiration that still exists for him today.'

(October 2007)

Hotels

AB Bejerano
Founder of AB Hotels

With a small collection of properties, including Sopwell House in St Albans, Hertfordshire, AB Berjerano's most recent creation, the Arch Hotel in London, is a case study of his entrepreneurial skills. Like many entrepreneurs featured in this book, family involvement in running the business is a common factor. Why? In the case of the Berjerano family, it is evident that AB's two sons, who are both directly involved in the business, have a great deal of empathy with their father's vision, arguably allowing a venture which is inherently bound by risks and obstacles to be turned into a success. The development of a hotel is a complex, meticulous process and requires a degree of dedication that goes beyond a simple 'conversion', and this is not easily understood by those who have not been through the process. There are few who can truly appreciate the skill and tenacity required to transform an historic building into a luxury hotel, and it takes great vision and foresight to make it happen.

More than just a hotel

It is often said you should never mix family with business but in some instances this mix seems to work. In January 2010 Abraham Bejerano, an established hotelier and founder of AB Hotels, and Alon and Rafi, two of his four children, opened The Arch, an 82-bedroom boutique hotel in central London. Abraham and Rafi met at The Arch to talk about the highs and lows of realising Abraham's dream of transforming seven listed town houses and two mews houses into one unique hotel.

According to Abraham there are three elements to a good hotel operation that if you get right, you cannot then fail. These are: design, location and service. This may sound obvious but these three elements all cost money and the larger the project, the larger the investment, something

Abraham is all too aware of, having invested his own money into the build with no external backing. In a market that has been volatile, this was a bold initiative.

For many years, Abraham had London firmly in his sights. Rafi remembers days spent viewing endless properties with his father in search of that perfect opportunity. Finally eight years ago, Abraham's dream started to become a reality, as the family secured the first house a stone's throw from Marble Arch. But this was just the start of a distinctly bumpy road which would include squatters, bankrupt contractors, planning regulations, legal issues and a flooded ground floor four days before opening. All challenges that would make even the hardened of hoteliers want to pack up and go home. As we walk around the hotel, Abraham points out the time lapse renovation photographs hanging on his office wall. The room we were having coffee in is hard to recognise from just two years earlier and suddenly the scale of the project becomes clear.

'Planning and space issues were some of our biggest obstacles; we couldn't put a skip outside the building for an hour without applying for a permit first, something we took for granted when extending our other two properties where we have acres to play with. Here we were constantly on site and wrestling with planning permission. We wanted the main entrance in the middle of the building but couldn't because of damaging the facade of a listed building; we couldn't remove the staircases because they were listed – all five of them. We would have lost too much space if we had used them so we had to board them up, which means we have some interesting storage cupboards.

'Half way through the building work our main contractor went bust. We had no roof, no project manager and no architect, and it was costing us a lot of money just to stand still, so we sat down, regrouped and decided to hire the same project manager and surveyor of the company which had gone under. We thought we needed a new contractor regardless so we might as well employ the people who already knew everything about the building.'

Abraham is not a property developer, he is a hotelier – a fact he readily admits – so this family-funded project has also been a family-run project.

'My sons came on board a few years ago, Rafi was already working in hotels and Alon was in finance but wanted a change. Even my
daughter has had a hand in choosing the artwork. We share the same
values and ethos and instead of working hard for someone else they
might as well work hard for the family business. They have their
opinions and I have 30 years' experience, I know how to adapt having
worked through three recessions, the boys are learning as they go, they
have complementary skill sets with Alon as project manager and Rafi
as our sales and marketing manager.'

The hotel reception, lounge and restaurant are relatively small, but well
designed, the place feels private and relaxed which is helped by the
casually dressed staff. There is a real feel of 'home away from home', but
with the touches you would expect from a five-star hotel.

'We have a great management team, so we don't have to be here all
the time. Our culture is embedded in the team. Our staff are our DNA.
We let them express themselves and allow them a certain amount of
empowerment, which is working as we have a 75% staff retention rate
in our first year.'

Abraham and Rafi are, as one would expect, an interesting combination.
Abraham is charming, very calm and measured. Rafi is full of energy and
has a passion for the project that seemingly brought the three men closer
together. One can imagine that they were always a close-knit family unit
but somehow this project has meant more to them than just a hotel development – it has been a personal and testing challenge for each of them.
Each of the three has had their sleepless moments.

'We have built the hotel from scratch and everything you see has
been picked out or designed by us. The Marriotts and InterContinentals
have the edge with finance and resources, but as a small business
we are able to deliver a more personalised service. It is funny when
customers who have traditionally stayed with the larger groups come
here, they will not go back.

'You can't go head to head with the larger players and actually
there is no need. We offer something very different. The key here is
informality. The life clock of our customer means that we don't restrict
our services – we have no opening or closing times for our dining. We

are individual and are able to respond quickly to customers' needs. We needed to mould our philosophy to compete with the big boys in the areas we can really shine in.

'What differentiates us from others? Our customers want to feel at home, that's why we built a gym and have all the mod cons in rooms. We were the first to put Sky HD in all rooms. More importantly we have no time limits in the restaurant; if they come in at 1 a.m. and want eggs Benedict that's fine, or if they want to sit at the bar with a glass of champagne they can do so without feeling they need to be rushed out, they can sit there all night if they want to. The cost of staff is a concern but at the moment this is necessary.'

With work on the hotel complete and four days to go until their soft opening, disaster struck one evening when a burst water pipe flooded the ground floor with boiling water, ruining tables, carpets, floors and walls. As Rafi showed us pictures of the damage it was clear to see that this had to be one of the toughest times to see through, especially so near to completion. Ten months after opening, Abraham, Rafi and Alon are working harder than ever and already have a good base of returning customers consisting of hedge fund companies, the entertainment and film sector along with banking and corporate.

'We are not a big hotel. We are an unknown and we don't have a brand name like Marriott to trade off. A massive amount depends on word of mouth and partnering with companies such as SLH, Hip Hotels and Mr and Mrs Smith. Our main markets at the moment are Germany, Switzerland, the US and France. You try and focus on the countries that are going to give you the most rewarding potential and give them what they demand.

'Every business must have a plan, and so far we are spot on with ours. Financially we are on track and we hope to have a return on investment soon. We only have ourselves and our team to rely on to make sure this hotel is a success.'

(January 2011)

Gordon Campbell-Gray
Owner, Gordon Campbell-Gray Hotels

Gordon Campbell-Gray is an entrepreneur in its purest sense. He operates on instinct, looks to take risks and seeks to pursue a vision which is over and above established convention. As a result, Gordon is someone whom others view as a trendsetter and visionary; he admits to looking for locations which offer a frisson of danger and as such appeals to the notion that travellers today are looking for different experiences.

Gordon's great escape

Gordon Campbell-Gray opened luxury hotel Le Gray late last year in the Lebanese capital, Beirut. The Scottish-born hotelier saw an initial two-year project turn into a four-and-a-half-year journey, set back by two outbreaks of war. Was it a step too far?

Individuality is a word that has been used many times to describe the works of Gordon Campbell-Gray. He pursues hotel developments as 'projects of passion', and there are few contemporaries who would have the nerve to discuss their future plans in the visionary terms Gordon prefers to use. An original and arguably experimental style has delivered new standards for luxury hotels, encompassing a flair for both design and good hospitality, the key to which is Gordon's personal style of hotel-keeping. So what took him to Beirut? It is a capital city that, at various points in history, has been revered for its architecture and elegance, but in modern times has been plagued by political instability and war. The most recent periods of conflict in the city took place in 2006 and 2008, halting plans for Le Gray on both occasions. Weighing up these options, some hotel developers would argue that the comparative frequency of such events presented too much of a risk. Yet, in November last year the doors opened and business has since been brisk, elevated by a whirlwind of global publicity. How has Gordon managed the scepticism and operational challenges?

On one hand there is much to entice international investors and hoteliers to Lebanon. Its economy has remained largely unaffected by the global financial crisis; it has a reputation for conservative regulation and has been forecast by the World Bank to grow by 7% this year. The services sector, which is dominated by tourism and financial services, accounts for roughly 67% of GDP, and the *New York Times* rated Beirut as the number one place to visit last year. Yet for all of this potential, the ravages of war have regularly undermined an economy so reliant on its services. The reconstruction of the city, which has been undertaken following the end of the Lebanese civil war in 1990, lay in ruins after the 2006 war. A well-worn globetrotter, Gordon had travelled to Beirut initially during a time when the city was still in a poor state, but was enticed to go back there following a recommendation from guests at his flagship hotel, One Aldwych.

'They suggested that Beirut might be a good idea for a hotel and, despite my earlier experience, within a week I decided to go. I was dazzled. The city centre had been beautifully restored in exquisite detail and was incredibly sophisticated. Virtually immediately I decided to take on the project. Beirut is a beguiling and uplifting city. It has a kind of magic – there is a frisson of danger, which makes it exciting.'

This may be the case, but with such a protracted build-up to launching Le Gray, didn't he question the project at some point?

'Let me give you an example. One day I left to return to the UK and that afternoon, they bombed the airport. I was just furious that I was not there because it felt as though I had abandoned it.

'For me, being a hotelier is like being an adventurer. Many people thought I was mad to go to Lebanon, but I didn't feel this, nor did I think I was being brave. If I thought it was genuinely too dangerous, then I would not have gone there. What we didn't expect was two more wars, which meant that we had to stop work on both occasions. The project lost momentum and you have to address issues such as building up a staff team all over again. I cannot pretend that it was easy, but I never questioned that we were going to build and open a hotel.

'To be fair, designing a hotel is an enormously long process, so we were able to utilise the time in revising plans. The fun part was when things began arriving – lamps that had been ordered four years ago! There isn't a pencil in a room that wasn't seen by me. My team are pretty tuned, but the minute that I get removed, it's not the same. Campbell-Gray Hotels have a sense of style – they are individual but they all are related.'

With supportive Lebanese investors, Gordon always had the weight of the city and its regulators behind Le Gray. However, maintaining a level of consistency and motivation among operational staff was a challenge. While the senior management team remained throughout the project, the core opening team had almost too much time for pre-training, as the opening got delayed.

'Throughout the project I was there a lot and just sought to remain visible. But the motivation of the team was terrific and the local population have shown that they can adapt their standards of service. For example, our philosophy is that all guests are treated with equal respect. This has actually been a learning curve as the Lebanese can be quite snobbish – in my view their attitude is very genuine.'

Le Gray's principle customer base is derived from inter-Middle Eastern travel, although interestingly the UK is now the fourth largest feeder market. Its success has already provided opportunities for capitalising on their presence in Beirut, and CampbellGray Hotels have plans for two further properties, including a beach resort about 25 minutes from Le Gray and another hotel just outside the city.

'Le Gray has been the first exciting, sexy thing to happen in Beirut for a while. The global interest has been phenomenal – we have never done anything that has caused such as storm. I think that people see it as a boost of confidence in Lebanon that we are there.'

It is evident that Gordon's passion for the location is as much part of Le Gray's inception and development as the journey of creating a new hotel. He has a unique visionary focus, which is supported by the capacity to deliver, unfettered to any great degree by what some would see as natural barriers to evolution. This has truly set Gordon apart from the mould of traditional hoteliers.

'The obvious way to develop a company is to be strategic, so you might think of destinations like London, New York and Paris. But that is not my style. If something exciting comes along, then we will look at it. It's an instinct. I am not ambitious or competitive and have no interest in 'winning', just doing things successfully. Many people suggested that I look beyond Beirut in favour of Dubai at one point, but this was never for me – there were already a number of hotels there. And I did not strategically pick the Middle East, I picked Beirut.'

Despite a fairly modest growth since its conception in 2003, CampbellGray Hotels is now preparing to extend its brand into other parts of the world, with developments in Montpellier, France; Havana, Cuba; an eco-resort in Grenada and a project in Scotland. Plans for a property were progressing in New York until the financial crash.

'To be honest I have so enjoyed the experience of being in the Middle East that not opening in New York is not a big deal. It's when places like Libya, Damascus and other parts of northern Africa provide potential opportunities that we may look there. There are so many undiscovered stretches that are accessible and have that little hit of danger. We are looking for something slightly unusual.

'There are so many places we could be, but our expansion will never be at a level that our small team cannot cope with. We want to love every minute. Twelve or 13 hotels is ideal, but it could be 10 or 16 – I don't know. CampbellGray Hotels does not think in short-term cycles, we are always looking 10 years ahead. We do not have a strategic plan to build a certain number of hotels; for us, everything we do is philosophised and built to last.'

As one who puts an extraordinary degree of his personal spirit into each hotel project, the core conclusion that I draw from meeting Gordon is that he is, indeed, a philosopher at heart. Passion is the overriding driver for his work. Renowned for his hotel art collections, he would never sell the works on display, for example, and he is a proven environmentalist and philanthropist. Perhaps it is this sense of sparkle that elevates the CampbellGray collection. As Gordon concludes:

'Life is not always good. We need to remember that it is just a hotel – it should be fun to work in. My dear friend Dame Anita Roddick said there is no great honour in having a company that makes soaps and shampoos but there can be great honour in what you do with the company. I feel the same about having a company which creates hotels. It is what we do with it!'

(July 2010)

Hotels

Peter Taylor OBE

Chairman, The Town House Collection

Peter Taylor's creation of the Blythswood Square hotel in Glasgow is a testament to his vision and tenacity as an entrepreneur. Like the Berjerano family, Peter's son is involved as a director of the hotel and his passion for the environment, a philosophy shared with his wife, was an important part of the hotel's formation. Blythswood Square was truly about the transformation of dream into reality, and required a depth of vision which many others could not see. Its development was beset my many challenges, including the most serious recession since the Great Depression and numerous construction issues; many would have simply walked away. Instead, Peter's strength and insight has created one of the most iconic and beautiful hotels in Scottish hospitality.

A perfect storm

The last two years have tested many people. For Peter Taylor the development and opening of Blythswood Square – a five-star hotel in the heart of Glasgow – was almost a trial by ordeal with construction failure and higher levels of investment at a time when the financial markets were in crisis and every penny counted.

Peter Taylor and The Town House Collection acquired Blythswood Square – the former Royal Scottish Automobile Club (RSAC) – in 2006 for £5 million with a vision to create a hotel that mixed the historical with the contemporary. The company planned to invest £15 million to create a high-end hotel and spa in one of Glasgow's most historical squares. The hotel was originally due to open in September 2008 and was eventually opened over a year later with a cost closer to £30 million – £10 million more than had been projected. It is worth noting that that the building had stood empty for four years and had two owners since it had been the RSAC. There were always going to be issues attached. However, as one senior industry player commented: 'Peter has been to hell and back in developing Blythswood and many would have given up.'

The major obstacles included the collapse of a back wall that caused numerous issues plus a construction company which eventually went into administration. This was in addition to working with the banks at a time when they were under immense pressures. Anyone who has overseen a redevelopment will understand the problems and issues involved but this period of time became almost a 'perfect storm' which tested the convictions of one of the industry's most experienced hoteliers.

'Yes, I am not sure anything else could have rained down on us', commented Peter quietly when we met. Peter is a naturally modest and unassuming man and as he spoke it was clear that this was as trying a period of time as he had faced.

'Oh it was not easy and we certainly faced many obstacles but we had a vision and passion for this property that we were determined to see through. And we probably didn't make things easy for ourselves as we wanted to go the extra mile and this does cost money. We could have invested less however we would not have achieved what we now have. It is a question of conviction and making judgement calls. I am very proud of what we have developed and I think that despite all the problems we faced, the hotel will be very successful... but yes, there were some dark moments.'

Peter is not new to working with hotels with history and therefore has some good insight into what could be expected. Peter is the owner and founder of the Town House Collection, a collection of luxury hotels – Channings, the Bonham, the Howard and the Edinburgh Residence all based in Edinburgh. The hotels offer their own individual character, retaining many of the period features of Edinburgh's historic past. So how did the story with Blythswood begin?

'I was originally approached maybe eight years ago to see if I would get involved when the club was in trouble. I did have some discussions and felt at that time that it would have been too complicated. However I guess that initial discussion had sparked a passion in me for the building. It is a building that is iconic in Glasgow.

'Late in 2005, I looked at the property again. It was just meant to be. We very quickly acquired it in January 2006, with a vision to create a five-star hotel but it needed defining, so we had much work to do.

'As soon as we got into the building we realised that much more had to be done – some of the plans for the rooms were too small and there needed to be a combination between the historical and the contemporary. We wanted this to be unquestionably the best hotel in Glasgow and therefore we needed to get the balance right.

'So we went back to the planners with a revised scheme delivering fewer and much larger rooms. We also created a luxury spa. We got planning permission in a record nine weeks. One has to say that despite all our problems, the City has been very supportive. The building had been standing empty for four years and had a number of owners who had attempted different solutions but had struggled.

'This created – as one would expect – a certain amount of cynicism about whether the figures would stack up. We started work in late 2006 and in November 2007 a back wall of the original building collapsed. The collapse delayed us by about 18 months. It couldn't have happened at a worse time and understandably it made the bank nervous. In fairness, they continued to fund throughout the project but it was not easy for either them or us. We invested £10 million extra into the project at a time when the financial markets collapsed.'

As others had struggled to make the property work successfully, one had to wonder what would make the difference.

'Everything in the building is bespoke. We have a passion about the environment. My wife and I built an eco-friendly house in Edinburgh and we used our philosophy to influence this build too. With the mixture of old and new, we had an opportunity to do something special – we have installed: rooftop solar water heating, Combined Heat &

Power (CHP) to cater for the base heating load and electrical demand of the hotel and ground source heat pumps served from an array of bore holes under the new build spa and bedroom extension which will provide heating and cooling to the bedrooms. This has resulted in a 43% reduction in carbon emissions. We have a sophisticated building management system. This alone cost an extra £1.5 million. We did this because we believed that it was the right thing to do.'

So have they been through hell?

'It hasn't been easy but one has to face these challenges. Our vision was to create a special hotel and I think we have achieved this despite all the challenges that we have faced.

'We have looked into every detail. The hotel placed the biggest order of Harris Tweed since the launch of the QE2. It provides vibrant colours that are key to the feel of the building.

'We paid homage to the history of the building, including theming the bar on the Monte Carlo rally which had started many times in the square at the front of the building.'

How had, I asked, the whole experience impacted on Peter?

'It has made me pause, take a break and consolidate before we push on. But how has it personally changed me? I am not sure it has. I have great pride in what we believe in and what we have achieved, and that we did it through a period of adversity. That happens in life.'

How is the hotel trading?

'We are delighted with how it is all going. It is trading well. The leisure market is strong. The corporate market is slower, but picking up. We are attracting celebrities and other high profile guests and feedback is good. We are delighted to have received several awards during our first year of opening including the prestigious Scottish Hotel of the Year which is a tribute to the team at the hotel and their continued passion and commitment. We are looking forward to good days ahead.'

(September 2010)

Ritz and Escoffier: two names synonymous with hospitality

It is hard to imagine two greater influences under one roof than César Ritz and Auguste Escoffier, the duo who opened The Savoy hotel in 1889 were a unique partnership. Both classic entrepreneurs, their union was a risk for the owners but they proved their skills at attracting a new mix of clientele and giving The Savoy a special reputation in hospitality. A key achievement was to spot the influence of women and they set out to attract more female clients to the customer base. Both gentlemen were pioneering in the hospitality industry.

Original role models

The influence of César Ritz and Auguste Escoffier on the London hotel market

When Richard d'Oyly Carte opened The Savoy Hotel in 1889 to wide acclaim, its reputation was founded on the work of two great professionals – César Ritz and Auguste Escoffier. Their influence upon the London hotel industry remains until this day. However, Ritz was not the initial choice of D'Oyly Carte for the role of General Manager at his new hotel but he was persuaded to appoint him on the advice on one Lillie Langtry who argued that Ritz would enable the hotel to attract female custom.

It is César Ritz who is credited with persuading gentlemen to dine in The Savoy with their wives, daughters and families. Previously, any socialising between families would take place within the privacy of their own homes. Lily Langtry believed that women were an untapped source of business and that an impressed wife would have great influence on making the hotel fashionable. Ritz achieved Langtry's vision with the aid of Lady de Grey who invited some of her friends to a banquet in the restaurant. The party was screened off from the other guests but people could not help but hear the laughter and music that ascended from the party and soon The Savoy was proclaimed as being both a respectable and fashionable place to dine.

However, Ritz could not have achieved this without the work of Escoffier in the kitchen. Theirs was a very special partnership, which had begun a few years earlier at the Grand Hotel in Monte Carlo. Both were original thinkers who emphasised the importance of comfort, cleanliness, service and acknowledged the influence of women. Escoffier once remarked that 'most of my best dishes were created for ladies'. It is an old story that Escoffier invented the first peach Melba for a dinner hosted by Dame Nellie Melba.

So who were these two great men?

César Ritz was born in Niedewold, Switzerland, in 1850. He was the thirteenth son of an alpine shepherd and began his career as a simple wine waiter at the Hôtel de Trois Couronnes et Poste. His early career was not heavily marked with distinction and he was sacked from a number of establishments for displaying a poor attitude, but he continued to work and his breakthrough came when he was made the Restaurant manager at the Grand Hotel in Nice in 1873. At the age of 27, he was made General Manager of the Grande Hôtel Nationale at Lucerne. In the 1880s, he became the General Manager of the Grand Hotel in Monte Carlo which is where he met Escoffier. Madame Ritz wrote that this was 'one of the most fortunate things that ever happened to either of the two men's lives'. In 1887, César Ritz acquired his first hotel, the Hôtel de Provence in Cannes. Ritz's reputation in Europe grew rapidly, so it was understandable that he would be recommended to Richard D'Oyly Carte. Upon taking up the challenge of managing The Savoy, he insisted upon bringing with him his trusted friend Escoffier as well as his cashier from Monte Carlo, Ajostini, and maître d'hôtel, Monsieur Echenard.

Whilst managing The Savoy, a Ritz Hotel syndicate was formed with the aim of building hotels named after Ritz himself in Paris, London, New York, Madrid and Johannesburg. The first venture was the 'Paris Ritz' which opened in 1898 to huge acclaim. The key financier was a wine merchant called Marnier Lapostolle who believed himself to be in Ritz's debt as Ritz had introduced Lapostolle's own invention to The Savoy and had hence created a market. That invention was a liqueur called 'Le Grande Marnier'.

Ritz was involved in the creation of another new quality hotel in London named The Carlton. These two ventures, together with the management of The Savoy marked the peak of Ritz's career. However, the storm clouds began to gather and by 1898 he had left The Savoy. Some say he was dismissed for covering for his friend Escoffier who has been taking backhanders. Officially he resigned on a matter of principle – for not being allowed to dismiss a housekeeper who disagreed with Ritz's methods. In 1902, aged 52, he suffered a nervous breakdown and he was never to fully recover. He died in 1918 in his beloved Switzerland at Kusnacht near to Lucerne. It is ironic that his name will be forever associated with the 1906 London Ritz when his role in its development was minimal.

Auguste Escoffier, the son of a blacksmith, is known as 'the king of chefs'. Escoffier was the complete professional who treated his kitchen as though it was a sacred temple and who introduced to London's kitchens, new efficient methods of improving service. He also possessed a huge ego which is why he created his best dishes for women as he believed that they really appreciated his work whilst men viewed their food more pragmatically. Escoffier never could speak more than a few words of English and he would joke that if he spoke the English language, he might also learn to cook in the English fashion.

The great Escoffier died in Monte Carlo in 1935.

EP magazine would like to thank Fairmont Hotels for their support with the writing of this article.

(April 2005)

Hotels

Robin Hutson
Co-founder, Hotel du Vin

Robin Hutson made his name as an entrepreneur for co-founding Hotel du Vin with Gerard Basset in 1994. Spotting a gap in the market for a relaxed, casual approach to hospitality and a new style of hotel, the pair set about creating a provincial hotel brand. Hotel du Vin was founded at the same time as Malmaison, and Ken McCulloch ultimately acquired the business in 2004. Robin has since gone onto pursue other entrepreneurial ventures, and although he looks for a certain amount of risk, his story is interesting because it is grounded in true hospitality foundations through his formative years spent at the Savoy Group and Chewton Glen.

It's not as easy as Monopoly

With the emergence in recent years of high quality, mid-market hotels and the refining of the budget hotel offer, not to mention the recently refurbished grandeur of famous London five-star operations, the industry has been constantly evolving. Now, it seems, we have something for everyone. Robin Hutson, director of Soho House and co-founder of Hotel du Vin talks more about the role he has played in these developments, and what he glimpses of the future.

I'm curious, that after 10 years building his own company – Hotel du Vin – Robin Hutson was able to walk away and become chairman of Soho House. So despite my overwhelming desire to ask him about a reported description of him as 'right flamboyant, just like Richard Gere', I resist and cut straight to the chase: how did it feel to walk away into something new?

'I think we really did sell Hotel du Vin at the right time', commented Robin, 'I'm one of those in-the-trenches operators. I enjoy smaller businesses where I can actually know everyone by name and it was getting to the stage where I couldn't do that anymore. The business had a strong base and a lot of growing still to do and it was right that there was new ownership to do that. As for staying on: I'm either in or out and I was upfront about that, it wouldn't have been good for me or the new owners to stay on after the sale. Natural progression…

'I had been involved with Nick Jones' Soho House group for eight years as a non-executive director,' explained Robin. 'So when he asked me to spend a little more time on the business and 'how would you like to be Chairman?' it was a natural progression and a great chance to get stuck in again, at first just one or two days a week, but now really most of my time.'

I'm equally intrigued by the beginning of Hotel du Vin, which must have felt at the time, like a departure from the tried and tested. In 1994 when Robin and Gerard Basset teamed up to launch Hotel du Vin such concepts did not exist. How do some people have the ability to see what is around the corner and act on it? It all looks so easy in hindsight. Robin put this into true perspective.

'It's really hard to imagine isn't it? But in 1994 there was no good coffee on the high street. In fact, it was really quite difficult to get an espresso. Other things were very different too. I remember our first advertising campaign telling people that there was no dress code! Can you imagine that now? It would just sound crass.'

Then there is the simultaneous development of Malmaison. Today the two names are usually said in a single breath. Ken McCulloch and Robin Hutson know each other well, but in 1994 as the two brands were developing at either end of the country, neither knew of the other's plans. How did Hotel du Vin actually come about?

'I was Managing Director for Martin Skan at Chewton Glen, and Gerard Bassett was Head Sommelier. We could feel a change towards a more casual, relaxed approach to the industry, so we left to set up Hotel du Vin.'

'At that time, like Ken I suppose, we felt that there was really room for a new style of hotel. As well as the move towards a more casual approach to hotels and dining, there was a real need for a quality, affordable offering in provincial towns. Apart from the beautiful (and expensive) country house hotels there were really only the run-down, crusty coach house hotels on offer.

'When we started out we had a very simple concept in mind; for example, no room service and no cooked breakfasts. We wanted to offer a pared back version of an excellent hotel. Well, that was the plan! After fantastic press coverage from day one we were pushed both externally and internally to stretch ahead and add things to the basic model, but the core values and plan remained the same.'

The decision to have a sommelier as a business partner is also slightly unusual?

'Well I suppose most people opt for a chef in order to get the food side right and that makes sense. In our situation, Gerard and I knew each other well and really saw a great opportunity. We wanted the restaurants to be a feature but didn't want to be a slave to the food or for the hotel to be known for the chef rather than the whole. However, as it turned out, a 21-year-old James Martin was our first Head Chef!'

So let's return to the start, where did this well known hotelier begin? Like many it was in the training grounds of the Savoy Group, at Claridges and The Berkeley that Robin launched his hotel career.

'I had a good time at school, but I suppose you could say that it never really held my attention,' smiled Robin. 'I realised that I quite enjoyed cooking and the kitchen and so went on to train in that area. The next natural step was a hotel management course and it was then that I really understood that if you are passionate about something your interest increases and performance follows.

'After graduation, I joined the Savoy Group and really learned how to do it all properly. I also had a great time, as the reception manager at The Berkeley. I met all the celebrities and that's exciting for any 22-year-old!'

The Savoy Group and Forte have produced many of today's leaders who have gone on to do all sorts of things. I'm interested in the reasons for this. Is it that this training gives you the foundations to build upon?

'Absolutely,' replied Robin, 'it's only when you really know how to do things properly that you can start to muck about with the concept and change all the things around the edges – like we did with Hotel du Vin. I can still see it in the younger ones coming through today. People who have had that formal background and training have a different level of confidence; they know that they have that base to work from.'

Robin, like many strong leaders, is also quick to point out the others who have inspired or guided him at different stages of his career, like Martin Skan at Chewton Glen who he describes as 'a real taskmaster who taught me a lot'.

'After The Berkeley and a year in Paris with The Savoy, my wife and I decided to travel and I spent two years in Bermuda as an Operations Manager of a resort there. It was in Bermuda, working for John Jefferies, that I learnt all about marketing – that certainly wasn't 'the done thing' at the Savoy Group, but in Bermuda we marketed the heck out of it!

'On my return to the UK, I took up the position of General Manager at Chewton Glen, where I learnt a lot from Martin and got a recession and a few more projects under my belt.'

And we all know where the story goes next and how the Hotel du Vin chapter ends. After a lot of good press, many accolades, seven hotels and exactly 10 years later (to the day) Hotel du Vin was sold to MWB. After a short break, Robin became chairman of Soho House. Then history repeats itself, in January this year the Soho House group was bought by Richard Caring, of Caprice Holdings fame and this time Robin agreed to stay on as a director.

Soho House comprises a number of members clubs in the UK, including the original Soho House in Greek Street in the West End as well as a club in Manhattan. In addition to this, the group owns Cecconi's and other restaurants in London, and the Cowshed range of products. So what are the plans?

'It's a crowded market. You begin to get the feeling that everything has been done,' said Robin. 'We have a mix and match approach to this business, with the members clubs as the core. We can add anything from cinemas, to hotel rooms to spas to fit the space and offer a complete lifestyle club. But we can't afford to stand still.'

In a market that has just been described as crowded, I'm keen to hear where Robin thinks the industry will head next?

'I think it will all be about a return to traditional values and substance. The days of form over function are passed. It's simply not good enough to over-design a concept and expect it to overcome shortfalls in the core service and product. You just have to look at where the celebrities are heading. It's not the super trendy, over-designed destinations. The current favourites have traditional values and service such as the Connaught or Claridges. You can't just buy a hotel like you do in Monopoly.

(October 2008)

Hotels

Sonu Shivdasani

Founder and CEO, Six Senses Resorts & Spas

Sonu embodies many natural entrepreneurial traits. He is open to taking risks and is prepared to use intuitive thinking to make business decisions. Sonu readily admits that might prove to be 'a step too far' for some people looks more like a safe bet to him. He is a visionary thinker who seeks to push boundaries in an intelligent and inspiring way.

Pushing the envelope

Founded in the mid-1990s, Six Senses Resorts & Spas has become recognised as one of the world's leading luxury resort operators. The company has operations based in the Indian Ocean and South East Asia with openings due in Oman, Jordan, Spain and Greece, which will make the company a truly global player. After this expansion, the aim is to open in the Americas. Six Senses is led by Sonu Shivdasani, an individual who has developed a reputation for being a very modern and insightful thinker.

What helped make Sonu become a global entrepreneur? Did being educated within two of Britain's leading establishments leave a lasting impression? How important has his family been in his development? How has he changed whilst developing Six Senses?

Since opening its first location in the Maldives in 1995, Six Senses Spas and Resorts has developed a reputation for offering some of the most well-thought-out and creative destinations for the high-end tourism market. Its present expansion plans will result in a total of 18 resorts by the end of 2008, adding a further five to seven new destinations in the following years. As I discover the story behind Six Senses' conception and development, I gain insight into its founder's business philosophy.

British born and educated at Eton College and Oxford University, Sonu Shivdasani possesses a striking energy and conviction in his approach to business. His father – too, was an entrepreneur and built up the family business in Nigeria across a range of trading activities, moving to Switzerland in his later working years. Acknowledging that he grew up in a 'pretty entrepreneurial environment', I am interested to learn how Sonu's observation of his father's experience has impacted on his own approach.

> 'We often talked through business issues around the dinner table and sought to analyse the particular incident or situation that needed to be decided upon,' notes Sonu.

Discussion and reasoning are clearly intrinsic values to Sonu's philosophy, not just skills learnt through familial and academic teaching. His entire approach is driven by the desire to test judgement and theories where others may choose to run with a safer option. With this in mind I move on to ask Sonu how his British education has influenced him.

> 'Without doubt I believe that the course I chose to study at Oxford – an MA in English Literature – was extremely helpful. Because it was not practical as such, the course taught you to develop a thinking mindset of critical reasoning and not to take things for granted. You also learnt a lot about people and I believe that understanding human nature is very important. My tutor at Oxford was, also an important part of my learning.'

Some of the significant milestones for launching Six Senses were the considerable steps involved in bringing what could be considered serious hurdles, into a saleable idea for investors and consumers alike. Initially these steps included regenerating an unused and isolated island, resolving transport logistics to and from the island, and seeing off the threat of bankruptcy from the operating company with whom much of the financial security was linked. Yet, Sonu relays these events with the character of one who sees the cup half full and not half empty; any perceived hurdles were resolved and this questioning approach remains a central element of the Six Senses ethos. An open-minded, rational and relentless thinker, Sonu is consumed by the vision for his business. I am intrigued to discover how Sonu views the notion of risk and its importance to his success?

'Without doubt you have to take risks in business to be successful. In my career some risks have proven to be successful, whilst others have not and I think that you have got to keep a sense of perspective about your failures. In addition there are some risks which I took early on my career which I would probably not take on now. However, risk is, in a way, a slightly subjective term. Some initiatives which may otherwise be perceived as risky are, in another sense, a sure bet. For example, we are developing a resort near the Cambodian border and our investment is US$75 million, with an average of US$1.5 million to 2 million per room. To me, this is not a question of risk, when you consider that the cost of land and access to the island (which is provided from Bangkok) is easier than travelling to other destinations in Thailand. I always seek to push the envelope to ensure we are making decisions which take on all the facts, and challenge conventional wisdom.'

Sonu also credits his wife, Eva, a former international model, as having great impact on the progression of the vision for Six Senses. With a shared love of travel and new experiences, Sonu refers to her often during our discussion.

'We can bounce ideas around and particularly around design and creative elements; Eva has an amazing attention to detail. We have always been happy in different cultures and stayed at numerous interesting hotels around the world, and we both share a passion for environmental sustainability. However, I think the fact that we both initially believed in the potential of the Maldives and that she encouraged and supported the idea of developing a resort there that has been hugely important in the early days. We felt that a resort offered an opportunity to provide an experience for the private, leisure consumer that would contrast to what was generally provided by the corporate hotel brands. These tend to be orientated at the business traveller and centred on a smaller length of stay.'

Sonu's vision for establishing Six Senses Resorts and Spas has been to 'provide innovative and enriching experiences in a sustainable environment.' He comments:

'At some stage, zero emissions will become a qualifier, not a differentiator and I hope to ensure that Six Senses sets an example for others to follow by our programme of by reducing emissions. We are, for example, working on initiatives such as the creation of an Eco-Suite to be completed by 2010.'

The company's current expansion is partly premised on opportunities that it will provide for leadership and career development amongst employees. I comment that it must have been challenging, at least initially, to approach the task of attracting talent willing to work with such a different vision. Sonu notes, 'Ownership and accountability are vital to our business' success. We have between 20 and 30 incentive programmes and the key is to motivate people about the vision. I am also seeking to reinvent the idea of the regionalised business. We like to add more twists all the time, constantly redefining the notion of intelligent luxury – by which we mean providing what the consumer wants in as luxurious a setting as possible – and I believe that by operating in clusters we can achieve this more intimately for our guests in different locations throughout the world.'

Six Senses have developed a unique and innovative approach to their business, and Sonu is the driving force behind its vision and ethos. It is also evident that there is real innovation behind his approach. The desire to ensure new boundaries are set down, continually creating new possibilities, are fundamental to his philosophy.

(October 2007)

Surinder Arora

Chairman, Arora International Hotels

Surinder Arora is one of the most successful and respected hoteliers in the UK. His vision was to spot a gap in the market for a hotel which catered to airline staff, and Surinder has since gone on to develop Arora International, whose hotels include a partnership with Sofitel. His success has been the result of great personal sacrifice into a venture which was entirely driven by his sheer determination and hard work. An extremely ethical operator, Surinder has a strong value set; amongst these are integrity, loyalty and tenacity. Having manoeuvred his hotel business into the mainstream, Surinder has gone onto become one of the most respected entrepreneurs in the industry.

A farmer's market

Recently, there has been much written about the impact of British entrepreneurs, of Asian origin, on the UK economy and the positive impact that they are having. There have been many factors stated for this occurrence – work ethic, family values, and culture. What are the true factors that lie behind this success? Surinder Arora, Chief Executive of Arora International tells us his story.

The proliferation of Asian entrepreneurs currently making their mark in the UK comprise a portfolio of strong commercial performances and sustained business growth, seemingly able to outperform standard market expectations. There has been much written in the media about the impact of these men and women, with a recent feature in the *Daily Telegraph* (April 2006) stating: 'their extraordinary achievements over the past two decades bears testament to the much lauded "Asian business values" of sustained hard work and family enterprise.'

Specifically, there is a prevalent view that the rise of importance of Asian businesses in the UK coincides with a weakening in the work ethic of the UK as a whole. One of the other points often raised is that the concept of family businesses, that have been built over the years, are the foundations of their success. Many have been built over a long time, not seeking quick success, but building a sustainable business that has strength based on longevity.

In July 2006, *En Passant* had the opportunity to meet with one such entrepreneur to hear his views on these issues – Surinder Arora, Chairman and Founder of Arora Hotels and the Arora Family Trust. Currently guiding his business through an impressive expansion programme, his projects include a £180 million deal to build a Sofitel at Terminal 5 (the only hotel group to be granted a franchise partnership with this five-star brand), the acquisition of a further nine hotels following a £300 million agreement with the BAA Airport Hotels Unit Trust and the purchase of a portion of the exclusive Wentworth Club. It is therefore somewhat startling to note that Surinder built his first B&B in 1999, and less than seven years later, aged 47, he is estimated to be worth £127 million.

Honing in on the idea to develop an airport-specific hotel brand, Surinder's initial set-up was to acquire a row of houses opposite the BA crew's check-in centre on the Bath Road, Heathrow. He garnered support and recognition for the idea through writing a letter to both BA and the crew themselves. With support for the concept in place, Surinder set about personally meeting all of the people whose homes he wanted to buy and develop, actively working to attain planning permission with local councils. Understandably the B&B he eventually built was highly popular with BA crew, not just for its convenient location but also for the friendly and welcoming service. Having established this initial success, Surinder decided to build and run a hotel on the same site. Single-handedly managing the construction project, with an initial, small investment from a friendly bank, he had little by way of experience in such a risky undertaking. Leading this first hotel project to completion has been the biggest challenge that Surinder has faced in his career. He 'lived and breathed' the project spending seven days a week on-site, eventually opening three days ahead of schedule.

Today, the Arora International Hotel is a 360-bed operation. In the lobby we see that it is buzzing with activity and there is a sense of family atmosphere. Surinder's view that all customers should be treated 'like royalty' is clearly embraced by staff in the hotel. In this case, with the majority of customers air crew, the cabinet of 'sensible shoes' in the foyer and diverse range of airline uniforms represented are both strong testaments to how well the founding vision has been successfully translated.

Surinder arrived in the UK at the age of 13 unable to speak English and having to learn a new way of life, eventually finishing school with O Levels. Prior to 1999, he worked for BA as an office junior and also as a wine waiter at an airport hotel in the evenings; as much to learn more skills, as to make a living for his family. He has no qualms about such modest beginnings and it is fascinating to hear how Surinder has methodically and carefully evolved the vision for what is a growing and highly successful enterprise from scratch. We discuss the arguments presented by the *Daily Telegraph* article, which argues that a combination of 'very, very hard work and strong, family-minded culture' is the common theme of the success of many successful Asian entrepreneurs.

Surinder's own view is that the hallmarks of his own success can be found in any entrepreneur. Hard work and tenacity are characteristics of many successful business people. Yet, it is the difference in Surinder's approach to building and developing his business that sets him apart. In his own words he is a 'farmer, not a hunter'. By this he means that his business has been evolved within an infrastructure that has been with him since the beginning when operating the B&B business; his lawyers, accountants and banks have not changed as the business has grown and in his view this has brought about relationships based on respect and mutual trust. In speaking with him, it is also abundantly clear that Surinder's own strong value set has given him what can best be described as a 'humble presence of mind' gained from his strong and integrated family network. These values are principally to work hard and not rely on government handouts for financial support, to 'not forget where you came from' in life and to keep going no matter what, especially in the dark and difficult times. 'Don't ever give up in life' is a simple philosophy that Surinder refers back to throughout our meeting, and it is a straightforward but relevant mantra. He believes that it is easy and often tempting for people to just fail to persist with their goals when things get difficult in life – and that now, more than ever, times are tough for many people. As someone who has gone through some personal and professional struggles in his life, Surinder's deepest message is that there are plenty of mountains and valleys to navigate throughout one's life and, it is while we are in the valleys, that our character is truly tested. These are the times, he says, where we must hold on to our beliefs and principles.

Family values and a strong, vibrant influence from his parents and wider familial network are clearly a bedrock of Surinder's success. A close knit family is a 'big plus' and he is greatly indebted to his late mother, Shila, for her role in driving the importance of sheer hard work and tenacity – a plaque is dedicated to her in the lobby of the Arora International Hotel and his jointly owned Manchester Hotel is a partnership with none other than Sir Cliff Richard (his mum was a lifelong fan), complete with themed rooms. Shila herself worked in supermarkets when times were tough, and did not shy away from embedding the propensity to do the same in her own mentoring and teaching of her son. Surinder too, almost matter-of-factly, acknowledges that, if he had to do it all again in the way that he has, he most certainly would. This contrasts sharply with the emerging generational issues impacting on recruitment and retention within the UK, where a significant proportion of younger people leave the back-of-house roles regarding them as inferior, preferring to get further up the career ladder from the outset. Surinder himself acknowledges this problem stating that fewer nationals are prepared to 'roll their sleeves up', which has certainly contributed to a rise in the recruitment of Eastern Europeans into his hotels. It is interesting to note that one of the underlying issues associated with this 'resistance' from UK nationals is higher levels of personal debt incurred by young people who must earn bigger salaries and who have grown up without the same worries over recession and interest rates experienced by older generations.

We discuss Surinder's own view on the UK economy. He believes the economic situation is genuinely 'scary' and this is mainly driven by the high levels of debt incurred by both corporations (in the pursuit of major growth programmes) and individuals, meaning that not even a major hike in interest rates, rather just a fractional increase, could initiate serious problems. Yet, Surinder believes that the economic stability brought about through the current government, notably in keeping interest rates low, has helped him in his own considered business endeavours. He does not believe that the UK will get back to the 'crazy old days' of high interest rates of the 1990s.

The fruits of Surinder's success are clearly defined by immense hard work, hands-on involvement in his business, and a strong support network of both family and trusted business partners. His personal commitment to the construction of his hotels is absolute – Surinder meets *En Passant* in between frequent trips up and down the Bath Road to T5. This is clearly how Surinder likes to lead – from the front, and in a manner that ensures his business investment is sound and communication as transparent as possible.

Our time with Surinder is both constructive and an opportunity to take stock of what is genuinely an inspirational success story. Whilst it is possible to argue that his own success as an entrepreneur is indeed characteristic of such people generally, Surinder's charisma and propensity for business success is also drawn from his humble and unpretentious approach to leadership. This difference is clearly attributable to his family and the hands-on, hard work put in to build the business to where it is today. Undoubtedly the positive results that the Arora Group are experiencing, including a rate of business growth which exceeds standard forecasts, denotes some important messages to the wider community. The harvests being reaped by successful Asian entrepreneurs looks set to continue.

(October 2006)

Food Service

Marc Verstringhe

Founder, Catering and Allied Services International

Marc founded and led one of the major foodservice catering forces of the period from 1975 to 2000 – Catering and Allied. At its peak, Catering and Allied made contract catering almost appear to be sexy and this was quite an achievement as back in the 1980s; contract catering was seen to be the poor relation in the industry. It is due to the work of the sector's leaders of this time that brought up the profile and reputation of the sector.

Catering and Allied was a company that stood for high but sound principles such as great people being empowered to deliver great food and service. The highest compliment probably ever paid to the company was that one of its fiercest competitors once banned its employees from ever mentioning their name.

For many of those employed by Catering and Allied, it has been hard for many to find a similar ethos or culture again and they will often be found still talking fondly about the governing philosophies that stood behind the company. There are others that will say that the world has changed and that a company such as Catering and Allied was right for its time and could not operate in today's market. This is simply not true. What made Catering and Allied different – for the good and the bad – was Marc. Marc was its soul and driver and without him, in truth, the company would not have been seen in the same light, as it was Marc that embodied and walked the high principles that the company stood for. It should also be noted that Marc would be the first to disagree with this comment as he would point to his colleagues.

It can be argued that the culture of the company became its weakness over time for as Marc took a step slightly away from the coal face, others tried to copy Marc's approach but it could not be achieved as it was more than just a philosophy or an approach. It was a culture glued together by his spirit and generosity.

This may sound over complimentary towards the man himself. This may be half true but the reality is that Marc's strengths and weaknesses were the company's strengths and weaknesses. Again Marc will argue – correctly – that he had strong beliefs, principles and strategies that he brought to the company. This is absolutely correct but the question is whether the next layers down in the company drivers really understood Marc's thinking. As will often happen, as Marc and his closest team took a step away, the culture would become gradually compromised as the principles were subtly changed and altered and of course as this happened the company became slightly less competitive. It is a natural and common problem for 'generous' entrepreneurs who are very supportive. The company culture comes to rely too much on the individual and their generosity – so that when it is in not there, the founding principles start to be altered and decline sets in. But at its peak, the company was one which every competitor admired.

So what is the story of Catering and Allied?

Catering and Allied was founded in 1975 by three colleagues – Marc, Kit Cuthbert and Jan Joops. At its peak, the company was split into a number of sections:

- Catering and Allied London
- Catering and Allied Holland
- Catering and Allied Chiltern
- A shareholding in Digby Trout Restaurants.

Marc believed that directors should not build 'ivory towers' but stay close to their clients and hence believed that, as the old saying goes, 'small is beautiful'. Marc and the co-founders believed that to retain the core values of the company, it was important that the leadership teams were close geographically to its clients. This dictated the approach of the company to its growth in both London and Holland. Each founder had a clear remit and each was close to the coalface with no desire to leave it.

In 2002, there was a book published – *Managing to Serve* – which outlined the history of contract catering, of Catering and Allied, and also the management principles that lay behind the company. The irony, of course, was that the success of Catering and Allied was not about management theory or any textbook thinking but about very passionate people who enjoyed working together to deliver a top-level service to their clients. It was exceptional because the founders were exceptional.

However, it was a company full of contradictions. Many would say that the company focused more on standards, people and service levels rather than on profits. However, this was not true.

Marc would argue that Catering and Allied was very commercially focused and in fact outperformed many of the 'reputedly' more business-orientated concerns where it counted most. He will note that all the original investors had a return on their investment that was close to 1600-fold. He will also point to the fact a report in 1998, which calculated productivity of employees versus turnover, placed Catering and Allied ahead of all its major competitors with the average employee contributing £34,391, whilst their closest competitor was High Table with £32,391 and with Compass lagging behind at £25,154. He would also note that the company was market leader in London, Holland and had a shareholding in another market leader – Digby Trout. Chiltern was aborted as it was hard to translate the successful formula in London to outside the capital.

The company and its story was an undoubted success but so much of this comes from the man himself. Many have tried to copy Marc's approach and failed. Marc believed in freeing up the individual to perform and not in manuals. He would describe the company's approach as a 'patron driven' methodology whereby the manager on site was the 'patron' and could bring their own style/approach to the restaurant. This worked for a long period of time but arguably began to suffer as the market turned in the early 1990s and costs became tighter.

So what does make Marc different to others?

To answer this question, one needs to understand Marc. Even today in retirement the man is passionate about the industry. He will still attend many industry meetings and is still actively promoting the importance of strong links between education and industry. He speaks with an enthusiasm and passion that makes it very easy to understand why Catering and

Allied stood that one step apart from others. He is one of those exceptional people who will rarely be heard to utter a bad word about another and who are driven by a passion for food, wine and friendship.

To many discussing friendship in business may sound almost 'soft' but to Marc it is fundamental. I can almost imagine him scoffing at someone saying it would be soft to have a good relationship with a competitor and declaring 'Surely we are all bigger than that?'. Marc would often have lunch with key competitors swapping information and war stories.

Marc and I have spoken much over the past decade and so often he has spoken of the importance of strategic alliances. For much of this time, the economy was booming and I would find myself politely listening but ignoring as I could not see the value of an alliance with another company … that was until the recession came and the world turned upside down. It was only during the heart of the recession did it occur to me that, of course, Marc had worked and operated through three recessions and that, of course, during these times it was sometimes important to be able to work with others towards a common goal. It was not lost on me that I had been naïve.

What were Marc's origins?

Marc was the son of a Belgian hotelier and grew up in the seaside resort of Knokke le Zoute. He, therefore, understood early the importance of client satisfaction and how it would impact on business. His father encouraged Marc to think broadly and to be 'international' in thought and deed. He ensured that the young Marc was multilingual – which although common today was unusual in the late 1940s.

These two points do go a long way to understanding Marc as he wants his customers to be inspired and he has always looked beyond boundaries. Marc would note that he was driven from day one of his business by the question: 'Why should a client choose us?'. This is very similar to: 'What can we do to ensure that the client wants to use us?'. Marc was also ahead of his time with the Dutch company and working internationally. To Marc it was natural. To others it was radical.

The final point that can also be related to this period was Marc's thirst for knowledge. He takes great enjoyment from learning from new cultures and environments. He has a mind that wants to listen and learn and even today he enjoys discussing new ideas. Marc may be retired but he is still young at heart.

In 1954, Marc was called up to military service with the Belgian forces in Germany. He found this period useful as it helped him see life through different eyes and to plan and think strategically. After National Service in 1957, Marc moved to England and became Restaurant Manager at the Lygon Arms and his career in England was soon developing very fast. By 1971, he became Managing Director of Sutcliffe Catering and in 1975 founded Catering and Allied with his colleagues Kit Cuthbert and Jan Joops. He broke away from Sutcliffe because he felt that the company's principles had changed and was losing his creativity and focus on clients. With this in mind, it would be inevitable that Marc would break away as he could not be dishonest to his beliefs.

It is too simplistic to argue that Marc inspired many because he had strong belief and conviction in the things that others were also inspired by. This is certainly true and he created a structure that allowed good people to express themselves.

He understood creative talents and freed them up to be creative. He achieved this through a desire to exceed client's expectations and understood what this required but he also had empathy for the creative talent which could be difficult. It was this empathy and often generosity that allowed his team to trust him and want to be successful for the man ... but it was also inevitable that over time this would be hard to maintain as others would learn, catch up and bring new innovations through.

Food Service

Alastair Storey

William Baxter

Co-founder, BaxterStorey

BaxterStorey: the formula for success?

Alastair and William have established one of the most respected independent foodservice companies in the UK. Despite clear differences in their entrepreneurial characteristics, they both share common traits that contribute to the successful partnership. First and foremost of these is a shared vision, notably a commitment to retaining an entrepreneurial culture as the business grows. In addition, the duo have demonstrated their willingness to take managed risks, namely through strategic acquisitions such as the gourmet sandwich chain Benugo in December 2007, and both have fulfilled and active lives outside of work, with motor racing a shared passion.

Yet, they are both different in significant ways. Alastair is both leader and entrepreneur, and has arguably steered the embryonic BaxterStorey concept into a company of over £360 million turnover. On the other hand, William is a classic entrepreneur who prior to BaxterStorey had successfully established two other respected catering companies, Baxter and Platts and BaxterSmith – a feat unmatched by any other in the foodservice industry. This story is likely to be one of the most fabled ventures in future years.

Taking it to the edge

BaxterStorey has become one of the most successful companies in the foodservice sector. What next for the business?

Formed in 2004 by the merger of Wilson Storey Halliday and BaxterSmith, BaxterStorey has grown both organically and via its acquisitions of Holroyd Howe and Benugo in 2007 to become the largest independent player, and fourth in the market. There are many observers who speculate about BaxterStorey's plans for the future and, in particular, whether it will remain the leading entrepreneurial business for contract catering, or evolve into a larger, corporate player.

In a career spanning more than 30 years, Alastair Storey, CEO, has previously held positions with Sutcliffe Catering and Granada Food Services, before embarking on his own venture in 2000, initially as Wilson Storey. He is a shrewd individual, coming across as incredibly passionate yet possessing a steely grit and determination. Throughout our interview Alastair is very engaged, and willing to challenge assumptions and issues in a direct and honest fashion. He argues that market domination has never been the ambition of the business:

> 'BaxterStorey was established as the antidote to large multinational corporations, offering fresh food, local produce and getting back to the idea that frontline staff are the important people in business. We have grown as a consequence of having an interesting product, so having huge volume is not the most important factor. It's rewarding when people comment on how well we are doing, as we always think there is a lot we could be doing better. Yes, we are pleased with what we have achieved, but we are never satisfied.'

Alastair believes that BaxterStorey still has a fairly modest share of the UK business and industry market, and at present a core focus is on investment in regional representation, including Scotland, Ireland and Wales. Despite the company's concentration on blue chip B&I clients, a market which accounts for less than 50 per cent of the available market, Alastair argues that the business can substantially increase market share:

> 'BaxterStorey is always planning five to 10 years ahead. We are not interested in a flotation and we do not intend to sell.

'Having established our business in the south east we have steadily increased penetration into other locations and I think we are still very much underrepresented in these, so there is huge potential to take BaxterStorey to a broader market in addition to further potential in the south east. We do not want to do anything off-piste.

'It's very easy to look at things in a global way, yet we are in a relationship business: our clients have high expectations. There are short lines of communications in BaxterStorey and the board is literally walking the shop floor – we have a fear of becoming remote.'

Alastair's comments raise an interesting philosophical question, as there is an argument put forward by some that the business will naturally become less entrepreneurial in its approach as it grows. It is the question in our meeting to which Alastair has given a great deal of thought and he raises a number of thought-provoking points:

'I think that there is often a perception that entrepreneurs are always doing something exciting with no rules. However, I do not think this is true. Most entrepreneurs know exactly what they are doing and, if they are not following rules, it might be that they are not yet sure of their boundaries, are trying to find a pattern or rhythm coming out of what they want to achieve.

'I believe BaxterStorey is highly entrepreneurial. We give our management teams tremendous power to do what they want to do. Does this mean that they can do anything? No, because there is always legislation or other requirements which need to be taken into account. I would say that we offer our people flexibility, train them very well and give them the freedom to work within certain parameters. An entrepreneur operates in the same way.'

It has been noted that BaxterStorey has used debt to fund their growth and I am interested to learn how this has been managed.

'Even from my days with Wilson Storey, we have not been afraid of bank debt. I see it as similar to people needing a mortgage to buy their first home, not many have large funds available at the start of their lives. However, we are prudent and don't take excessive risks – we always set out to under-promise and over-deliver to our bank.'

The senior team of BaxterStorey is well-regarded and includes a mix of individuals who have run their own companies, and others with experience from other established operators. One might expect to find a degree of tension as the natural entrepreneurs in the business react to a more structured environment.

'I think this is a non-issue. The best businesses have got to have good strong personalities, and when you eliminate these you take away all the verve. I think that the board we have got is exceptional. They are their own people, so of course there is compromise involved. My job is to keep a reasonable balance, but ultimately these guys are all quite practical caterers and we all want the same thing. BaxterStorey has never done anything hostile or aggressive, the deals we have done were because we felt we needed more management expertise.'

With a Chefs Academy and Barista Training Academy launched in recent years, BaxterStorey is preparing to launch a management development programme this year to support the progression of future leaders in the business. Alastair believes that the biggest challenge in the industry is getting the right talent, particularly at senior level.

'Contract catering is a brilliant market and the challenge for BaxterStorey is that we need to be good champions of the industry. For some reason, once you get to a certain level, it can be a struggle to find the next generation of leaders.'

Having pointed out that his father has only just retired at the age of 86, Alastair is focused on creating a long-term vision for BaxterStorey and, in doing so, pushing the boundaries of what can be achieved. In his eyes it can be easy to get caught in the macho culture of business, focused on win–lose scenarios and the quick wins, but this is not his style.

'I just don't think you can take a short-term view. One of the great advantages of being privately owned is that if our margins are down a bit, it may mean that there is less to reinvest, but we do not need to report to a market that we are going up all the time.

'I love fast cars and F1 racing and there is a great analogy from that sport. Once you get to know the feeling of being inside the car you can constantly take things to the edge; the challenge is keeping it all together. This is the skill of running a business: keeping a lot of things organised and running to its maximum, so that you can take things as close to the edge as possible, without going over. And that takes leadership, enthusiasm of shareholders, doing what you set out to do and constant investment in training.

BaxterStorey has been one of the success stories in contract catering. In speaking with Alastair it is evident that he is working to evolve as a leading independent operator which sets new standards of in terms of quality and leadership. He concludes:

'This vision has not changed at all and is not going to change. Yet, BaxterStorey is growing and evolving. To me it feels like a better business than it was five years ago. In five years' time, it will be a better business, but it will be different. Now that is what I would call entrepreneurial – sensing movement around you and recognising when it is time to take bold decisions.'

(February 2010)

As good as you have to be

William Baxter has been one of the leading figures within the contract food service sector for almost 20 years. He is also a character that many see to be a role model for the sector. Yet few know much about the man that has stood behind three successful businesses in that 20-year period.

At times our industry can be full of 'hidden daggers' for those that have been successful and it is very rare to find anyone in such a position without at least a few barbed comments from the jealous and envious. When there is a character that is both successful and universally popular and respected, it is a remarkably rare feat and one that says more about that person than any accolade could. William Baxter is one such character and it is more remarkable for the fact that he has been a leading figure in three very successful business entities, who have all carried his name within the contract food service market over the past 20 years – Baxter and Platts (1987–99), BaxterSmith (2000–04) and BaxterStorey (2004–present day).There is literally no one else who can lay claim to such a feat.

So why is it that so few have anything bad to say about the man? Part of the reason is that it is very rare to ever hear William being critical of others. It is quite difficult to be critical of anyone who is never critical of others themselves. I remember taking a reference from William on someone that he had dismissed and he still had more good to say about the person than bad. It is a strange contradiction for a man who has achieved so much but he does appear to understand other's failings:

> 'Sometimes you just have to understand that not everyone can be as good as you want them to be', he commented. 'Generally, they will live up to 80% of what you want and you just have to accept that as good enough'.

William is invariably positive in his outlook and possesses an infectious charm that does make people feel good about themselves. Over lunch recently, I asked him why he was always so positive even when speaking about his fiercest competitors. He looked at me slightly bemused by the question:

> 'Because, I genuinely like them all. They are good people. It doesn't mean I don't want to beat them but neither does it mean that I don't like them.'

Maybe, this is also part of his secret – the fact that he has a clear perspective and lives a full life beyond work. One does get the feeling that work is just one of many challenges that he enjoys. Others include motor racing – he has competitively raced in karts, cars and on bikes over the years – fishing and golf. He has a boat moored near to Oban, on the west coast of Scotland, which he takes out regularly around the Hebrides. He is one of life's natural enthusiasts. If he had not found his success in the contract catering sector, he would have surely found success in some other discipline.

> 'At the end of the day, this is a business I enjoy because it revolves around people and good food. This industry is made up of people of all shapes and sizes and many of them are just genuinely good people who enjoy what they do. That has to be a good start for any business.'

In his younger days, William was one of four children and his brothers and sisters were naturally academic. The other three went onto become either lawyers or doctors. By contrast, William was dyslexic and worked to prove himself. He both worked hard and played hard. Despite his dyslexia, he still gained three 'A' levels in zoology, geology and art. He was offered two places at university to study architecture but turned them down and instead chose to go to Westminster College to gain a HND in Hotel and Catering Institutional Management. It was here that he met his wife and they married during their second year. Upon graduating he joined Sutcliffe Catering and was soon progressing. At the age of 23 he was managing 17 operations.

'I had a great time at Sutcliffe and they had an excellent team of characters,' recounted William. 'I remember once falling foul of a client and Don Davenport was called in. I remember thinking – that's it, there goes my career!' I had only been an Area Manager for a short while and had just received my first company car. Don handled the situation superbly and even had the client almost apologising. It was a real team at Sutcliffe in those days and you felt that people were there for you. There was a good banter in the office and good atmosphere throughout the operations.'

In 1987, William resigned from Sutcliffe Catering to found 'Baxter and Platts' with Robert Platts who had also been a colleague. Robert Platts was a different but similar character in many ways – the son of a military doctor, he dropped out of Bangor University where he had been studying biochemistry and soil science and went to Ealing College to study for his HND in Hotel and Catering Management. He joined Sutcliffe as an Assistant Manager but worked his way up and became General Manager for the caterer's City of London operations. Both men were charismatic characters in their own right and although, it may have appeared that they would be successful, it did not initially all go to plan.

'It was quite an experience and we were hardly an overnight success,' recalled William. 'It took us six months to win our first contract and we were probably one month away from giving up. At the time, Rob and I just went for it and it was nerve-racking as we could see our mortgages building up. But, fortunately, it did come good.'

'It was a real partnership with Rob as we both went through those really tough early years together and we had skills that complemented each other. He was superb at IT, accounts and administration. I was better at building up sales leads. We would make decisions together and we always agreed early on that we both had to be in agreement on an issue for something to happen. It worked for us, as we did not lose a contract until 1995.'

Baxter and Platts became an established player and they won the Food Service Catey Award in 1997. Turnover grew to around £25 million, and they were acquired by Granada Food Services in 1997 for an estimated £16 million. After their 'earn out' year, Rob Platts retired to Guernsey whilst William stayed initially within Granada Food Services before starting again with BaxterSmith. At the time of his departure from Baxter and Platts, the company had grown to a £90 million turnover, with over 300 contracts. William and Rob were two of the very few people to increase the value of their earn-out following acquisition.

> 'I could have retired but I have four children at school and I could either sit at home making myself some coffee or I could come to work and be somebody.'

In 2000, BaxterSmith was launched alongside his friend, former colleague and Director at Baxter and Platts, Mike Smith. Unlike the early difficult days at Baxter and Platts, BaxterSmith seemed to ease smoothly into becoming a competitive force.

> 'Yes, it was different as people knew that we had done it in the past and could deliver what we said we promised in the future. It does make it very different from starting from scratch. Mike had joined Baxter and Platts early on and we worked very closely together for a number of years, so we knew each other very well. Mike had been our Sales Director and then became MD when I became Chairman. We both knew what we could achieve and how we wanted to go about it.'

At the end of year two, turnover was £16 million with a profit of £400,000. When BaxterSmith merged with Wilson Storey Halliday in 2004, it created a business with a turnover of £105 million with over 200 contracts. It also brought together a formidable group of senior players including Alastair Storey (former CEO of Granada Food Services), Keith Wilson (Finance Director at Granada Food Services), and Linda Halliday (CE of Halliday Catering Services) as well as William, Mike and Sales Director Simon Esner. It was a board that matched most of those possessed by the larger, more corporate players in the sector. Cynics at the time suggested that the team would soon break up as they would find it difficult to work as a unified team but two years on, BaxterStorey is seemingly moving from strength to strength and has acquired even more senior talent to its ranks in Noel Mahony, John Bennett and Dawn Gallimore.

'Alastair and I have been friends for a long period and we trust each other in business. Alastair was CEO of Granada when they acquired Baxter and Platts. I have been friends with Linda too for a long time, so it was not as though we were all new to each other as happens with some mergers. Friendship already existed; we just needed to find the best methodology for working together effectively.'

Cynics also suggest that BaxterStorey is preparing itself to exit. William just lightly chuckles at this last assertion:

'People have always being saying that for the past few years but we have no exit strategy as we are all still relatively young, with young families and we are enjoying building the business. It is an exciting prospect at the moment. We are the biggest privately owned contract catering company and we are growing. We all want to know how far we can take it and that is a great challenge for us to have. We want to build a business that delivers for the client and that offers an excellent environment for talent to flourish.'

(December 2006)

Food Service

Robyn Jones OBE

Co-founder and Chief Executive, CH&Co

Robyn occupies the interesting position of being an entrepreneur who has made the transition into a leadership role with her business, CH&Co, a successful, independent foodservice operator. An unexpected redundancy proved to be a catalyst to launch her business. Supported by husband Tim, Robyn has carved out an extremely well regarded niche in contract catering, and the business has since grown under her vision and values. Robyn emphasises that she has needed to adapt her style of leadership at each stage of the business development, and she is without doubt one of the most tenacious characters one will meet. In May 2010 the company went through a major rebranding and now operates under the group name, CH&Co.

Coat of many colours

Robyn Jones is regarded as one of the industry's foremost entrepreneurs. She has built up Charlton House Catering Services since 1991 to be an £80 million business employing more than 2000 staff. Now step back 18 years. Robyn faced an entirely different set of emotions triggered by a redundancy and a recession. How did she make the transition from setback to Chief Executive?

'It was a very difficult time. My confidence disappeared completely, and I felt that my credibility was damaged. I asked myself: Why me? What have I done? What could have done differently? There were no answers of course. It was the recession starting to bite.'

The story of Robyn Jones' experience starting up Charlton House is well documented. Both she and her husband Tim worked in the backroom of their home to establish the business following her redundancy from the construction firm Higgs and Hill. She had her final pay cheque, a Thames Valley Enterprise Allowance of £50 per week and a telephone. The company has since grown to become one of the leading independent contract caterers in the UK. The decision to set up on her own was taken virtually immediately after leaving Higgs and Hill and, in speaking with her, she confirms that intuitively she knew she 'wanted to be her own boss'.

Further, in spite of the emotional upheaval of her situation, Robyn was able to overcome any sense of apprehension towards taking such a step, and develop some clarity on what she wanted to build.

'I have always been a very forthright, focused person with a definite plan and I don't accept failure. Yet, I felt the threat of redundancy was a threat of failure. It was not in my personal plan to have this happen to me. Originally I did go for other interviews with other companies, but was not inspired. I am not a good employee! I knew what I really wanted to do.

'We decided to setup Charlton House the day after I was made redundant. There was no holiday, no respite and I just got on with it. I kept going no matter what and did not give up. OK, I had received one knockback, but I knew I had to carry on.'

Prior to Charlton House Robyn's career had been dominated by large industry players, including Grand Metropolitan, Gardner Merchant, Compass and High Table. Higgs and Hill had wanted to establish a contract catering division alongside their existing business and Robyn had taken a step away from working with an established player to become involved in a new development which needed to be started from scratch. Operating with what she describes as one 'real' contract at the company's head office, she was also running building sites in the build up to winning new contracts.

'Literally as I was starting to move things forward the Board decided that they couldn't invest and needed to pull the plug. It was not one of the most pleasant experiences.'

Robyn sees the situation as partly her own fault:

'I had wanted to leave Compass, which was a secure job, to take on a job which had more risk attached. But I am someone who gets an idea in my head and has to do something, so I had to accept the consequences.'

Despite admitting her feelings of self-doubt Robyn states that she wasn't daunted by taking the decision to set up a business during a recession.

'I thought: I've got nothing, so I can't lose anything. I just had to get out there and win business – and at no point did I think that this wouldn't happen.'

Aiming for three contracts was the initial vision for a fledgling Charlton House, which proved difficult given her lack of reference sites.

'I would say to potential clients, we don't have any yet – but you could be the first! I had to sell in a very positive way. And I swiftly learnt to use the word 'we', so clients could picture a corporate company and that there were this feast of people behind the scenes.

'Our first contract was with Guide Dogs for the Blind. I put my heart and soul into it – the purchasing, HR, food safety, payroll and used to serve food to be with the customers and staff. But the telesales stopped. When I went back to do this, it became clear that I had missed opportunities, having not had time to return calls or follow up leads. I had to keep all the balls juggling all the time. It was a very steep learning curve.'

As Charlton House has grown, acclaim for Robyn's achievements has also increased. Looking back, what has she had to learn?

'You have to be a chameleon. My coat has changed many times and I have adapted.'

Though she had to gather the knowledge necessary to run the administrative side of a business, she regards this as 'building time'.

'At the time of setting up the business, I had only ever worked for my competitors up until that point, in operational roles. In many ways Compass would never have let someone get close to this other side of business, so it was very new being able to build processes and systems from the coalface. We had to be capable of covering all the jobs and be seen as professional.'

Robyn doesn't see herself as an entrepreneur but a 'caterer through and through, which is about delivery. I make sure that we deliver all the elements of our success, but I am not a Richard Branson.'

Yet, when reflecting on how comfortable she has been with taking risks in building the business she acknowledges that there have been a few.

I mean, who would have set up a company in the last recession? But I didn't see it as a risk. In many ways, it was the safe option.'

As Robyn explains that Tim had suggested she put the house up as collateral, she provides further insight into her thinking at the time.

'To some degree I did lack a bit of confidence and didn't want to risk losing my house. It was a case of we can do this on a shoestring, but we will do it properly and don't ask me to do it completely on the cheap. I made sure we had systems set up properly from the outset – there was no cash on delivery.'

Charlton House has grown quickly since the beginning, reaching more than £300,000 turnover in its first year of operation. Her first Operations Manager – Caroline Fry – was recruited in 1996 and the senior team has grown since. Has Robyn found it difficult to let go?

> 'I have found it very easy to delegate, so adjusting to each stage of the company's transition has been quite easy. A lot is required to run the business and I have to entrust others with making decisions. We have always taken on senior staff with the same vision, so that's something I have always felt comfortable with.'

Given the economic climate, when many people will be questioning their job security and wondering what to do next, Robyn provides an example of not only what can be achieved, but something of the mindset that is needed to remain focused.

> 'Fear is a terrible thing. It destroys many things. I would say: don't fear, there is something positive in there somewhere, and you need to try to relax. Don't let fear take you into a frenzy. I certainly don't let people see my fear. There have been challenges along the way of course, everyone has them – it's how you deal with it.'

(April 2009)

Food Service

Chris Robinson
Chairman, Heritage Portfolio

Chris is a classic serial entrepreneur. In a 40-year career within the hospitality industry, Chris began his entrepreneurial career at the age of 27 to establish Lothian Catering Contracts Limited in 1978. In 1980 he changed the name of the business to Wheatsheaf Catering Limited to coincide with a strategic shift into a niche market, banqueting and outside catering. Over the next 18 years Wheatsheaf went on to become one of the most highly regarded operators in the Scottish hospitality market, winning prestige contracts at Hopetoun House, Signet Library at Parliament House and

Edinburgh Castle amongst others. The business was sold to specialist London based Ring and Brymer in 1996, a division of Gardner Merchant Limited, which had recently been acquired by Sodexo. At a young age, this move made Chris and his young family financially secure.

This comparatively straightforward narrative of start-up to success, belies a much deeper and complex individual story. As is so often the case with entrepreneurial characters Chris is an extremely driven individual, who always wanted to 'be his own man'. The pivotal moment in his career was when he worked for the Open Arms Hotel Group in East Lothian. It was Chris' first appointment following graduation from Edinburgh Napier University with a HND in Catering and Hotelkeeping in 1972. Just six years later he was offered a directorship and an equity stake in the family-run business. However, Chris chose to give up this secure position to establish Wheatsheaf:

'I went from 10% of something to 100% of nothing. I regard being an entrepreneur as a vocation.'

This turning point in Chris's career coincided with an appointment as a part-time lecturer in hospitality at Edinburgh Napier University, a post which he held for nine years. He has since maintained a strong involvement in education and gone on to become a guest lecturer at Cornell University in the USA and at Cornell Essec in Paris, France. In addition to numerous other roles on hospitality industry committees, including President of the HCIMA in 1992 (now the Institute of Hospitality) and board member of SCOTVEC the Scottish Council Vocational Education for five years, these experiences not only provided Chris will valuable networking exposure, but also a very clear insight and perspective on entrepreneurialism developed over time.

'My committee colleagues would give me friendly advice that my commitment in time to HCIMA would have an adverse affect on Wheatsheaf and that was well intentioned, but irritating. To my mind these experiences were essential as it was part of helping to grow my business. I always had the sense of perspective that I would need to change from being a hands-on operator to delegating jobs, so that the business could grow. It didn't mean that the business was not my baby but I wanted to bring people on and develop them, that was part of my enjoyment.'

In a further career twist, Chris was the major shareholder, Chairman and Chief Executive of the Heart of Midlothian Football Club from 1994 until 2005. Under his leadership the club rebuilt their stadium with three new grandstands, were club winners of the Scottish FA Cup in 1998 and participated in the UEFA Cup Winners Cup and UEFA Cup. He sold his shareholding to the Lithuanian/Russian businessman Vladimir Romanov in 2005. Chris has since held several senior appointments in Scottish Professional Football, including Professional Leagues Vice President of the Scottish Football Association, Chairman of the Referees Committee for the SFA and Director of the SFA as Executive Committee Member.

Chris is currently the Chairman of Heritage Portfolio, a specialist hospitality provider in prestige venues in Scotland. Founded with Alan Duff and Ian D'Annunzio-Green, the business sits at the top of its niche market with a client list and contract venues list that is incomparable. The business operates an award winning e-commerce division, Beetroot Blue and in 2006 acquired Ruthven's, a retail café operator in public art galleries, bringing another dimension to the business portfolio. What is interesting about this venture is that Alan Duff, Heritage Portfolio's Chief Executive, began his career as a student intern with Chris at Wheatsheaf. The pair share a degree of synchronicity and vision, which is unique.

'Although my role as Chairman was to be hands off from the operation, my outlook as an entrepreneur had not changed. Alan and Ian wanted me to be their Chairman and, in turn, we wanted to create something out of the ordinary. Our reputation for winning new business and putting on creative events was essential. We all had credibility. From my perspective it was an opportunity not to make the same mistakes, as with my initial experience of Wheatsheaf, by operating in too many market segments.'

As a character Chris does is thoughtful and concise in his communication style, and an intelligent, rational thinker. However, this again belies some of the cast-iron values that he has nurtured throughout his career.

'As an entrepreneur, you must be driven, have sticking power and be self-aware, as it is important to have the presence of mind to change direction where necessary. You need a degree of ruthlessness but having said that it doesn't mean you don't care. I've seen many businesses tread water because they weren't prepared to take the necessary risks.

'The UK business mindset regards failure as dastardly. In contrast, you may fail several times in the US but have one success, and that one time is regarded as important. People should be allowed to fail, but it is harder to fail these days and move forward.

'You must have an ability to share your vision with your people. Nothing replaces face-to-face communication. Even just a simple, straightforward briefing of staff to let them know how the business is doing and where the next opportunities are coming helps to bring people with you. Personally I like to be visible to everyone in any of the roles that I have had.

'You also have to do what is right for you at key stages. For example, when the moment came to sell Wheatsheaf it was not a prospect that I had not previously been contemplating. However, we had just won the contract with the Edinburgh International Convention Centre (EICC), only for the decision to be reversed the next day and this had bought out a certain degree of disillusionment. That, along with the numerous offers from external parties which were presenting themselves, made me take stock. In the end I had to do what was right for my family, and that was financial security at a young age.'

From a business perspective, Chris had worked with Cornell University for many years and has had the opportunity to engage in a serious intellectual debate regarding entrepreneurial behaviour. His key message is that an entrepreneurial business often goes in five-year cycles.

'The energy required in the first two or three years of a new business is considerable, so you naturally spend a period of time after this initial stage consolidating and recharging your batteries before moving into the next phase of growth. That's why some say if you can survive the first five years in business, you will be able to move on and be successful. If I look back at Wheatsheaf this is exactly what happened, and, in fact, Professor Kaven at Cornell uses this business as a test case.'

Chris Robinson's career provides a fascinating insight into both the personal and business drivers of an entrepreneur. He blends absolute dedication to his craft with a thoughtful, reflective insight on his journey.

'I don't think your vision as an entrepreneur is unique. It's the ambition and desire to deliver the vision which sets you apart.'

Chefs

Paul Bocuse
The Great Chef

Hospitality is a creative industry with food and wine standing at its heart. Exceptional creative talents, therefore, also lie at its heart and creative talent is rarely the full rounded businessman. They have often instinctive, passionate, egotistic, highly driven characters.

A great chef will often only be viewed as being great once they have had their own name above a restaurant. They are led towards having their own business and yet very few actually possess the skills and financial acumen to actually manage and lead a business. They are the creative force and, in truth, need capable advisors around them but this is often expensive and many of the great chefs have led difficult lives in the name of their passion.

It is, therefore, worth reflecting on the story of arguably the greatest chef of the last 40 years.

Paul is regarded as one of, if not the, greatest chef of his generation. He was really the first to bring the notion of a celebrity chef to the fore. He was one of the principal drivers behind the concept of Nouvelle Cuisine that became such a dominant theme in the 1980s and early 1990s. It is claimed the term was invented to describe Bocuse's work and approach. But as the man himself would say, cooking is about testing the boundaries and trying new ideas. He did not seek to create a concept, it happened naturally.

'I believe that in cooking like in music, one doesn't invent much. One makes interpretations but the word 'invention' for me is a bit pretentious.'

In 1975, Bocuse invented the now famous Truffle Soup – known as *soupe aux truffles* – for a presidential dinner at the Elysees Palace. His world-famous restaurant is based in Lyon which, in turn, is regarded as the culinary centre of France. He has received Michelin stars (his first in 1961) and won numerous awards including a medal of Commandeur de la Légion d'honneur. In 1961 he received the honour to wear the title of Meilleur Ouvrier de France.

Lyon even boasts one of the great food markets named after the great chef – Les Halles de Paul Bocuse. He has been nicknamed the 'Pope' of French Cuisine. Lyon is also home for L'institut Paul Bocuse which teaches and practises classical French culinary techniques. The research centre within the Institute is home to multi-disciplinary academic research into food and the food and hospitality industries. Much can be said by the chefs of today but Bocuse has been ahead of the game for quite some time and even into his eighties is still driving forward the agenda.

Without doubt, Paul has been one of the great chefs of the 20th century but it has not been an easy journey for the man. It has been very well documented that he has had a number of marriages and mistresses. His private life has been controversial and this has brought its own pressures but the man himself has continued to be driven by his passion. For Bocuse, there is no compromise on working hard and pushing the boundaries of his own talent and influence.

In an interview with Mietta O'Donnell (*Herald Sun*) in 1997 he described his belief that cooking is an art form that needs to be treated with great care and genuineness:

'It is an arrangement, one makes interpretations, but you must respect the basic culture. Asian and European cultures are completely different. You can't mix them. And the worst thing with Asian tastes is that the marriage of wine does not work at all.

'There are too many cooks trying to do new things and you know when one reads cookery books one always finds something which has already been done. What is invention? I think that is a very pretentious word. To mix chocolate with tomatoes or tomatoes with jam – that's not an invention. ...A sole with chocolate – the sole is a good product, chocolate is a good product, the two mixed together – give you shit.

'But people should be able to enjoy different experiences – there is good rock 'n' roll, good jazz, good opera. But not all on the one night.'

And his advice to chefs: 'they must work, and must work more, they must cook correctly and exactly and they must season well.' He scoffed at fears of salt and the use of butter and cream, 'the base of French cooking,' and is certainly not keen on change, 'what's new today is already old tomorrow.'

One of the contradictions of Paul is that he disregards the pretentious and believes in genuine craft and yet Nouvelle Cuisine is often viewed as being pretentious.

Bocuse will leave a legacy that many will try and copy. Many of today's chefs do but the difference is that Bocuse believed in almost traditional values but was driven to improve on what existed. For Bocuse, it was about authenticity and substance and from these foundation stones he built his career.

Chefs

Albert Roux OBE

Albert Roux is one of the most successful chefs of our generation and, along with his brother Michel, revered for engineering a revolution in UK fine dining. Having launched Le Gavroche in 1967, Albert has continued to create new dining experiences through his consultancy and strategic business partnerships. However, a look at his early experiences as a young man and chef reveal that, along with hard work and dedication, Albert maintains a real sense of perspective on life. Albert is both courageous and irreverent, a true character of the industry. He is fun, engaging and has clear personal vision which he translates into various projects.

59 years a chef

Albert Roux has been one of the leading names in the industry for the past 30 years. The man is legendary. But what were his origins and influences during the early days that helped to make him such a great chef?

We met Albert in Brasserie Roux at the Sofitel St James in central London. For a change it was a pleasant summer's morning, and he looked relaxed and slightly tanned. We were greeted with immaculate courtesy. Most have heard of the great man's achievements and successes, but where did his story start and how did it unfold in the early years? This is a story that perhaps few people know.

'I was born (1935) in a very small village – one that is almost unnoticeable – in the region of Saône et Loire in France. My family were pig breeders and we had a shop attached which sold pork. In those days there were no supermarkets and shops only had a licence to sell certain products. A shopkeeper would not be allowed to sell more than he was licensed for.

Food was also in short supply and my mother somehow managed to cook dishes that were full of flavour and taste. I guess it was this that fuelled my love for cooking. She was so creative. I always got a lot of enjoyment from cooking as it gave me freedom to be creative, although it also requires discipline. To be a great chef one has to have imagination and not be afraid to try new things. I say that I cook with my right hand but have the cookery book close by in my left hand. It is about striking the balance between being classical and creative.'

So, I asked, how did Albert's career begin?

'Becoming a chef was not my first ambition,' he replied recalling those earlier days. 'I attended the local school until the age of 12 and then moved – at 12 – to live with a family in Paris. At the time, I was studying to become a priest and I had started working towards this since the age of 6. However, I soon discovered the church was not for me and I turned to my second love – cooking. As chance happens my godfather was chef to the Duchess of Windsor in Paris, so I went to talk to him. He advised me that I should start with an apprenticeship in pastry and, if after four years I was still keen to become a chef, he would help me. Within a few weeks I had started my apprenticeship. My godfather was right to start me with pastry as it teaches one both the need to be creative and disciplined. Pastry comes after the meal – it has to revive the appetite and has to be pleasing on the eye and in taste. After the four years I spoke to my godfather and told him I wanted to be a chef. I was determined and sure enough, he found me a job in England with Lady Astor at Cliveden.'

Did Albert's brother Michel follow a similar route?

'He was always going to follow what I did. We had no father and I acted as the father figure; he was going to follow in his brother's footsteps. It was as though we were linked.'

How does the story continue?

'I moved up the ladder and spent one year at the French Embassy in London, followed by a time with Sir Charles Clore, who was then one of the most powerful businessmen in Europe. At the age of 22, I was called up to do military service in Algeria. It was funny but when I returned to the UK after completing my service I was immediately deported as my permit had expired. Years later, when I was receiving my OBE, I joked to Jack Straw that it was not too bad an achievement for a man who had been deported! Back in Paris, I found a job as sous chef at the British Embassy and then I had one of my greatest breaks of luck. One day at the Embassy, I met Lady Cazelet. What a lady – beautiful, such elegance, great manners. It was love at first sight.

'I had eight very happy years with the Cazelets. I used to go riding in the morning with the 'old man' (Major Peter Cazelet), as we affectionately called him, and he often took me to the races. It was one of the happiest periods in my life.'

Albert Roux has such a distinctive face – one that almost tells a number of stories without a word being uttered. It is a face that says 'I have had a full, rich life – one that has experienced the good and bad.' Whether he is listening intently or considering a question, it is full of character. When smiling it is full of warmth and his eyes sparkle with fun. He is a natural story teller. The movement of his arms is to emphasise each point. It is very engaging. It was the Cazelet family and many of their friends who helped Albert and Michel open Le Gavroche. Albert smiled as he recalled how it came about.

'One day the old man said to me 'I know of your desire to open your own restaurant. If you stay with me for the next two years, I will invest £500 into it.' And he was true to his word. The £500 was a third of the money that we needed. Another £500 came from other members of the family. When we opened, my brother and I owned 70% of the business and the investors had 30%. But we could not have done it without their support. They invited 500 people to the opening – people from the highest levels of society and stood at the door acting as hosts. We could have asked for no more.'

How were those early days running Le Gavroche?

'Hard work and fun. We had to learn very fast – especially portion control after coming from working in private households. We would often overbook the restaurant and send customers across the road to the pub to wait with a complimentary bottle of champagne. We soon learned. We had so much fun and so many good stories. I remember the Rolling Stones once arriving and the Maitre De thought they were hooligans. I recall turning to my brother saying that we had the Rolling Stones in the restaurant, to which he shrugged his shoulders and simply said 'Who?' He would so often not know who someone was. He once asked Princess Margaret if she had a reservation.' Albert laughs at the memory.

'I also recall a young couple, clearly deeply in love, who both, shall we say, left the table at the same time to visit the same toilet. We had to quickly cover for them and have a waiter stand in front of the door to say that it was out of order. They returned to the table 20 minutes later with no one any the wiser.'

Albert's story is remarkable and one that confirms all the old adages about hard work, determination, perseverance, luck, and love of his craft. As we finished I asked how he viewed the London market today.

'With great pleasure. My ambition was to have trained one English chef to three-star Michelin standards and I have had three. That is my greatest achievement.'

(October 2008)

Anton Mosimann OBE

Anton is one of the most influential chefs in British cooking whose culinary services stretch from serving royalty to the Olympic Games. As an entrepreneur, Anton has evolved a distinct set of values in the pursuit of his passion for food, and that is first and foremost about treating others with respect. He uses food to engage and delight both customers and staff, but has a shrewd business mind. Latterly, Anton has included his sons, Philipp and Mark, in the business and as a team they have much promise moving forward, with Anton guiding his sons in a similar value set.

Cooking for friends

Over the years, Anton Mosimann has been one of the true figureheads and ambassadors for the industry. In 2005, he was awarded with the Catey Lifetime Achievement Award. We were delighted to have the opportunity to interview one of the most influential chefs of our time.

You have been one of the most influential chefs of our time – where did your fascination and inspiration of food come from?

'My parents owned a small local restaurant near Berne, so I grew up in the restaurant and even did my homework at the tables whilst my mother worked all around setting up. I learned at an early age – going to the market, selecting the best, freshest ingredients and then rushing back home to cook. I still remember the wonderful smell of freshly baked bread and of fruit fresh from the tree.

Where do you continue to find your inspiration for food and where do you believe the food sector is moving towards?

'I have been fortunate to travel all over the world and I draw inspiration and ideas from my travels. Earlier this year, my wife and I were in South East Asia – 14 different places, 18 different flights! Cambodia, Laos, Shanghai, Myanmar – some of the fresh herbs, spices, wow! We visited Bali and I did a cookery course for a day, just to learn a little bit more about Balinese food and the way they cook. You never stop learning. Food I believe is going back to basics, people are looking for simple dishes using the freshest and best ingredients possible, cooked in a healthy way keeping the natural flavours and tastes as much as possible.

What impact do you believe supermarkets and media have on our food values and consumption?

Supermarkets and media together with newspapers and magazines have made an impact on their customers. What is fantastic to see is the emergence of farmers' markets, particularly with organic products, which is encouraging more people to buy the freshest produce possible.

As one of the very first TV chefs, how do you believe the media (in particular TV) has changed over the last few years? If you had the opportunity, would you film another series and if so what angle would you take?

The media has made food and cookery into a form of entertainment these days. It is wonderful that there are more television programmes, books and written articles than ever before on the subject. It is fantastic to see so much about lifestyle, quality of produce, ingredients, restaurants. As a chef, I think it is great that people are much more aware and inspired by this media. My policy has always been to keep it simple and let food taste of what it is. I would do a television programme concentrating on very fresh, simple and healthy food.

What led you to leaving The Dorchester and creating your private members club, The Belfry?

It was a bold step! I felt it was the right time for a change, after 13 years, five general managers, I gave back the two Michelin Stars and set up Mosimann's. I wanted to create an environment where members could come and dine in relaxed yet luxurious surroundings and have the finest of food and wines. It is like cooking for friends and we still have members today from the very beginning in 1988.

How do you pass on your inspiration of food to your team?

Every morning when I am in London, I go into the kitchens, shake hands with all of the kitchen staff and look at the produce coming in. I keep them very involved, we discuss ideas, new menus, changing the presentations of dishes. I am passionate about my work, therefore it is much easier to pass it on to your team in order that we all believe we are creating the finest and most wonderful food for our guests to enjoy, using the best ingredients possible.

You have worked with the Prince's Trust for several years and have given many the opportunity of training within your kitchen during this time. How did you become involved, and have some of these trainees pursued a career within the hospitality industry?

We have worked for the Prince of Wales for many years and in 2000, we were awarded a royal warrant for catering services to HRH The Prince of Wales. His Royal Highness has done a huge amount through his Trust and I felt that we could also offer an opportunity to assist with encouraging disadvantaged young people to take a look at the hospitality industry. We have now run the *Get Into...*Cooking pro-gramme for three years, where the young people spend a week with us both in the kitchens at the Club and our Party Service. From each course we have then offered two students a place at Mosimann's and we have three at the present time. The week can literally change their lives and it is an incredibly rewarding and humbling experience for my whole team.

You have achieved world renowned recognition and through your events business orchestrate events on a global basis, what do you still aspire to?

I am still young, energetic and luckily in good health. I love what I do, I get up each morning and cannot wait to get to work – there are many things still up my sleeve. Watch this space!

(August 2005)

It's in the blood

In 2007, after close to 20 years operating the iconic Mosimann's members club in Belgravia and the associated Mosimann's Party Service, Anton Mosimann was joined in his venture by his two sons, Philipp and Mark. The next generation have come on board to help continue to drive the business forward and build on this well established, quality brand. Is this a case of strength in numbers, or a classic 'recipe for disaster'?

Many will be familiar with Anton Mosimann and his distinguished career. From an OBE and a Catey Lifetime Achievement Award to honorary professorships, his work has achieved acclaim around the world. For those of you who are not familiar, Anton has been a staple in the London dining scene for many years. Since his days at the helm of catering at The Dorchester at the tender age of 28 he has arguably impacted London, and indeed British dining, more than any other individual. And to top it all off, he is a true gentleman. Welcoming me into the small dining room overlooking the kitchen, Anton and his sons Philipp and Mark are the model of chivalry, civility and service. I'm interested to learn whether this chivalrous exterior is reserved for guests or carries into their day-to-day lives.

In 2007, both Philipp and Mark returned to London from their careers overseas and joined the family business. As Joint Managing Directors they have been careful to define overall responsibilities with Philipp overseeing Mosimann's Party Service and business development, and Mark at the helm of the club dining and sales. This arrangement allows each to breathe and grow; yet, they are careful to communicate well and to clearly stand as a united front in any major decision making or changes in direction.

As Philipp explains:

'Nearly two years before we joined the business we discussed this and put measures in place – not only to prepare ourselves but also the team here. We had to be mindful that there are people here that have been part of the Mosimann business for 20 years and have seen the two of us literally growing up as children. We didn't want to cause problems by simply walking in, assuming responsibility and demanding respect.'

Mark elaborates:

'It is really important that if someone asks any of us a question they will get a similar answer, and also that people are comfortable that if they provide one person with information that this will be shared. I suppose it's what you hear from many businesses – communication is so essential. Of course, it isn't always perfect,' he admits with a smile, 'but we really try. We have meetings every Monday with the 3Ms – Father, Philipp and myself. We discuss our plans and to agree any strategic decisions among ourselves before we move any further.'

It is this dynamic that I find fascinating. After 20 years at the helm of the business, with two vibrant sons who have new ideas and have just joined the business, is this a harmonious relationship or are there tensions?

'It's never a boxing match, but we do need to get everything on the table so that we can discuss it all and by the end we pretty much agree,' Anton insists (this is met by wry smiles and raised eyebrows from his sons).

'We all have to be mindful that there are different generations, different schooling and different ideas. There might be a suggestion that comes up that I've tried before, but we need to try it again as it might be right this time.

'Respect is a very important word in a family business – in any business. We all love Chinese food, including the youngest member of the family – 10-month-old Conrad, who already loves Chinese crackers. No matter what, every Sunday we meet for lunch, always at the same Chinese restaurant, Shanghai Knightsbridge, and there is no talk of work – it's family time. Little Blake [Philipp's eldest son, aged 3½] has been coming along since he was one week old – and now he can use chopsticks,' beams Anton.

'People have often asked me why this is a membership club, why didn't we open a restaurant and go for stars?' comments Anton. 'Part of the answer is that it was already a private members' club and we offered for the existing members to join us. However, it is more than that. I really believe that we all like to have things that we can't have – that great car that you can only dream about and have to work towards. Well it's the same policy here. There is a waiting list and although there could be a temptation to put up the prices and admit members with cash in their wallets, we have never been hungry. There is a process and we follow it and people have to wait.

'I also believe in value for money. It is only if you are serious about it and value-driven that you can hope to last through this generation and the next. Take the past year for example, yes we have suffered a little, along with everyone else, but we have members that have been with us for 22 years and they still believe in what we are doing here.'

'We have spent a few years now learning from Dad and seeing how the business runs before we try and take on the world!' explains Mark, 'I think it helps that Philipp and I spent time living entirely separate lives. When we left for Lausanne Hotel School Dad told us not to come back for 10 years, to go and see the world and learn different things. I think he wanted us to master profit control while we were practising with someone else's business! So we had not even lived in the same city for that time. Because of this, there has also been an element of getting to know one another other again. Now two years on, we are in a situation where we are all bringing different experiences to the table.'

Anton is the son of two restaurateurs in Switzerland, and as he puts it he was 'born into the business and has never left the kitchen floor'. He recalls, with a sparkle, his memories as a child tasting fresh, seasonal, honest food and selecting produce at the markets. I wonder if Philipp and Mark have the industry in their blood like this as well. Was this joining of forces inevitable?

'We have always been surrounded by hotels and restaurants,' agrees Philipp. 'It was simply always part of our lives. When we went on holidays, they might be summers at Lausanne Hotel School while father was teaching summer school, or they would revolve around produce and going out to eat.'

'Food critics at the age of 4,' Mark grins and the others laugh. 'But the decision was never forced onto us at all,' explains Philipp. 'In fact I think that if anything it was the opposite as we could see first-hand that it is not an easy industry and we know the passion and dedication that has to be put in.'

Dedication certainly runs in the family. In their 'spare time' both Philipp and Mark are involved in ultra-marathon running, in which they run 155 miles over a period of six days. Races take place in such inhospitable places as the Sahara and more recently the Namibian Desert. Anton runs as well, but admits that he prefers slightly shorter distances. So, with two years settling in and consolidating the club dining and Party Services businesses, where to next for the Mosimann Group?

'The club will always be the core of the business, and we will not lose sight of that,' says Mark. 'Our members are really important and the Party Services aspect of the business is about providing our catering wherever our members might be around the world.'

'It began that way many years ago,' agrees Philipp, 'as home catering for our members and it has snowballed from there to include international commitments such as our contract at the Beijing Olympics and prestigious local events such as a seated dinner for 1400 for Prince Philip's 70th birthday.

'There are many more opportunities for Party Services. This year we are taking five well-known chefs to Vancouver to the Winter Olympics and will run a pop-up restaurant for 17 days with only a week to set up and prepare. It's a situation where service levels and expectations are high and it is a great opportunity. We are lucky that we can draw on previous Mosimann staff from around the globe that will jump at the chance to take part.'

'We have spent many years establishing a strong brand and a reputation for quality,' concludes Anton, 'and we are comfortable with where we are. If partnerships or other business opportunities come along and feel right then we would certainly consider them and we will always seek to maintain a presence internationally, be it through our events or otherwise.

'We are open minded about the future.'

(February 2010)

Richard Shepherd CBE

Richard Shepherd's transition from chef to entrepreneur is bittersweet and compelling. He does not befit the natural entrepreneur mould, and was thrust into such as role after joining forces with another legendary entrepreneur, Peter Langan, at Langan's Brasserie. Realising shortly after joining that the business was going bust, he set out to build bridges with the banks and pay back debts rapidly, a feat which he achieved. The toll on Richard was immense and he notes that it is not a risk he would be prepared to take again, but he has nevertheless capitalised on the opportunity since. With the support and help of his brother (who sadly passed away in 2004) managing the accounts, Richard has carried on at the helm of Langan's and his other restaurants for more than 30 years and is a true giant of the hospitality industry.

True courage: Richard Shepherd's Great British odyssey

Michael Caine hosts a table, Dudley Moore plays piano, artists exchange pictures for food — all in a day's trade for Langan's Brasserie during the late 1970s and early 1980s. Richard Shepherd was first its rescuer from insolvency and then its visionary. His story is one of high stakes, personal sacrifice and enduring passion.

'I had been friends with Peter Langan for a while. The reputation that he had was an act. He was not an alcoholic then. He was highly intelligent and well read, with a lot of taste and style. Peter asked me to come on board and I thought 'why not'? I felt I had been kicked in the guts after a disagreement at the Capital Hotel. Of course, people thought I was mad and I knew I was taking a risk. Three months after joining I realised that the business was insolvent, there was no money. So I went and made a deal with the authorities to get some time to pay back monies owed, writing £268,000 of post-dated cheques. I paid it back within two years. It is not a risk I would be prepared to take again. My son has told me that he wouldn't want to come into the business as he saw what it had done to me.'

Following on from this tricky moment, Richard Shepherd CBE has been at the helm of the Langan's restaurant business for more than 30 years. He presently owns five London establishments with an annual turnover of over £10 million. Awarded his CBE in 2000, Richard has also won a Catey Award three times. With Michael Caine and Peter Langan as his original business partners, Langan's Brasserie became the first London restaurant to attract celebrities in abundance. From actors to royalty, Michael played 'an amazing part' courting the famous, whilst Peter would provide the public face. Richard, evidently, was unfazed by the limelight; a character trait which must have proven a major factor in the lasting success of the restaurants today.

'For ten years there were a minimum of 20–30 paparazzi outside the front door for lunch and dinner. However, I knew that it would not stay fashionable forever and set about ensuring that we developed a regular clientele from TV, sport, media and radio to create a popular 'club'. This was helped by the likes of Tony Vickers, John Bromley and John Hockey. We turned the business around from being 80% celebrity and 20% business to 80% business and 20% celebrity.'

Following the tragic death of Peter in 1988, Michael and Richard had by then established ownership of the Brasserie plus two other restaurants originally owned by Langan – Langan's Bistro and Odin's.

'Prior to his death, Peter had told me he wanted to go to America and set up business there. We had made arrangements to support him by buying out his shares in these other restaurants. So it was a very tragic loss and a sad time.

'Around 1993 I found a property called Greens in Westminster through Simon Parker-Bowles, which we bought and it became Shepherd's. Michael and I went to look at it together. With time to kill he suggested that we go for a walk. We ended up on a council estate and Michael said: 'Do you know the last time I was here? It was picking up a cheque from the dole office. And guess who was behind me? Sean Connery! In 1997 I bought out Michael's shares. There was no fall out and we are still on good terms.'

Keen to build up 'asset value' Richard acquired a site on Old Brompton Road in 1997 which became Coq d'Or. He also did a deal with P&O Ferries to set up floating Langan's Brasseries on 10 ships.

Richard knew he wanted to be a chef from the age of 12. He believes it was a logical decision due to his early experiences of work. At the time Richard could not have stayed on at school and learnt the necessary skills to become a chef, as this was not part of the curriculum.

'I had a happy childhood which was not privileged. I had to take on part-time jobs in cafes and hotels and that is why I chose cooking as a career path. My parents were always supportive and at the age of 15 I left home. I was not prepared for leaving home. The job was with a hotel in Great Malvern and I had the attic room. I can remember not even unpacking my suitcase, lying on my bed and crying for two weeks. However, I knew that giving in was the easy option.'

After his apprenticeship Richard moved to London working at both Simpson's-on-the-Strand and The Savoy, before leaving to work in the South of France.

'In France I had an education on absolutely everything about cooking and food. It taught me that the French had a respect and love for cooking which came from the heart and culture, not a textbook.'

Upon returning to London Richard commenced the next phase of his career, first working at The Dorchester.

'I was not welcome by the staff as I had been brought in from the outside by Eugene Kauffler. This was unusual at the time as most staff had to start at the bottom and work their way up. I discovered all sorts of theft and, having been approached to join the union which was a closed shop, I refused. My colleagues sent me to Coventry and it was a difficult time. When I left to start at The Capital I was asked if I would consider returning at a later date as Mr Kauffler's successor. After being approached and declining, Anton Mosimann was brought in and in my consideration he did a better job than I could have done.'

Richard then recruited Brian Turner to join him at the Capital Hotel and achieved recognition by attaining one of the UK's first Michelin stars in 1974.

'We worked very hard and were two young lads who had developed a good reputation,' recalls Richard. A disagreement prompted his departure and Brian's promotion to Head Chef. Richard joined Langan's in 1977. Richard has no current plans to expand and is focused on stability.

'I am very happy with the company's performance at the moment. It is a very sound business and I want to maintain that.'

Shortly after he joined Langan's Richard brought his brother into the business to look after the accountancy and set up the administration correctly.

'It was a great comfort to know that my back was covered. He was my greatest confidante and when he died in 2004 it hit me big time. I had lost my best friend less than 18 months before in 2002. In 2005 my General Manager Peter also left to emigrate to New Zealand after 26 years service. It felt as though I had lost both my left and right arm.'

An original member of the chefs Club Nine, which included the late Peter Kromberg, and Michael Bourdin, Richard is passionate about his heritage and the education of future chefs.

'Club Nine was a very proud achievement. We became friends meeting up to talk together about our problems. And it emerged that we shared the same problems. The Club was the forerunner for the Academy of Culinary Arts.

'The industry has moved on. You can eat as well in England as you can anywhere else in the world. Yet, I am nervous that it is becoming too fragmented. It is splintering off into too many different directions. I think people experiment with food before getting the basics right. People take a bit of this and a bit of that and the purity has disappeared.

'It is easy to knock colleges. But we need to put more apprenticeships into place; teach stocks, sauces, fish and meat. Many cooks today cannot bone a side of meat and often use boil-in-a-bag sauces. I have tried to have the courage to create fabulous dishes of real British food like bangers and mash, fish and chips which have been on our menus for over 25 years. Customers like it and it is done well. I do not like what I call 'lego on a plate' where the food is piled up and falls apart the moment you cut into it. There is too much snobbery. With the media's help we are likely to start believing our own hype.'

In a career spanning nearly 50 years, Richard has carved a place in culinary history. From humble beginnings to the risky business of creating a restaurant group, he has stuck to his foundations and never forgotten that love for what you do is essential. His passion, reflected in both joy and worry for the future of cooking, is evident in equal measure.

'The fun is no longer there. Bureaucracy has taken over by people with clipboards ticking boxes. Industry had a reputation for developing on the job and I believe apprenticeships should be used as a way of teaching students how to do something well. It is not just a job, it is a way of life. It is my life.'

(October 2008)

Restaurants

Michael Gottlieb

Managing Director, Christopher's Group

Michael has been one of the hospitality industry's central characters over the past 20 years – Founder and Managing Director of Smollensky's until its sale in 1997; Founding Partner of Café Spice; President of the Restaurant Association; Managing Director of Christopher's Group (2005–present); Managing Director of Restair UK (2000–05) amongst others.

One of the reasons for the central role played by Michael is not due simply to the positions that he has held, but also he is one of the most thoughtful and considered of commentators on the industry. Michael is one of those characters who has great clarity of thought and is able to dissect a situation very effectively. He thinks and talks in a very straight-forward, commonsensical fashion. He has no agenda and just plays – as the old saying goes – 'what is in front of him'.

When I first met Michael, I was told that he was a tough, no-nonsense operator. This was true and especially so in 1991 when the market was in recession. But Michael was never tough for no reason. In fact, quite the opposite. He is a deep thinker who really cares about those that work for and with him. He never seeks to belittle but neither does he shirk from a difficult conversation.

Michael in many ways is a contradiction. He could be called a man ahead of his time. He was truly international in focus before it became the vogue. An American who has lived in London for many years and who is married to a Swedish lady. Café Spice was a concept that was ahead of its time. And yet this is a man who is detailed and has guided a number of companies through difficult times.

'I am not convinced I am an entrepreneur. I think I am quite a good business manager. I suppose I had to run my own company as I was pretty unemployable. I was fired from quite a few jobs. I was not a good employee. I think I was just always my own man and my thinking did not always suit corporate companies.

'I remember working as a marketing manager of Hertz. Car hire is an interesting business model at times and certainly was in those days. I remember we held second position within the market in Europe. Avis were the clear market leaders. I rewrote the pricing manual with the objectives of making the pricing structure far easier to understand and with fewer grey areas. It would, I believed, have given us a step forward against Avis but the leadership team at Hertz was not overly impressed. Why? Because it meant that we many have become more customer-friendly but we would have lost margin in certain situations.

'I suppose I had the traits to be an entrepreneur but to me it was all common sense. I remember running my own venture on the side selling Tie Travel racks to the BA magazine before they became com-monplace. I did it on the weekends with my wife and it paid me more than my salary.

'When I applied to work for Bob Payton, I negotiated a stake in the business. It just seemed natural to do so and Bob unders tood how I worked and thought. I had become tired of just being an employee and I wanted to be part of a business. I replied to an advert in the paper and Bob rang me up and offered me the job without even meeting me. That was typical of Bob. Anyway, I asked to meet him before accepting and we discussed things through and we agreed that I would get an equity stake (8%) if we increased profits in the first year. We did – we doubled the profits but in fairness it was not that hard as Bob was brilliant in many ways, but he was not the best business manager.

'However, as we grew and became more successful, Bob's behaviour became more and more eccentric and it was becoming increasingly difficult to work effectively with him. I think that often entrepreneurs need a catalyst to make them take the step to become the entrepreneur. The catalyst for me was the Finance Director who suggested that I worked on a business plan. I drew up a short paper and sent it to a friend that I had, who was a venture capitalist. I just wanted his thoughts on the idea and approach. I rang him up a couple of weeks later to see what he thought and he told me that the investment had been agreed. So we were off.

'Of course, it was not that straightforward. The overall investment was £1 million which in those days was a lot of money and I had to invest £50,000 plus place our house on the line. For someone who is naturally cautious, it was quite a risk but it just appeared to be the right thing to do.

'One of the reasons that I am not convinced that I am a natural entrepreneur is that entrepreneurs often push for growth. I didn't, I was quite happy with the few restaurants that we operated. I found opening the business was very emotionally draining. We opened in the April and were making profit by the December. In January, I feel into a deep black hole – a depression – for three months. The reason was simply that I had put so much into the previous nine months, and now the business was profitable, my body just let out all the emotions.

'I am not the most naturally driven character. One key factor is the influence and support of others. I think some entrepreneurs like myself are significantly encouraged by the belief others have in us and our assumed abilities … be it friends, relations, even employees. It's a bit like sucking up energy from an audience if you are a stage performer say. It may not be the prime driver of entrepreneurial endeavour but to me it's very important, especially as I hate to let people down.

'I enjoy running businesses. I am not really an operator or a marketer – I am a generalist. I like to see the overall picture.'

These are very candid thoughts and paint a picture that many entrepreneurs feel – that they had no choice but to do setup their own business. It was a decision that they had to make because their convictions drove them down that road.

Michael is a man of convictions and values who simply does not compromise on what he believes not to be right. Michael's strength came from the fact that he was – at the core – a very able business manager who did understand exactly what he was doing. It was, therefore, almost a natural conclusion that he began his own business.

Restaurants

Des Gunewardena

Chairman and Chief Executive, D&D London

Des occupies the dual role of chief executive and chairman of D&D London, a collection of restaurants, including Skylon and Launceston Place, which were originally owned under the Conran Group. In creating a separate restaurant business in 2006, Des made the transition from Sir Terence Conran's CEO, with whom he had worked since 1991, to lead role. It is this unique combination of his experience with Conran, one of the most revered entrepreneurs of our time, together with the rigour and discipline applied through his training in finance that defines Des as a corporate entrepreneur. Des has a controlled and methodical approach to risk, which he applies to good effect in making strategic moves within the business on matters such as service charge and his partnership with the Modern Pantry. His vision is to create a culture which places entrepreneurialism at the heart of the business so that D&D can evolve and grow organically, and he actively encourages new ideas from his management team.

Better by design

D&D London owns and operates more than 30 restaurants including 23 in London, in addition to operations in Paris, New York, Copenhagen and Tokyo. What has been their strategy post Conran? Des Gunewardena, Chairman and Chief Executive, with David Loewi, Managing Director

In 2006, when D&D London was formed through a management buyout, the move was viewed with interest by many. The name Conran had become synonymous with a cultural design evolution and is one of the most established and iconic UK brands. So what was the motive? What would be the changes? Inevitably, the answer appears to lie in maintaining a balance between old and new. On one hand there is the legacy of an individual who changed the face of eating out in the 1990s, on the other is the focus and determination of two restaurateurs aiming to challenge standards both in their business and the wider industry. With aggregate revenues of £75–80 million, the company reported a profit before taxation of £2.8 million for the year ending March 2009. Of the persistent and inevitable characterisation of D&D London as 'the former Conran' restaurants, Des and David – who have worked with Sir Terence for 21 and 15 years respectively – recognise the value this brings:

Des: 'To me the association is entirely positive. I'd much rather people say they came out of Conran, rather than D&D – who? The correlation means that D&D is a great brand. Does it matter? It does not really matter to a customer. Does it matter to staff and suppliers and business partners? Maybe a little more. I get feedback saying, 'you feel like a very different company, but in a positive way'. We were a bit like the BBC of the restaurant business. Conran Restaurants was successful, but perhaps a bit of an establishment. The reality of how we do business now has given us slightly more dynamism.'

David: 'D&D was about having a name in our own right. It's positive. We have done a lot of development, but we are proud of where we have come from.'

Sir Terence appears to share a similar view. Asked about perceived tension between management teams following the MBO, which saw 49% of the business sold to Des, David, the Management team and investors, he said: 'It had got too big for me to get pleasure out of it. Restaurants need constant loving care and I couldn't give that.' The new ownership structure has resulted in changes to the running of the restaurant business, and the crux of this has been to put operational control into the hands of managers and chefs. Des and David want to ensure that the quality of their food and leadership gets the highest profile as they pursue a strategy that ensures that each restaurant is recognised by customers as a destination in its own right. Since the MBO, D&D's two openings in London – Skylon and Launceston Place – have attracted considerable attention; last year's Professional Masterchef winner Steve Groves resides as senior sous chef at Launceston Place. D&D has also opened three restaurants in Copenhagen and two in Tokyo (including Iconic, which won a Michelin Star this year), as well as the 50/50-owned Modern Pantry in Clerkenwell with Anna Hansen.

Des: 'One of the things we have tried to do is bring a bit more personality into the restaurants, so the business is much more hands-on, fast moving and more foodie. Conran was always a people business, but D&D is much more about the energy and quality of people that we have. I think this is generally a level above where we were.'

David: 'The focus is really about our chefs and whom we are attracting to work with us. In the past we have talked about design and having great places, but not as much about food and service. Obviously that is what defines a restaurant business. D&D does not have a big, heavy structure. There are no tiers among operations – managers and chefs work together with our support and guidance.'

Des: 'David and I made a very conscious decision about how we would work. We have an open-plan office and see and talk to each other a lot; previously this was not the case. What this means is that there is a very clear development strategy.'

With Conran Holdings Limited retaining a non-controlling 51% stake in the business, and Des remaining involved in the parent company, D&D retains a platform for design-led projects. Its vision is to own and operate high quality, modern restaurants and hotels in the major cities of the world. D&D is presently working on an 80-bedroom hotel development due to open in London Moorgate in 2012, with long-term plans for UK growth. This is not a new direction, as the business previously had great success with the refurbishment and sale of the Great Eastern Hotel – for a profit of £35 million – while trading as Conran. For David, whose hospitality career was founded in the hotel industry, it is an exciting step.

David: 'There is a natural evolution to this stage. People thought I was mad to leave hotels, yet so much has changed in 15 years. Some of the best people that I have worked with have come from restaurants. It is a career, not a job. D&D can offer the opportunity to be part of the growing organisation, international travel and the chance to run restaurants as independent businesses.'

Des: 'I think we can bring something different to the UK hotel scene – a small group of luxury high-end modern boutique hotels in big cities.'

Restaurant development is planned for the UK and internationally, with Des and David acknowledging that much of the long-term growth is likely to be focused overseas. They already have established operations in Paris, New York, Tokyo and Copenhagen. A major project is underway in Birmingham, while a joint venture has been struck for new sites in the Far East. However, London remains a central focus.

Des: 'One of our big mistakes in the nineties was believing all the media hype that there were too many Conran restaurants in London. That is why we diversified into the international market and hotels – but this thinking was completely wrong. London is enormous and a big eating-out city. There is no reason we could not have doubled the number of restaurants, so we can continue to do more. Are we really the Waitrose of the industry? No, and we are not trying to be that. We are a £75–80 million business – that is not big.'

David: 'Opening abroad is more challenging, but you learn a lot. Customers are different; so are reservation systems, eating styles. But this adds great knowledge back into your core operations. We are looking for the right partners and right space.'

DES: 'The constraint on growth is not the lack of cities. It is how fast and how much can we grow and retain the entrepreneurial philosophy that makes us who we are now. Yes, we look for quirky spaces, something different, but we also want to be known for having the best people.'

It is this philosophy that, in part, drove D&D to make one of their most controversial decisions to date, scrapping service charge. Des and David did not see the move as too risky – and the result has been that tips are well ahead of expectations – but it's clear they are intrigued by the debate that ensued following the announcement.

Des: 'Conran actually pioneered the discretionary service charge, but it was only ever meant to be discretionary! In practice it came to be regarded as almost compulsory. So we wanted to change this and believe the change will improve service. Whether a restaurant is left with 5% or 15%, the important thing is that customers will think they paid a fair price.'

David: 'It is working as it should do – staff providing really top-notch service and getting rewarded. It's nicer for customers to decide.'

D&D London may well continue to attract comparisons to their days as the former Conran, but it is clear that Des and David embrace the heritage and strength that such a connection provides. The evolution is clearly in the focus of the leadership team towards innovation and reinforcing the individuality of the eating-out experience across all elements of their operations. Having already garnered considerable respect, moving squarely into the hotel market is sure to reflect the blended philosophy D&D is seeking to create.

(July 2010)

Restaurants

Ian Neill
Former Executive Chairman, Wagamama

Whilst Ian prefers to be thought of as a businessman, his career is distinctly entrepreneurial. Acknowledging that he has benefited from learning the discipline of more formalised processes, Ian prefers to keep his own counsel rather than bow to convention and prefers to keep his style somewhat detached. As a restaurateur he has been involved in the evolution of a number of successful concepts, notably Wagamama which at the time of its conception was revolutionary in its shared eating style; Ian acted as the driver to grow the brand into a household name. Ian has a clear vision of what a restaurant business stand for and is regarded as an innovative and intelligent role model for others.

Marching to the beat of a drum

In the mid-1960s, Ian Neill followed the classic Mod bands such as 'The Small Faces' and wanted to go to Reading – at the time, the heartland of the movement. However, life is rarely as accommodating and instead he settled in Leeds, undertaking a two-year catering course, followed by an HCIMA diploma and then embarked on a career that has seen him head up several restaurant companies that have become household names – Pizza Express (1978–86) Rank Restaurants, where 200 units including Sweeney Todds, Oliver's Hot Bread and Prima Pasta came under his auspices and more latterly and currently, the very successful Wagamama (38 sites in the UK, 57 in total including international franchises). And yet Ian remains, as I remember him on our first meeting at his Pizza Express office in Soho in the early 1980s, modest, amusing, open-minded and thoroughly enjoying himself.

A role model to countless successful operators he seemed genuinely surprised when I told him that others, when asked whom they most admire in the trade, regularly mention his name.

Ian describes his career progress as one of continual discovery. Any regrets?

'Nobody ever told me when I was young that I could invest.' No matter, he discovered he could anyway and partnered the legendary Peter Boizot in restaurant ventures, a business relationship that continues to this day. His mantra is to 'operationally deliver an experience that people want to repeat.' He admits to mistakes. He has sold some sites that didn't work for him but where other operators have come in, re-branded and been successful. I asked him if he had enjoyed his corporate life and his response was measured: 'you take the good bits, gain great experience from it, the structure and systems and adapt it for your own business. Most people who have been innovative or entrepreneurial have benefited at some stage from more formal procedures associated with the bigger Companies.'

So who were his role models?

'The guy who launched Viking Direct, what a great idea!!! Also Phillip Green, such an amazing instinctive business flair.'

I pointed out that Green never uses a computer, 'Says it all,' replied Ian. He also admired the late Bob Payton who 'stimulated the whole theme driven restaurant scene, but it was Pizza Express that defined social dining in a totally unique way in the 1970s and Peter Boizot deserves a lot of credit for that.'

In recent years, Ian has enjoyed great success with Wagamama, which is pledged to grow at the rate of 12 new sites a year from 2006. I pointed out that it was very formula driven:

'I defy anyone to successfully roll out a group of restaurants without proper systems.'

Fair point and one that the private equity players have not been slow to recognise. Currently Ian's star is as high as it has been throughout his distinguished career. He sits as a non-executive on the Board of Paramount Restaurants (formerly Group Chez Gerard), which recently acquired

Caffè Uno. One gets the impression that offers abound to both advise and add weight to the board of numerous independent and publicly quoted businesses. He is understandably choosy and has no need to spread himself too thinly. He started his career working as a waiter at the Imperial Hotel in Blackpool where his early orientations towards hotels began and ended. The faster pace of restaurants and the fact that people 'went home afterwards' held greater appeal. He had grown up in Los Angeles from the age of 4 to 15 when he was sent back to England to boarding school in Kent. The story from joining Pizza Express in 1978 to the present day runs like a restaurant equivalent of 'rock family trees' as so many of the peer group have become synonymous with success, as well as brands (as opposed to bands) which have come and gone. Ian's trick has been to be one step ahead, constantly anticipating the trends and eating desires of the public.

I asked him why the larger multinational chains often failed to break through with new brands.

> 'Clearly there have been successes like Tony Hughes with All Bar One but too often the big plcs reshuffle and move people on before they have had sufficient time and ownership of a brand. Short termism undermines the likely chances of success. UK plc is not noted for its patience. People rarely get the chance to clear up their own mess and put it right.'

James Dyson, I mention, has stated that success is 98% failure and people need to dare to fail.

> 'Correct but large companies don't usually give that opportunity, their shareholders or the city don't allow them the scope.'

I ask him to tick a multiple-choice question; do you see yourself as (1) businessman, (2) entrepreneur or (3) restaurateur. He goes for the first and expands on businesses being his fascination. He is very well read and informed on who is doing what in a whole range of different sectors. I refer to his reputation for fair mindedness, a point he embellishes with his attitude to references.

> 'So often people seem to get rubbished if their tenure in a job ends poorly and the full perspective is not taken into account, i.e. how they

have performed over the full period of that employment, I prefer to judge people over their entire time in a company.'

Finally I recalled his office in Soho in the early 1980s where he proudly hung a photograph of himself with Margaret Thatcher at a meeting of the Finchley Conservative Party. He recalled the photograph fondly and said he was a great supporter of the former first lady of Downing Street. He had however, long since lapsed as a member of the Conservative Party during its years of relative oblivion. Would he now be returning to the fold with its new dawn under the charismatic David Cameron?

'Definitely, he strikes me as honest and genuine with a great opportunity to grasp and provide real leadership.' Ian could have been describing himself and his own ongoing opportunities, but of course he is too modest to ever bang his own drum, preferring as always to march to the beat of it!

(February 2006)

Restaurants

Roy Ackerman OBE

Roy Ackerman has had an extremely diverse career in the industry, which befits his entrepreneurial traits. He is the consummate serial entrepreneur with ventures ranging from media to restaurateur to personal assistant. Roy has strength of character, together with a great deal of personal passion and tenacity. These behavioural traits are what drive him, and have latterly been recognised in numerous roles chairing leading industry associations such as the Academy of Culinary Arts and Academy of Food and Wine Service.

From the beginning...

Much has been written about Roy Ackerman in the past. As a well recognised face in the international hospitality industry, is has been noted that Roy has 'held more posts than a fence builder's assistant'. However, what was the career that originally made the man?

From Chairman of the World Master of Culinary Arts and Chairman of the Restaurant Association of Great Britain, to Honorary President of the Henley Festival of Music and the Arts, Roy Ackerman has been involved in various aspects of the hospitality sector for many years. Researching about him before we met, I read numerous articles about his passion for the industry, his involvement, and indeed leadership, of many industry associations and also his impact on the industry as the author and publisher of guide books such as *The Ackerman Guides*, *Egon Ronay Guides* and *Cafes of Europe*. Yet, despite a broad range of articles and interviews, I came across very little about Roy's time in the industry. I wondered – how did he get here?

So I ask Roy to start from the beginning:

'Okay then. But please don't ask me to name any dates,' quips Roy, with a grin. 'I always say that everything happened 10 years ago and quite clearly that is not the case!'

I'm quite content with this arrangement; after all in a career as broad as Roy's it is the experiences that are really important rather than the dates.

'Initially I was attracted to the industry for the core reasons: food, drink and shelter,' explains Roy, 'And they pay you at the end of the week! But more than that, it was an opportunity to meet people – people who had travelled and have the opportunity to travel myself – it seemed glamorous and I was interested in who they were and what they did.

'I was 14 when I started as an apprentice chef. Of course I lied and told them that I was 16 and went on to do a five-year apprenticeship. I really enjoyed it, the food you cooked and ate, the lifestyle and I still really love that aspect of it and love working with younger people with the same enthusiasm – all the competitions are great for that.

'After the apprenticeship I worked with a number of different people and they were all 'mad' men. First for an Italian with a bakery and outside catering company, then with a man named Ronald Avery who was a wine merchant, and then in a company with a number of coffee shops. After that I worked as a PA for a man named George Silver who was an ex-army Major with between 40 and 50 restaurants. He really taught me what it meant to be tenacious and to never give in. As it turned out, he went on to be an actor and was in *Victor Victoria* with Julie Andrews, *Gumshoe* with Albert Finney and many other films.

'I found myself working in London with a multiple caterer and at the same time I was living in Oxford and had a few bistros there. I would work in London during the day and then return to Oxford to open up and operate the bistros at night and during the weekends, working both front and back of house. They were long days, but it was wonderful and I still meet people who were undergraduates and customers from that time all over the world.

'The favourite encounter of my career happened in Kakadu National Park in Australia. I was with a group in a small air-conditioned restaurant there. During the meal the waiter came up to me and asked me if my name was Roy. He told me that there was a lady in the corner who would like to say hello.

'I was surprised to find that it was a customer from Quincy's Bistro in Oxford from nearly 20 years earlier. She introduced me to her new husband and explained that her previous husband had passed away, but that they had frequently dined with us in Oxford. She specifically remembered one evening when they had come by after the theatre to be told by the maitre d' that there were simply no tables left. Apparently I'd come along, and as all the chefs were about to have supper in the kitchen insisted that they were welcome to join us if they wished. So they propped themselves on stools in the kitchen and remember that meal to this day! I really love the fact that such small gestures can make people feel great.'

I can certainly imagine the situation as I sit there interviewing Roy, as on our arrival for the interview a fellow diner called out 'Is that Roy?' and settled in for a 10-minute catch up. But, back to the story:

'So, I had four bistros in Oxford and Michael Golder, my soon-to-be business partner, had two restaurants so we decided to put them together and form a public company. Over the next nine years we opened over 50 restaurants and also grew by acquiring other businesses. We ended up with 130 restaurants and hotels around the country and were eventually taken over by Forte.

'When I think back I always remember Derek Pain, the financial journalist, saying that we had come into the market on 'a menu and a prayer' which is probably true. It all just moved so quickly – in the late 70s and early 80s there was a new deal every week and it was hard to catch your breath, but by the time we sold we were really doing it for different reasons than those we set out with. I was very lucky, as operations grow you really need to have that business element and Michael took that role while I got to do the 'fun' bit.

To bring the story to the present day, Roy then bought some new restaurants and established more including: Simply Nico with Nicola Ladenis, 190 Queens Gate with Antony Worrall Thompson as Chef Director and Elena's L'Etoile in Charlotte Street, with the then 70-year-old Elena Salvoni, who 'now 18 years later, still does it with style' insists Roy. Next follows Roy's move into publishing and producing guide books with *The Ackerman Guides, Egon Ronay Guides, Cafes of Europe* and *Martell Guide to Europe.* How was it to suddenly find himself on the other side of the equation?

'I have a frustration with flippantly written comments from one off visits,' admits Roy, 'particularly in guides. A newspaper review is tomorrow's fish and chip paper, but guides stay around for a long time and in the end they can really impact on people's livelihoods.'

At present Roy is involved with both Tadema Studios, his design and consultancy business that works mainly with international hotel and restaurant groups, as well as coolcucumber TV, a monthly online half-hour web TV programme in which Roy visits and profiles various restaurants and chefs and shares his experiences with the online viewer.

'With *coolcucumber*, I wanted to do something positive, there is too much that focuses on the industry in a negative light – it doesn't all have to be about bad language and stress. Really we are here to look after the customers and the people who work in the industry. I just wanted to show the best of it.'

(December 2009)

Restaurants

Sir Terence Conran

Sir Terence Conran's experimentation with restaurant design has been the inspiration for many, and his influence transcends generations. An inquisitive nature has given him a certain approach to life in general and together with a flair for design, he has applied this to numerous entrepreneurial ventures. From a hospitality perspective this meant that Sir Terence completely changed the eating-out experience in Britain. His story is a hallmark to power of vision above and beyond established thinking.

A burning flame

For the past 50 years Sir Terence Conran has had an impact on the way we live. Born in 1931, he studied art and graduated from the Central Saint Martin's College of Art and Design. In 1953 he opened the Soup Kitchen with friends and the rest, as they say, is history. So what are the passions behind the man?

I meet Sir Terence on the same day he flies to New York to open the new Conran Shop on Broadway. Aged 79, he remains at the centre of his business world and exhibits a huge amount of passion for his work. 'Sir' Terence fits his title well. When speaking with him, there is recognition that this is an individual who has achieved something special, and he commands respect. A teenager during the post-war years, Sir Terence emerged as a young man during the beginning of a decade that was to become the age of the consumer, and a period of immense societal change. For the UK, the 1950s was the beginning of a period of increasing prosperity, the end of rationing and it was in this context that Sir Terence's pioneering work in shaping Britain's lifestyle and attitudes were formulated. His innate connection to France has driven many developments. However, as becomes clear during our interview, it is the vividness of his memories and power of observation that characterises Sir Terence and underpins his success.

Born in Kingston-upon-Thames, Sir Terence attended Bryanston Public School in Dorset. It was during this time that he discovered his passion for design, and the pleasure of working and experimenting with different materials such as pottery, metal and wood. A naturally inquisitive individual, these early years inspired him to look at all aspects of living in a new way.

'I always loved making things, understanding the mechanics and purpose, and knowing how things work. I used to start up the kiln in our family garden, building the fire up to reach the right temperature while drinking beers. It was here that I fired my first pottery and it was very rewarding to see the final result.

'Then, when I was living as a student in London during the late forties and early fifties, I became friends with a doctor who had just come back from Korea. We were sitting in the kitchen one evening, wondering about the world, having no money and what we could do about it. As students we could not find a place to have a simple meal at an affordable price, so we decided to open a café. But no one knew anything about running a café; I mean where do you start?'

This episode drove him to travel to France for the first time in 1950, after graduating from college. It was a seminal experience and Sir Terence became an advocate for the French lifestyle, in turn igniting his mission to share this passion and vision with Britain. At the time England still had rationing and the quality of food and produce available was limited.

'It was a breath of fresh air. France was such a huge farming country and I was amazed by the markets. Everything smelt different, the quality and abundance of produce was inspiring. At the time you could eat four courses for one pound in a Routier restaurant and the people were so kind. So naturally I wanted to bring back some of this lifestyle to England. I think that has to be the heart of what I do – the ambition of every designer is to improve people's quality of life.'

However, Sir Terence's love for France went beyond the detail. His introduction to the French eating-out experience became the basis for evolving the design elements that would come to define a style of restaurant that would change the eating-out scene in London.

'I went to stay with my girlfriend in Paris and wanted to get a job in a restaurant. Eventually I found work as a *'plongeur'* [kitchen porter] and it was like a new world had opened up. People worked in the basement, in very difficult conditions. However, despite these challenges, the kitchen was well organised and disciplined, similar to an army in some respects.

'Working in the back of house really struck a chord in my mind. In those days front and back of house were two different worlds. It was a constant battle; chefs were spending hours and hours completely cut off from the restaurant ambience and this created a difficult rapport. For me, it was a huge problem, so this was my inspiration for creating the open-plan kitchen.'

Returning to London in 1953, Sir Terence opened the Soup Kitchen near Trafalgar Square. A bowl of soup cost a shilling and sixpence and it was the first opportunity that he had had to experiment with a new style of restaurant design. The total build cost was about £247 and fixtures included the prized asset, a Gaggia espresso machine – at that time only London's second.

'Designing a restaurant adopts the same principles as any type of design. It has to work from the point of view of the staff and customers. To deliver the workability of the place, you try and work out which areas are going to have dense usage, the number of people who may use that area and what they need. Personally I always take the view that the kitchen staff must see the diners and vice versa. It's important because it removes the barriers between front and back of house.

'In Paris both big and small brasseries were able to combine speed and efficiency in very confined spaces. During my time there I observed how one waiter was able to manage and serve 27 covers. This was incredible efficiency, but it was because everything was roughly where it needed to be and I realised that a waiter's station was equally as important as a guest's table.'

Sir Terence opened his latest venture, The Boundary, with Peter Prescott in January last year and it includes three restaurants and bars, 12 guest bedrooms, five suites, a bakery and a food store. It is the epitome of Sir Terence's vision for a lifestyle hospitality concept. However, the restaurant industry currently faces numerous challenges including high rents, skills shortages and an increasing cost base. What advice would he give to entrepreneurs thinking about getting into restaurants?

'I would tell them to go work in the type of establishment you want to open and learn before you launch yourselves into the business. I think to have a bar today is very important. A café operation works well with a small food shop, if possible with British products.

'There are so many good chefs and operators who fail because they thought they could design their restaurant or spend a fortune on a designer, but the end result did not work because the kitchen was not properly set out, or the chairs did not fit under the table. These are the little details that create huge operational problems on a daily basis. The materials used are equally as important; some come better with age and are able to absorb the usage demand and retain their patents.

'And finally, a restaurant is at its worst on the first day! A new restaurant does not yet have a soul, it is not worn in yet. Bibendum is 22 years old this year and it's better today that it was when it first opened, because it has aged well; it has been well looked after by the staff, and this shows.

For Sir Terence there is a reason for everything in restaurant and each detail is essential. Throughout each of his restaurants, he has never compromised on the quality of design for the front and back of house and always sought to deliver a wow factor, providing a unique guest experience. So what would he like to leave as his legacy?

'I hope I have demonstrated that a good restaurant is part of one's quality of life. Going to a restaurant is like going on holiday; it's partly aspirational and you look forward to getting there. The experience and the ambience should all come together and improve your life, and that is partially intellectual and partially physical.'

Peter Lederer, chairman, Gleneagles on Sir Terrence

'Many people talk about innovation and many more indulge in 'CASE' (copy and steal everything) – few are genuine innovators. Sir Terence is certainly a creative innovator in everything he does. Furniture, lighting, food, beverage, training, style – he understands customers and has the ability to give them what they didn't know they could have, and all at a fair price. Brilliant.'

(July 2010)

Restaurants

Iqbal Wahhab

Founder, Roast Restaurant

Iqbal fell into restaurant ventures through his early career in public relations and media. He possesses a strong character and value set, including a keen awareness of what customers desire from an eating out experience, and this shapes the culture of his business. Iqbal is a classic, serial entrepreneur and likes to take risks in order to challenge conventional thinking. He has suffered several setbacks in his career but has continued to move forward despite this. Of Bangladeshi origin, Iqbal was raised in the UK and arguably his greatest success to date, Roast in Borough Market, is an extremely well regarded interpretation of modern British cuisine.

Life is a rollercoaster: Iqbal's amazing adventure

Death threats, the Cinnamon Club, shareholder fallout and Roast – Iqbal Wahhab is one of the industry's most unique restaurateurs.

'It was February 1998. I woke up one morning and turned on the morning television. The presenters were reviewing the morning papers, The Times, and so on. They had their finger pointed at a picture of me and were gesticulating madly. From this point on I started to receive death threats and was advised by Special Branch to leave my home. It's such a bizarre story that I wouldn't blame you if you didn't believe me. But it actually happened.'

And so begins one of the more startling anecdotes of Iqbal's career. Having written a stinging critique of his experience at an Indian restaurant for his column in *Tandoori* magazine, Iqbal's life changed dramatically. The review sparked national outrage amongst the Indian restaurant community and, obviously, many negative headlines. This included accusations from the Bangladeshi Caterers Association that he was collaborating with supermarkets to dishonour Indian restaurants. A libel suit swiftly followed, which Iqbal won. Later in the interview I will comment that he seems utterly unfazed by the rather 'up and down' journey of his entrepreneurial career. He has since gone on to create two of London's most celebrated restaurants, the theme of which has been the sophistication of British food concepts – Indian and the traditional roast dinner.

Following the incident with *Tandoori* magazine, a venture that he owned and had set up in partnership with Cobra beer, he left in order to 'disown' himself from the enterprise. Iqbal 'needed something to do' and decided to transform his words and beliefs into action with a restaurant. After 18 months and £2.5 million of investment, which should have been eight months and £1.7 million, the Cinnamon Club was born in 2001.

'In my previous role I had handled the PR for both Indian and French restaurants, one of which was Pied à Terre. Their Executive Chef would be sourcing ingredients at 6.30 a.m. and have created a new dish to serve by 11.00 a.m. that day. At this time chefs in Indian restaurants were only just walking in the door. I started to question my clients about new ways of doing Indian food. I wanted to know why they couldn't do wine matching or create the beauty of a Michelin starred restaurant. The consistent reply was that 'this is not what the public wants from an Indian experience.''

The restaurant, set in an old Westminster library over 12,000 sq ft, was a massive financial and conceptual challenge. Highly successful, it raised the quality of Indian food and dining experience – as was the vision. It is no secret that Iqbal fell out with his shareholders at the Cinnamon Club in

2005 and left the business. Iqbal's flair for creativity and passion for food was pitched against the cold hard reality of investment banking. Though Iqbal had endeavoured to ensure his financial awareness was up-to-date, it was never enough to satisfy the board.

'There was a tendency to apply the same rules for making financial investment decisions to a restaurant environment. You may be delivering on one day, but not the next and if you were not delivering then you were immediately in trouble. They applied these rules to me. It is true that I did not understand the figures 'off the top of my head' initially. Yet, I was pitched against young investment bankers who had made millions in the City but were not used to running a business such as this.

'The Cinnamon Club offered something different that had the potential to be developed as a concept. But it needed long-term vision. Ultimately I did not want to kowtow to the Board anymore and moved on. It was a very open and public split. Yet, leaving the Cinnamon Club was a turning point for me; I remain on good terms with the chefs and eat there regularly.'

Whereas the Cinnamon Club had taken the nation's favourite pub grub and transformed it in an entirely new way, Iqbal's next venture was the essence of simplicity. Roast opened in 2005, a successful conceptualisation serving the nation's favourite British dinner, which has seen 20% growth in the past year.

'It is an utterly straightforward concept. The idea is that people are happy to pay a premium provided they know that they are getting the best available produce. However, we opened to the worst reviews from restaurant critics in ten years. It was zero out of ten every week. And no, we were not perfect in our first few weeks, but who is? However, people actually ended up coming because of the bad reviews, as I think they simply couldn't believe we were that bad. We ended up turning customers away on day three. I think that the negativity was partly driven by resentment behind the idea that I could make British food innovative. The reality was that it was partly a reflection of my experiences of school dinners whilst growing up. I loved the simplicity of the idea.'

Iqbal is presently looking at his options for future developments. Roast is set in the ideally matched environment of Borough Market and he sees this is a unique trick. Whilst he is not planning another Roast, Iqbal does not rule out another British restaurant of some kind. Roast-to-Go is a concession concept that Iqbal has developed for staff restaurants or as an outside catering option. Presently in discussions on a partnership with a contract caterer, Iqbal feels that 'there is so much more life in a brand'. An American restaurant appeals to him, and that may be an option for the future, possibly in locations such as Dubai or New York. He recently sold his stake in three restaurants at the O2 Arena.

> 'I do not believe that upmarket restaurants will work at the Arena, most people arrive only 45 minutes before a show. My partner and I got an offer that was too good to refuse and I felt that my energies could be used better elsewhere.'

Iqbal's non-commercial interests are many. Two of the most high profile of these are his work as Chair of the Government's Ethnic Minority Advisory Group, which gives him a place on ministerial employment Task Force, and Skills Ambassador for the 2012 Olympic Games. One of the more challenging questions that the Taskforce has grappled with is the question as to whether the government has done the right thing by restricting visas for Indian chefs.

> 'It may be controversial but I do not believe that the government needs to change their policy for Indian chefs. I think restaurants should look to train other chefs and make use of the various programmes available. For me it is untrue to say that Eastern Europeans cannot cook Indian food.'

We go on to discuss how this issue may affect the development of other cuisines in the UK, noting Japanese in particular. Iqbal acknowledges that it can take up to seven years to qualify as a sushi chef. However, he believes that we must 'tackle the challenges for developing chefs full on and make restaurants aware of programmes such as Train to Gain or NVQs.'

Iqbal arrived from Bangladesh with his family at the age of eight months. His parents were both academics – his mother a school principal and his father a professor of philosophy.

'My brother and sister were 5 and 7 when they came to Britain. So whereas I had no notion of Bangladesh culture, my siblings did, could speak the language and appreciate the food. When we got to the UK the notion of multiculturalism at that time was quite different: it was about integration, the monoculture and assimilation into society. I spoke English and no Bengali, ate school dinners and was viewed as slightly odd by family. I think they felt sorry for me. Mum was a strict disciplinarian but my dad believed in free will. I was the youngest child and my dad wanted to raise me with the experience of free will. He made a pact with her that I would be left to work out right from wrong myself with no discipline. Though I was a bad boy at school, the lack of mental discipline helped me to process different experiences such as bullying or racism with no practical sense of my Asian culture. I always saw myself as British.'

It is at this point in the discussion that I share my view that Iqbal Wahhab does not really seem fazed by setbacks or controversy.

'I love being a master of my own destiny. I do not want to get to a point where I have to question my legacy and if I could have done more. I am always doing something that I shouldn't. But then if I didn't there would be nothing left to say.'

(June 2008)

Restaurants

James Thomson OBE
Scottish restaurateur–hotelier

James Thomson is a classic entrepreneur who developed a love of hospitality at an early age. He has dedicated his life to the pursuit of developing unique and beautiful experiences in a series of highly creative restaurant and accommodation settings in Scotland. An abstract and considered thinker, James is extremely intelligent and a hallmark of his success has been translating his personal passions into business entities, to great effect.

History, art and theatre

Research has indicated that most entrepreneurs sell their businesses after 8–10 years. Goals have been achieved; motivation falls. It is a natural cycle. Yet James Thomson, owner of Edinburgh's The Witchery and Prestonfield House, has been leading his own businesses for nearly 30 years. Why is James an exception to the rule, and what the drivers have been to ensure he has stayed at the top for so long?

'My grandmother worked in an old fashioned tea room, a lovely business with beautiful polished silver cake stands, high tea and the average waitress in her early 60s'.

This is clearly not the traditional place for a young boy to discover his love of hospitality. However, after a number of years filling in as a kitchen porter, when the regulars failed regularly to show for a Saturday shift, James began to discover the theatre of a kitchen. Then, at the age of 15 when he began working as a waiter, his love of the industry deepened... from the beautifully decorated dishes, to the starched crisp table linen, his attention to detail was well honed from the start. James was educated at George Heriot's School in Edinburgh, the son of a banker and brother to a lawyer. James' parents had made many sacrifices for his schooling and had thoughts about the sort of profession that a young, well-educated James might go into. However, as the self-professed dreamer and 'black sheep' of the family, James had other ideas. His love of catering and hospitality had been ignited and he 'horrified' his father by expressing an interest in going to catering college. Mr Thomson Sr, a reasonable man, saw his son's keen interest and obvious dedication to the concept, and cut a deal: a full season at an acquaintance's establishment in Jersey, the Hotel Atlantic. If, at the end of the season, his passion had not diminished then catering college it would be.

Nearly 30 years on James' passion for the industry shows no sign of waning. An entrepreneur at heart, James established a side-line whilst studying, providing catering for friends and fellow students' 18th birthday parties. So perhaps it is no surprise that at the age of 20, he became

Scotland's youngest licensee, when he opened the doors of the Witchery by the Castle.

'I had to take out three personal loans to get it started. I was so determined to prove to my family that I could do it there was no way I was going to them for help. But even with the loans, things were tight at first. My great aunt had sadly passed away and she left a number of things to me, most precious of these to me personally are some old family medals, but also her old furniture. It was about this time that I discovered my love of history, art and antiques. Her furniture, along with some other discarded furniture purchased locally, formed the basis of the restaurant. Having always been involved with the theatre from behind the scenes, and in a design capacity, I also drew on my ability to create striking, theatrical settings for customers to experience.'

This dramatic effect has become a hallmark for James' businesses. In addition to the Witchery Restaurant and accommodation suites, James has established the Secret Garden Restaurant (also based at the Witchery), The Tower on the rooftop of the Museum of Scotland and the stunning Prestonfield House Hotel. In each situation, the words used frequently to describe these establishments are those such as 'magical', 'dramatic' and 'designed to impress'. Sitting in a decadent room at Prestonfield, with a crackling fire and lovely antique furniture, I can feel the effect. But I'm intrigued to know, in this increasingly disposable world, how James manages to keep the venues and offering fresh and appealing.

'I simply offer an environment that I would like to spend time in and, in a city that originally enjoyed only about three months a year as a tourist destination, I also saw the necessity to appeal equally to the local community. Fundamentally, I believe in the importance of travelling a different route to the norm. Since the Witchery first opened there have been many external events that have put pressure on our industry. There were the miners' strikes, which led to power cuts and three-day working weeks, the Gulf War in '91, which really affected the economy, and so on. I've learnt that in a recession, don't cut back like everyone else – spend!'

Whilst this may sound counter-intuitive, it actually makes sense. As James explains:

'When money is tight and the pressure is on for families and individuals, then the frequency with which people dine out decreases dramatically. This really means that when people do eat out it is often for a special occasion and their appreciation of all the little things increases. In these situations the nice touches really can make all the difference. So I never cut down on flowers or the linen or the other 'non-essentials'. In fact with many establishments selling their own cellars to purchase special wines, I also took the opportunity to build the cellar at the Witchery during these periods. I want to make sure that customer celebrations are always special.'

The grounds and buildings of Prestonfield have an elegance and atmosphere that seem timeless. James bought the property in 2003 and has since restored the buildings, along with decorating and furnishing the hotel in that unmistakable dramatic, antique style. This, he says, is the easy bit:

'Investing in the property itself is not so hard, it's the people, the team that are more of a challenge'.

To add a little background, after his time in the tearooms as a teenager, James worked at Prestonfield House as a waiter whilst studying at college in the 1970s. So in neat, storybook fashion he returned to the hotel some 30 years later to lavishly restore and regenerate his old training ground.

'The challenge here was to take the whole hotel through that period of change. Some of the people working at Prestonfield had been here since I worked as a waiter in the '70s and it can be difficult to introduce new systems and take staff successfully through that process of change.'

Attention to the training and development of the teams is clearly something that James believes in. As the first independent Scottish restaurant to be accredited in 1998 with the Investors In People award, and numerous study trips to Disney in Florida to learn more about development and team building, customer service and innovation, James is never idle in this area.

'You can never underestimate the importance of a good team. Everyone must know what the business is striving to achieve, and it is important to work with people to find the right person for the right job. We have a range of skills and abilities within the team from those with first-class honours to those with language difficulties or dyslexia. However, if you really take the time to get to know people and treat the staff well you can help each person to find the right fit'.

So, where to now? James had mentioned at the beginning of our conversation that his early plans were to work hard until he was 40 and then retire. Yet at 40, the Tower was just arriving on the scene so this clearly didn't go according to plan?

'I was thinking of retiring at that point, at the very least I was quite content with the restaurant and accommodation. But then I was approached about the Tower and had a dream of creating a destination restaurant in the museum. In hindsight it was like having a difficult child at 40 – lots of sleepless nights! Now, I don't think I will retire at all. I'm a city person at heart and Prestonfield gives me this fabulous opportunity to experience 20 acres of property right near the middle of Edinburgh. Scotland and Edinburgh itself have such a feeling of optimism, we have learnt to celebrate success and not to be so cynical. It's an exciting time.'

(December 2007)

Restaurants

Drew Nieporent

Owner, Myriad Restaurant Group

As Drew states here, 'It's like sometimes being an entrepreneur, you have extra vision. You can see how it would work.' This sentiment is, in fact, echoed throughout this book and Drew is no exception. A native New Yorker he a respected restaurateur in the most trend-setting eating out city in the world. Having established the original Nobu restaurant, with Robert De Niro and the unknown Nobu Matsuhisa, Drew cemented his entrepreneurial credentials. Cornell educated, he has continued to push boundaries for eating out in the USA through the Myriad restaurant group. A classic entrepreneur, Drew argues that knowledge of local market is critical in new ventures, and, whilst he is not afraid to push boundaries, takes a managed approach to risk. Thus his decision to launch Nobu in London remains what one of Drew's riskier moves to date, but highlights how such a choice can pay off if the circumstances are right.

'Restaurants are a bit like theatre'

One of the most prolific US-based restaurateurs, Drew Nieporent was responsible for the launch of Nobu, together with Robert De Niro and the then unknown Nobu Matsuhisa. A hallmark of innovation in Japanese cuisine, Nobu London became the first American-owned restaurant to achieve a Michelin star in 1998. Yet this is only part of the story. As Founder of the Myriad Restaurant Group, Drew has opened 31 restaurants in 23 years and remains one of the leading innovators in new concepts.

'Initially Robert held his own casting for the opening of our first restaurant together, which was the Tribeca Grill. At the end of the day this is what he is used to doing; even as an actor he is involved in all decisions. He introduced me to Nobu Matsuhisa, though I had known of him since 1987. Matsuhisa was not right for the Tribeca Grill, because it was an American restaurant. However, Nobu and Robert had a kinship and I wanted to try to make a business with him. We started talking about a Nobu restaurant in 1988, eventually opening in 1994.

'If it is a choice between John Doe and Robert De Niro it is better to have someone with notoriety, especially 18 years ago when celebrity was more downplayed. Robert is subtle and low key. There is a tremendous advantage with the association.'

Drew Nieporent has developed a respected reputation both in the US and in the UK. In addition to Nobu and Nobu London, he operates two other versions of the restaurant – Next Door Nobu (which operates a no reservations policy) and Nobu 57 in New York's uptown district.

Globally the brand has 20 locations, including a second in London, which Nobu Matsuhisa operates with a variety of business investors. The first Nobu Hotel is due to open in Israel in 2010 and a second is planned for New York within two to four years, with De Niro on board as partner.

It is interesting to learn that Drew had to convince both Robert and Nobu to make the decision to open in London.

'It was tough initially to get the buy-in as it was such a huge risk. We were doing things at that time that had never been done before. It's like sometimes being an entrepreneur, you have extra vision, you can see how it would work. For me we were entering a market without competition and we had a superior product. Our partnership with Christina Ong at the Metropolitan Hotel has been central to our success. Nobu London is not the same as Nobu New York, the feeling is uniquely British.'

Drew opened his first restaurant – Montrachet – in 1985 and the Myriad Group also includes Centrico and Mai House, a modern take on Mexican and Vietnamese cuisines respectively. In October this year he opened Corton, a modern version of French cuisine, in partnership with British chef Paul Liebrandt. An award winning wine and spirit business – Crush – completes the current Myriad structure.

'Really a restaurant business is not one that lends itself well to extrapolation. I believe that our longevity has been remarkable. We are in our 18th year at the Tribeca Grill and our 14th year for Nobu. I compare restaurants to movies – can you watch a movie over and over, or do you become so fed up that you want a new one? Well, we have been doing the same movie for a long time.'

Born and bred in New York, Drew graduated from Cornell University with a degree in hotel management in 1977. His career includes time spent with Maxwell's Plum and Tavern on the Green, and the prestigious Manhattan-based restaurants Le Perigord, Le Grenouille and Plaza Athenee's Le Regence. He has previously said that 'chefs are the new models' and Drew's knack appears to push cuisine towards more contemporary boundaries, describing the creation of new restaurant concepts as 'very rational' and a reflection of his experience to date.

'Having grown up in New York I was exposed to a great theatre of food. It was so authentic, literally right off the boat. My father was an attorney and my mother was an actress. I knew immediately that I wanted to do this as my profession; I think that restaurants are a bit like theatre.

'Cornell was the eminent school, with students coming from all over the world. It was the first time I had spent so much time with people from the Caribbean or Europe or Asia. The exposure to so many cultures was tremendous.'

A passionate and direct character, Drew reflects that an early experience working on luxury cruise liners as a student was a defining moment in his career.

'My biggest breakthrough career-wise was when I was 18 working on cruise ships. I was one of 60 waiters for 600 passengers, serving three meals a day. It was a real proving ground and gave me a lot of exposure. You knew you were privileged in a certain way, and it gave me the confidence to understand what it takes to inspire people.

'Ultimately, I want to be seen in the mould of Gordon Ramsay or Marco Pierre White; somebody who works with the best people and top talent. People do not want to be manipulated – there needs to be a level of respect and trust.'

The Myriad Group's other ventures have included the now closed Rubicon where Drew partnered with Robin Williams and Francis Ford Coppola, and there was even a venture at the Marriott Grand in Moscow. Montrachet was recently reopened after a complete remodelling as Corton, which he describes as 'a little like learning to walk again.' Drew is reflective when considering plans for further expansion.

'We were going at a pretty fast clip until 9/11.The uncertainty that then arose meant that we had to adopt a wait-and-see attitude. I see Las Vegas, Puerto Rico and Louisville, Kentucky as potential areas for growth. In New York, other factors weigh in when you are deciding to launch new concepts. People are loyal to their neighbourhood, especially in local Manhattan. At this point in our development I actually think we would be better off outside New York.

'Government regulation is challenging. From the minute you open there are health, labour and environmental officers on your doorstep and there is an attitude shaping America which is that they will look to shut you down if necessary. In addition you have a number of food critics plus the impact of blogs and other Internet sites which are not always accurate. So there is constant negativity.'

It is difficult to ignore the now ubiquitous topic of global finance in our discussion. One industry leader recently commented to me that the current crisis would 'change the face of the industry, as we are an industry that relies upon debt'.

Drew comments:

'The US is riddled with uncertainty. Everything is capitalised. It is extremely hard to borrow money and yet banks appear to have been getting away with poor investment decisions. In a way I knew this would happen. My approach is low risk/high return. You have to really drive the business to your door. I would open 20 more restaurants if the rents were more reasonable. But greed exists.

'Our industry is the best at policing itself but small businesses will be suffocated as prices escalate heavily. I am not optimistic at present.'

(December 2008)

Concession

Adrian and Ian Willson
Founders, Creativevents

Adrian and Ian Willson are classic entrepreneurs who embody the traits of commitment, hard-work and dedication. A young, dynamic duo, they have established their place in the event catering market, having taken on a high degree of personal risk to pursue their vision for Creativevents.

Two brothers, one ambition

In December 2007, the Sunday Times Fast Track 100 listing was published with only one catering company recognised. Creativevents, founded in 1997, stood proudly at number 52 with sales having increased at an average of 85% year on year since 2003. The two brothers who founded and continue to lead the business came across not only innovative, focused entrepreneurs, but likeable, genuine people.

We are sitting at one of Creativevent's new food outlets at the Olympia Exhibition Centre. It is one hour until doors open at the London International Horse Show (a major annual event at the venue), and all is calm. Staff were relaxed and confident, as were Adrian and Ian Willson – founders of Creativevents.

'We have no secret ingredient,' Adrian explains, 'with us, what you see is who we really are. We just work very hard and will do whatever it takes to make sure that we deliver. It may be an old cliché but we will go the extra mile; not just today, but tomorrow, the day after and the day after that.'

'We are competitive,' interjects Ian, 'because we are passionate about what we deliver to the customer. Sometimes we perhaps care too much, but I think that's how it should be.'

The brothers founded Creativevents with £5000 funding from the Prince's Trust. 2007 will see Creativevents turnover £10 million. They are specialists in providing bespoke food and drink at indoor venues and outdoor events throughout the UK. Currently their contracts include venues such as Earls Court, Olympia, the NEC and Excel London. As well as the indoor market, Creativevents provides high volume liquor bars for events such as Henley Regatta and Cartier International Polo, and festivals and outdoor concerts such as the 02 Wireless Festival in Hyde Park and the Red Hot Chilli Peppers in concert. New clients have helped to raise sales 85% a year from £1.2 million in 2003 to an annualised £7.6 million in 2006. In 2007, turnover topped the £10 million mark, so momentum is certainly building. I put it to Adrian that, clearly, so is their profile.

'Profile – that's frightening!' he jokes. 'This sort of thing is outside our day-to-day; we are much more at home when faced with 20,000 people wanting to be served at once!'

Down to earth… But it was only half a joke. These are two of the most genuine, straightforward people you could hope to meet. Originating from Yorkshire, they possess the character traits one would expect from a traditional 'Yorkshireman' – honesty, integrity, and straight talking. I have been to interview many of the industry's leading figures and all possess certain qualities to be respected or admired. The differences with Adrian and Ian are that, first you would trust them and second, you would be happy to stand with them and share a pint. They are no stereotypical characters and are very different to each other.

Adrian is the extrovert; Ian, the thinker and planner. Adrian is the older brother who is the natural leader. Ian observes and analyses first. Both are very open, and friendly. Even as we spoke, their eyes were casually watching the events unfolding about us. However, this was not through concern, they clearly had a very able and confident operations team in action. It is just their nature.

'Again, I know it may sound clichéd,' notes Ian, as he observes something which needs changing, 'but the devil lies in the detail. It is the small things that make the difference.'

It is no surprise to learn that they have built a business on a strong set of values in which relationships stand at the core. It is also no surprise that they have faced many difficult moments over the years and tackled them through those same values.

Neither Adrian nor Ian are originally from hospitality backgrounds and yet they are competing in an industry dominated by very established large catering businesses. In fact, they almost accidentally fell into the business. Adrian worked at Earls Court during his university days to earn extra money and enjoyed the work so much that he was drawn into the industry.

'Yes, they were good days,' says Adrian, laughing as he recalled the memories. 'I didn't take it too seriously, although I do remember thinking that I was really enjoying my time working behind the bars and wanted to see if I could build a career in this field.'

'We are very conscious that we are not traditional caterers,' notes Ian, 'but this acts as a motivating force. We work twice as hard to make sure we get it right and see things in a different way.'

'Have you noticed how we keep mentioning how hard we work?' joked Adrian. Getting it right… Ian smiles and nods in agreement. 'We take great pride in what we do. Don't get me wrong, we have made mistakes along the way but we take the lessons on board, learn from them and move on. We often do innovative things almost accidentally because we don't know anything different and then we smile when we see these ideas taken on by others. We don't take offence, it is reassuring and tells us that we must be getting it right. It is exciting when we see a competitor watch what we are doing closely, because it means we are really in the game.'

2007 was a landmark year for the company. Beyond recognition on the Fast Track 100 list, and securing the Excel contract, they took two decisions carrying high potential risk. In May, Creativevents recruited John Uphill from Sodexho Prestige to oversee expansion into the hospitality arena. This was a major step as the business was importing expertise from a large operator, and someone who had developed a career within a very structured, corporate environment. It is a challenge for such individuals required to transfer their skills into a more entrepreneurial environment, which by nature is less structured and relies upon informal communication. As Ian explains 'we realised that we were very good at retail catering, however to truly go forward as a competitive catering company we had to offer a one-stop-shop catering solution. John was the perfect choice as he had a fantastic reputation in the industry.'

Adrian comments that John has been a breath of fresh air.

'He had a hard task ahead of him, but he has just come in, rolled his sleeves up and got on with the job. He has brought a new dimension to the business.'

Creativevents has also substantially increased its presence in the summer festivals and concerts market. The company has invested a significant amount of money (in the high six figures) into this marketplace including marquees and equipment. The enterprise was not made easier given the wet weather. It was a high-risk strategy but, using the same ethos as with their other interests, the strategy paid off and the investment returned – with profit. Adrian and Ian may be good company but they are no-one's fools. How have these two decisions impacted?

'With regard to the outdoor market it was a big investment but sometimes you have to take risks to prove that it can be done in a different way and that we should never be satisfied with the norm. It has been great to offer customers a good product and service outdoors as well as indoors. The weather was not overly helpful but it was a success and we learnt lessons which will make it an even smoother experience next time.'

'It has been quite a year,' laughs Ian, 'we opened eight fixed sites at Excel whilst maintaining a high investment strategy within the overall portfolio. Market share increased in the concert and festival market and we achieved sustainable growth meeting financial expectations.'

'As Ian said – we have learned our lessons the hard way over the years but every company has to go through growing pains to succeed' comments Adrian. 'I think, because we are passionate about what we do, we are driven by wanting to do the best that we can and are also prepared to take risks to move the business forward.'

And the future? Adrian considered the question carefully before responding.

'We want to offer the customer what they should expect in this day and age and we want to be the best at it! We want to grow this business to maximise the potential of our team, who have grown with this business all the way. We are very ambitious and have lost not one ounce of drive. We are fully focused on what needs to be done. 2007 has been a good year for Creativevents but it is only a staging post in our development. We still have a long road to travel but at least we know we are on the right road with the right people around us.'

(February 2008)

Concession

Oliver Peyton

Founder and Chairman, Peyton and Byrne

Oliver is a serial entrepreneur whose latest venture, Peyton and Byrne, has won much praise from the industry. He has been beset by many setbacks and criticism, but has been able to move on and overcome these hurdles. Oliver's passion and gut instinct are what drive him. He is now supported by his sister in his current venture, and many are watching this company as it expands further into the culture and heritage sector, and the broader catering market.

Thinking, moving and evolving

Oliver Peyton is one of the industry's more colourful figures and attracts great interest. He is said to be difficult and demanding by some. He is certainly charismatic, innovative and slightly eccentric. Some say he is a Great British foodie. Others say his businesses are built on weak foundations. So what is the truth?

Oliver arrived in London in the early 1980s, with no money. It was before the great boom days and there were limited opportunities for people who wanted to make their fortune.

'Back then you had to make your own luck and find ways in which to establish yourself in the market. Nightclubs were the easiest way to do this. I knew clubs and I knew cocktails, so it was a good way in for me. I was able to do a few nights a week and then with a few friends we started a bar in Brighton.'

Oliver is very open and forthright as he talks. He is full of energy and constantly moving. One can imagine his mind works at equal speed.

'Brighton became too small, so I came up to London and started club nights. I started importing alcohol, including Absolut Vodka, to bars and sold directly to the bar scene, which was a good way to get to know a lot of people. Then the culture began to change. The drug scene was huge. Clubs turned into sweaty drug bins that were not nice places. You couldn't go to a club without it being full of the young set who were off their faces all the time.

'I thought what can I do that is different? That's when I opened the Atlantic Bar and Grill, and made a lot of money. At the time it was really one of a kind. We were one of only two bars in London that didn't charge people who came in after 11 p.m., which discouraged the ones who only wanted to come in to get wasted. People started talking about it. New York was seen as the cutting edge of the bar scene, and we were getting reviews that the Atlantic was like being in New York. At the time it was really seen as the place to go and very innovative.

'The Atlantic worked because it was a model that catered for everyone – be it young kids, transvestites or bankers. It offered somewhere to go clubbing or just have a nice meal. It really broke the mould.'

Following on from the success of the Atlantic Bar and Grill, Oliver opened up further restaurants that were equally successful –Mash, Mash and Air, and Coast. Then suddenly things changed again.

'I suppose I just grew sick of it all. Everyone started copying us, rich investors started opening clubs and restaurants as a bit of a plaything. Half of them can't have made any money.'

So wanting to do something different again, to innovate, Oliver opened Isola in Knightsbridge, which he viewed as his most ambitious restaurant. This was a flagship that would set him apart from the others, but one that would cost him everything.

'I wanted to do something really different and it cost a lot of money. Our plans were ambitious. For example, we had about 60 wines by the glass. A truck would come up from Italy each week to deliver the wines. Everything that could have possibly gone wrong went wrong, from building the restaurant to the reviews.

'When I lost everything I was disillusioned about it all. It was not a nice environment and people were not nice either. There was nothing new out there. So I changed tack, I started thinking what I could do to make a difference. If it wasn't on the high street bar or restaurant scene, where could it be? That's when I got my first contract at Somerset House. At that time, and to some extent still, visitors' experience of food in museums and culture and heritage venues was terrible. Food was overpriced and either soggy or rock hard. I could make a difference. I could see what was being done wrong and I knew I could fix it.'

Oliver is now heading up his second culture and heritage business. The first, Gruppo, was sold to Compass Group back in 2003. It was an experience that he found difficult as the contract demanded a 'lock out', although he retained Inn in the Park in St James's Park. Today, Peyton and Byrne has a turnover of £22 million and 300 employees. Oliver Peyton and his three sisters run a tight ship, possibly learnt from his earlier days in the industry. In 2006 Oliver opened four restaurants: the National Dining Rooms at the National Gallery on Trafalgar Square, the Wallace Restaurant in the sculpture garden of the Wallace Collection, Meals in the Heals flagship store, and the National Café at the National Gallery. Since then, the company has opened a range of cafés and restaurants including in the British Library, Kew Gardens and the Royal Academy of Arts.

'The restaurants and cafés we have at the moment are the ideal environment for me. I love culture, history and arts. Absolutely love it. So I love where the restaurants are. I am not a contract caterer. I hate that label. I am a restaurateur in venues and constantly competing with the high street in price, quality and ideas. I would never go back to the high street. I like our shops and that is about as far as it goes.

'We have made sure that no two venues are alike. We have an original look for each site and that is important to our clients. It's not just one size or model that fits all. The Wallace Collection is a testament to that. Everyone is our competition. It would be stupid to think otherwise but that is good as you need to continually adapt, and make your offer better, different. Business can be great, bad or fine. Stop moaning about it and adapt to it, it's just business.

'I really admire Alex Ferguson, he has been top of his game for so long and he continually adapts through the good and bad. That's what makes a good businessman; you suck it up, make changes and continue. Otherwise it would be easy and no business is easy.'

I can understand why Oliver has found his way into the culture and heritage sector, and why he feels at home here. He shares the same qualities as academics. He likes being challenged and having problems to think about and solve, but he doesn't go to bed at night without constantly wanting to learn about things and here he is able to mix with people who are experts in their fields. Maybe the time he spent working so hard in his career left little time for other interests, so who can blame him for now wanting to combine the two? Like most chief executives, he doesn't have time for the trivial. Their minds are elsewhere. Whereas some would politely end a conversation, I think Oliver would just walk off, leaving you talking to yourself. Maybe this is why he is seen as hard to work for.

In a career where Oliver has constantly changed his businesses time and time again to be different, is it little wonder that the man himself is different? Not many CEOs take the time to wander around a gallery with a client and take as much genuine interest as Oliver clearly does. He combines his passion for culture with business. I suppose it's the same as doing business with a client on a golf course, except Oliver wouldn't keep his eye on a ball for long. Maybe the test will come when he tries moving into the business and industry world as is the plan. I can't quite see him cycling up to Barclays in Canary Wharf. Or maybe I can? With any contract, Oliver brings his own energy and style. Some will want this personalised attention.

'I love people. I will often speak to customers to see what their thoughts are and if I get one or two too many emails from a site I will go there and ask what is going on. That's why I cycle everywhere.'

So what does the future hold? Surprisingly, stadiums are on Oliver's to-do list.

'Why are we serving rubbish in these places? We don't have the infrastructure at the moment to be able to do stadia but we are growing and probably looking at two contracts a year depending on size. We are looking at another level of business with B&I restaurants. We are also looking to roll out more Peyton and Byrne shops. We have one opening in Covent Garden this June, but it's finding the right location at the right price which is the difficulty. That side of the business is good, and when we feel like it we open another shop.'

He comes across as an opportunist. If he wants to do something, or feels he can do it better or add something somewhere he will do it and give everything. Oliver is not arrogant. He just believes in what he is doing and constantly thinking and innovating. He is very candid but also hardened to the views of others. He understands that the views of others can be fickle.

'When I was younger I read a lot of bad stuff. If you believe the bad stuff you become depressed, if you read the good stuff you become egotistical, so you can't win.'

Oliver clearly needs things to do and problems to solve constantly.

'For me it's not about growing or making money, it's about what can I figure out to fix or change or develop so it's better. There are always problems going on in this business and that is why I have stayed in it for so long. I need to always keep thinking and moving.'

(April 2011)

Corporate entrepreneurs

Food Service

Bill Toner

Chairman, Host Management

'The Chef who rose to become a CEO'

Bill has been one of the food service sector's most central characters over the past 20 years. He is presently Chairman of a growing independent – Host Management – but he is best known as the former UK CEO of ARAMARK (2000–05) and a key leader with Gardner Merchant/Sodexo in the UK.

Bill's story is one of many questions. This is a man that became a CEO at the age of 41 after beginning his career as a kitchen porter at the age of 14. He is a high achiever who is unflinchingly loyal and supportive to those that he is close to. He built his career within a corporate environment but he has always been almost a natural entrepreneur with an eye focused on growth. This is a story of a devoted family man with an almost traditional high value set.

Bill is one of the biggest characters to have walked the food service stage in the past 15 years and also one of the most controversial. Often these two factors are interlinked as it is well known that the British mentality is often critical of the biggest characters. When Bill joined ARAMARK in 2000, one of his senior UK colleagues remarked: 'ARAMARK wanted to change their approach in the UK and wanted a real leader. They have got the right man but I do wonder if they can handle it? He is a lion and they will be holding him by the tail. It is exciting but anything could happen'.

It was a very apt comment for Bill changed the face of ARAMARK in the UK swiftly and effectively. ARAMARK has been a sleeping giant in the UK and he swiftly changed the mentality and culture. The company grew apace. And he led from the front with a high work ethic. He would often start work at 6 a.m. and still be in action in the evening. He once remarked: 'I have seen Phantom of the Opera over 32 times with clients but if it is what I need to do to grow the business, I will happily see it another 32 times.'

One of the core traits about Bill is his high energy and work ethic. Very few could keep up with him and it was clear to all those that worked closely with him that he did love the battle of growing the business that he led – that was until he left ARAMARK in 2005 following tensions with the person he reported into in the USA. He was just nor prepared to do what he was asked to do: so he just walked away from the industry for five years before his return with Host.

During that five-year period, many asked why Bill had not returned to another company as he had been so driven but in truth, he just wanted to spend time with his wife, Suzanne, and family. He reflected and re-energised. The truth is that he gave so much to moving ARAMARK on that he was probably left disillusioned by internal company politics and infighting that he felt took his eye away from leading the business forward. He commented that 50% of the job had become political and it was already hard enough ensuring that ARAMARK was competing with the key players in the market without this added burden.

Bill once remarked:

'My aim was to compete very effectively with the key players in the market and to achieve this, we had to match them in every department and openly display that he really care and have a passion for excellence. This does not happen overnight. It does take time and a lot of commitment and work. We all have to be on the same bus, working towards the same goal if we want to be the best in the market. I will work from early until late towards achieving this and I only ask that others work with the same energy so we can all be successful. Then we can enjoy the fruits of our success.'

This high work ethic came from his humble beginning, when he decided to enter the hospitality industry rather than follow his four brothers into mining. He started in the industry at the tender age of 14 at as small hotel in Bathgate (West Lothian). His initial ambition was to become a chef and he worked hard to achieve this goal. He moved to France to work as a *chef de partie* for Hôtels Frontelle, and then on to South Africa as a sous chef at the Royal Hotel in Durban.

At the age of 23, he returned to Scotland in his first management role with Gardner Merchant at the Royal Bank of Scotland. Over the next 18 years, he rapidly rose up the ladder to become managing director of the UK operationat just 36 in 1995. In 1999, he was headhunted by ARAMARK to become the CEO for the UK. Sodexo did not give up Bill without a fight and there was a famous board meeting when the founder of Sodexo, Pierre Bellon, openly countered-offered Bill. But Bill is a man who is true to his word and he never flinched. Sodexo were hurt as they knew that they were losing a man who had shown his entrepreneurial and creative streak by bringing Gary Rhodes to the company and opening a restaurant – City Rhodes – right next to their City head office. It had been an audacious move that caught everyone by surprise. It was the start of a new trend as four more Rhodes restaurants followed and the other players copied the strategy.

It is now almost a legend that Bill was a sous chef who became a major CEO by the age of 41. He could not have achieved this without Sodexo/ Gardner Merchant's belief in training and development that allowed him to thrive but without doubt, the greatest feature was his drive to be successful. Many will say that Bill has a high ego and he is undoubtedly a big character but much of this drive is driven by values that are very pure. He has always struggled with people who did not care for the business as much as he did which was a problem as he cared very deeply and was naturally driven to excel through high energy.

High ego individuals are often very self-focused but the contradiction with Bill is that his focus is not so much on himself but on the business he leads and those close to him. Bill would often stand up and defend his trusted colleagues even if it proved to be a problem for him. There are many that will argue that Bill was ruthless and there is evidence for this but often for those that did not meet his standards. He was never ruthless with those that he believed in and would often place himself in the firing line.

Bill is not a complex character. This is a man who has built his career from the ground up through hard work and delivering. He was driven to build a better life for his family. This is the CEO whose daughter used to work on reception. This is the highly driven CEO who walked away for five years to spend time with his family. But the key to success lay within the man himself. He had this inner belief that he could lead and make change through the strength of his character. When people talk about Bill, they do not talk about him as a strategist but as someone who led from the front and almost carried an organisation on his own shoulders.

Food Service

Vince Pearson

Chairman, Waterfall Group

Vince is a driven and determined character who possesses the ability to remain largely unfazed in the face of adversity. He has an active and fulfilled life outside work which gives him a sense of perspective. Vince is an opportunistic character who successfully transformed himself from a role in the army to a board level role in Sodexo, one of the UK's largest foodservice operators. Vince's story proves that going off the beaten track can be worthwhile in the pursuit of a personal success.

A life less ordinary

Vince Pearson's career has been a blend of corporate achievement and following the 'road less travelled'. Author, entrepreneur and caterer, he believes it has been down to circumstance.

For more than 25 years, Vince Pearson has proven to be a resilient and competitive operator, who relishes contract catering for the variety of experiences it offers. Having worked in the healthcare, defence and education markets, he is today chairman of the Waterfall Group, a business created from the merger of Caterplus and Taylor Shaw in 2008. With a turnover of £40 million and 2500 staff, Vince believes he has found his dream job. He previously led a major portfolio of business in Sodexo as a board director during the late 1990s, following their merger with Gardner Merchant, and has also written a novel during a period spent in Australia. Despite inevitable setbacks, including a failed investment in Duchy Catering, Vince's personal passions and discipline have underpinned his approach to business, and remain central to his outlook.

> 'It may be a generalisation, but you will enjoy life and business if you are true to yourself. This is what energises me. I live by the motto work hard, play hard, whether in a business or social context. I am competitive, like being part of and building teams and ultimately, I think life and business is all about people.'

A major sports enthusiast, Vince realised early on that he did not have the potential to pursue a professional career. In his teenage years, 1973, his parents bought a fish and chip shop and a young Vince and his sister earned extra money on Sundays by opening at teatime. It is an experience from which he still draws inspiration. During this time his ex-Royal Marine father suggested the services as a possible career and soon after he had dinner with an army recruiter, whom his mother had met by chance. In 1977, at the age of 17, Vince became the Army's first bursary scholar at the University of Surrey studying tourism and hospitality. On completion of his degree, he joined the Army for three years, going to Sandhurst in 1981. This was followed by a period at Aldershot, where he was based in the Army Catering Corp Apprentice College as a subaltern, working as a platoon commander in charge of 60 apprentices between the ages of 16 and 18.

> 'The Army was a lot of fun; I got to play a lot of sport and met Lynda, who was also a subaltern, and who I was to marry some 25 years later! However, it was not my long-term career choice and I left after my three-year commitment ended. In retrospect, I didn't realise how fortunate I was until afterwards. The Army was instrumental in shaping my leadership style, which is about being decisive, looking at the bigger picture and thinking about how to get people motivated.'

Vince is a rational and thoughtful individual who believes that his catering career has not been really about choices, but sets of circumstances, leading him to get involved initially in defence. Upon leaving the Army, he was introduced to Tom Pearce, the owner of TAPPE Catering, based in Dover and a catering specialist for the MOD and Home Office. He joined in 1984 and helped grow the business from £1 million to £10 million turnover in five years. The business was sold to Pall Mall Services Group in 1989, part of the Davis Service Group, and Vince spent a further five years there, during which time his first two children were born. The turning point came in 1994 when Vince was headhunted for a role in Sodexo, based in Glasgow, and he ran the UK business, then a loss-making subsidiary of around £15 million turnover. However, fate intervened and after six months Gardner Merchant merged with Sodexo, providing a crucial platform for Vince to consolidate his experiences, becoming the only person in the new management team from the French arm.

'It was a bit like running Watford FC and being told by the owners, as we were about to play Manchester United in the semi-final of the FA Cup, that Elton John had bought Manchester United. Gardner Merchant were about 50 times bigger than Sodexo in the UK. I spent eight years there and it was a fantastic journey. There was lots of growth in healthcare and I worked with some great people like Ian Sarson and Wilson Barrie.'

In 1999 Vince realised a major achievement and was appointed to the Sodexo board looking after healthcare, education, PFI schemes and defence. It was a significant role, responsible for around £300 million turnover, and a period in which Sodexo were heavily pursuing their early interest in securing PFI contracts. Vince spent three years in the role heading up a team that included Andrew Leach, Jim Brewster, Michelle Hanson and Wilson Barrie. After a controversy over Sodexo's Land Technology subsidiary (a grounds maintenance division), incumbent CEO David Ford departed and was replaced by American Mark Shipman. It was at this point that Vince decided to move on.

'I had been looking for an overseas adventure and was having a midlife crisis. Divorced and with a new partner, we decided to do something different, relocating to Brisbane, Australia. I took up a project director role for a PFI Group at one of the local universities, heading up a bid that included the Commonwealth Bank of Australia, Walter Construction and Sodexo.'

With a beachfront house and new baby daughter, Vince spent two years abroad. After the PFI project finished, he took time out and wrote an adventure novel entitled *Time for Living*, eventually self-published for friends and family.

'It took about three months to do and was a lot of fun. However, towards the end of 2004 I was looking to return to the UK. We struggled with the distance away from our family support network and the relationship did not work out.'

Returning to the UK in 2005, Vince began a consultancy project with Duchy Catering, who had asked him to help them grow and find acquisition targets. The outcome of this period would prove to be the biggest learning curve in Vince's career and, as he puts it, the episode was a rude awakening about entrepreneurialism.

'In effect, I had been a corporate entrepreneur for 15 years. However, this experience involved entrepreneurship at the start-up phase of a business. Along with my current partners – Jim Lovett and Gary Palmer – we had invested money in Duchy but, when we understood what was going on, our plan of using that business to acquire Caterplus was no longer an option. Fortunately, we exited well before Duchy got into its difficulties and ultimately it was sold to Graysons.

'Nevertheless 2006 was a challenging year as we were funding ourselves, while trying to negotiate an acquisition. Although our original financiers dropped out, we did get venture capital backing from Yorkshire Fund Managers and bought Caterplus in February 2007.'

A specialist care and welfare catering business, Caterplus lost 25% of its turnover shortly after the acquisition as a major client gave notice, but the team had negotiated a protection clause in their deal. Having rebuilt volumes, the business acquired and merged with specialist education business Taylor Shaw and rebranded as the Waterfall Group.

'It has been refreshing for us, as the owners, as we can be very straight with clients and our people. For me, that is the difference between working with a larger corporate. But I have loved every minute of what I do and would not change any of my experiences. Contract catering has a fabulous diversity and I derive a huge sense of personal satisfaction serving old and young people at work.'

Having married his wife Lynda in 2008, Vince now resides in Norwich but spends about one week a month at their holiday home in St Mellion. With six children between them, Vince acknowledges that life is fun, if a bit complicated. In his position as chairman, Vince is actively involved in charity work, and he continues to abide by the mantra of work hard, play hard.

> 'I like the sense of team and challenge. I feel privileged in my role and want to put something back, particularly for some of the disadvantaged people in our society. My passion and competitiveness is always there and I am widely regarded by friends as someone who will fight until the end. I simply don't accept being beaten.'

(July 2010)

Restaurants

Robin Rowland

Chief Executive, YO! Sushi

The story of YO! Sushi in two halves; first there was its innovative conception and launch by Simon Woodroffe in 1997, the second has been the consolidation and expansion of the business under Robin Rowland, who joined the business as chief executive in 2000. YO! Sushi remains an entrepreneurial business and Robin seeks to foster a dynamic culture, whilst still building on core brand values. His vision has seen YO! Sushi grow from start-up to global entity. The journey has not been without its challenges and Robin has placed a high personal stake in the business, yet his vision and tenacity have remained throughout.

YO! Sushi now operates 55 UK restaurants and 11 internationally, and continues to pursue further expansion

A rollercoaster

The story of YO! Sushi, the Japanese-inspired conveyor belt restaurant, is in many ways one of the classic entrepreneurial business – one of an innovative business that was launched into the market to huge acclaim, to suffer growing pains, to come through with a view of a golden horizon lying beyond. It was a great idea that was launched at the right time – a time when the customer was becoming interested in Asian cuisine. It was also a concept that had not been witnessed ever before and one that many cynics had believed would not work – yet work it did, very effectively. Once this point was proven, few doubted that it would move on to greater successes. A recent article in The Times noted that YO! Sushi had 'arguably done the most to convert the British to a Japanese diet'.

Yet, successful businesses need more than just a good idea and an interested customer to succeed – good management, good people, and good locations – and it has taken time to get the blend and infrastructure right. What is particularly interesting is how the YO! Sushi senior management team have been together for the past five years, and have seemingly never lost faith in what the business could achieve. Often management teams change as a business goes through its stages and different skill sets are required, but in this case, the management team has bonded as one and grown together.

In 2006 the business has a projected group turnover of over £20 million, delivering circa £3 million EBITDA. Currently, they have 20 UK sites with four more opening by May 2006 and a view to double the number of UK units by 2010. They also have franchise partners in France and in the Gulf. More dramatically, they are looking at real expansion within the US market – which for many years has been a 'bridge too far for UK businesses'. They have a big vision of a US business with up to 200 sites. There have been many that tried to conquer the USA but have struggled. However, in recent times, there have been signs that this is changing as UK companies have begun to successfully expand into this market.

Wagamama and La Tasca are recent examples of two restaurant groups that are planning US expansion. Why the change? There is a whole range of reasons and perhaps it is of little coincidence that the businesses that are able to do well in the USA, are those that offer an internationally orientated product and this bodes well for YO! Sushi.

It is an understandably attractive market to enter as almost half of every dollar that Americans spend on food is spent within restaurants. In 2006, restaurant sales in the USA are expected to pass US$500 billion but competition is fierce with over 900,000 food outlets. YO! Sushi's aim is to open, with partners, 200 restaurants in the USA, which is a large forward step from the stable business base that they have built over the past eight years in the UK.

'We see ourselves as an international business,' commented Robin Rowland, the restaurant business's chief executive. 'Most of the senior team have either worked or lived abroad and we have an international outlook, which is important as we try to embrace and work in different business cultures. This fast casual concept will work superbly in the US market. Time will clearly tell if we are successful but all the signs are very good. We just believe in what we are doing.'

And the facts do support Robin's statement as the business has come a long way since Simon Woodroffe originally founded it in 1997. The early days were very encouraging as the first four restaurants performed successfully which encouraged Simon Woodroffe to go for further growth, including launching YO! Below bars. However, progress did not remain as smooth. YO! Sushi opened units in poor locations, they grew too fast. Robin Rowland took over management control as CEO in late 2000 and recognised the need to retrench before expansion again. Some of the second-phase sites were not as successful as had been hoped – and cash flow was tight. In 2002, the collapse of Fish stopped investment in the restaurant sector and these were dark days. However, the management team did not lose faith and pushed on opening two sites per year including Paddington Station and in August 2003, the tide began to turn. Primary Capital backed a MBO and acquired 60% stake from Simon Woodroffe and gave the business some real financial backing that allowed the management team to start focusing on building the growth that is in place today. The management team currently have a 17% stakeholding.

'I have tremendous respect for Simon, as he handed over control of 'his baby' and trusted me to get on with the job. He created the concept when many said that it would not work and he needed someone with experience to take it to another level,' noted Robin. 'The situation today is very good. 2005 has really been a strong year and we now have a strong pipeline of prospects for new locations; 2006 looks like another good year with solid like for likes and 4–6 new openings, plus 10 overseas with our partners.'

Robin joined the business in 1999, after working with Whitbread, Grand Met and Scottish & Newcastle and City Centre Restaurants. It was his time with the last two businesses that arguably gave him the confidence to take the YO! Sushi brand from where it stood in 1999 to today's promising position.

'I had some great early mentoring whilst at Whitbread and Grand Met,' noted Robin as we discussed his early influences, 'but Old Orleans from 1988 really allowed me the chance to learn as I was given great freedom to run the business. During my four year tenure, we took it from 5 to 20 restaurants and I was generally just left alone to get on with the business. I was given the same level of freedom by Andrew Guy at City Centre Restaurants in the mid 90s. He has a superb management style that gave me the confidence that I could really deliver as a business manager. After an initial operational role turning around Nachos, the board gave me a role looking for global franchisees for the company's 6 restaurant brands, which allowed me the opportunity to travel for 12 months meeting some of the best restaurant businesses around. I travelled to the US, South Africa, Hong Kong and Asia. It was a great education.'

So what tempted Robin to join Simon Woodroffe at YO! Sushi?

'I was attracted by the brand and its potential. This was a fabulous concept that could really be taken forward. But we had some challenges and we had to overcome some tough obstacles to make sure that we had the basis of a sound organisation that could be developed forward. When I joined, YO! Sushi had already made some classic mistakes of growing too fast and this placed great pressure on the business. I think that the real unsung hero for us during this time was Bob Silk, our bank manager at Barclays Bank who really did believe in us and what we could achieve. It is strange as there were some really quite hard times and yet we did seem to always retain our belief in the business. I remember in the middle of the financial 'workout' taking a huge risk in buying a large house, which meant that I had no choice but to succeed. I think that, plus three children at the time under the age of three and a half, ensured that I had the extra motivation to succeed.'

YO! Sushi was a radical concept that was launched onto the market at exactly the right moment. What, I asked, would make it stand the test of time and grow?

'We have a number of guiding principles by which we live and work. The first one is that we must constantly innovate and create. We must never stand still. There is no sacred cow in our business. Everything can be questioned and developed further. We also focus the key basics of what the business needs for sustained success – people, product, property and promotion. We have a strong relationship with our customer. I receive on average 10 unsolicited e-mails every day with constructive feedback. I would say that 70% are compliments and 30% are complaints but delivered in a manner that appears like they want to work with us. It is as though they want to help us succeed. I will always try and reply to each one within 24 hours. I believe that we enjoy a strong bond with our customer, which is built upon trust. We have a transparent product and there is nowhere for us to hide. I think that the customer respects this point.

'In January, we did a promotional offer of 50% off the price of food. We had 10,000 vouchers downloaded from the website within 24 hours and 50% of these were used within the first four days of the offer. This is a great sign that the business has built a strong relationship with the customer. We have also learnt to use our own skills as effectively. I believe in good third-party relationships and goodwill, so we will approach everything that we do in an honest, straightforward, decent way. We are loyal to those partners that work with us and we are prompt payers. I was once told about the seven-meeting rule, which I have used and really works. Just as you can't fold a piece of paper seven times, you find that as long as you are friendly and positive, you will often get a great deal in a negotiation on the seventh meeting. I don't know why but seven meetings probably wears down the negotiator but also shows our serious intent as we have invested so much time into the process. The result is that it has really helped the business as we have achieved great deals and working relationships.'

I noted that I was intrigued as to why he had never recruited an HR manager to work within the business, given the focus upon people.

'I am reluctant to assign the recruitment of our team to anyone outside of operations. I believe that 'people work for people' and the best businesses have enthusiastic teams. For this to happen managers need to recruit teams with the same values and drive and I didn't want line managers being influenced by a perspective outside of operations. It gives us the fluidity of moving quickly when it comes to recruitment. The same applies to training. The two trainers that we employ within the business are responsible to the operations director; 1½% of turnover is reinvested into the budget for the operations director to use for training. We want to up the ante on our investment in people. At present, our turnover for permanent monthly paid team members is around 30% and 90% for hourly team members and I want to bring this down.

Now on saying all this, I accept that there is a breakpoint where this might all change, needing more structure, but we are not at that point as we stand.'

And how does he view the future?

'I think that the company has moved through three stages. Its founding and initial growth, its stabilisation and then the MBO, growth and expansion. Now is a very exciting time and it is just great to see both how far we have all come over the past five years and how far we could all go in the next five.'

(April 2006)

Concessions

Richard Tear

Chairman, Searcy's

You need only go a few steps into a discussion about event catering before encountering the name Richard Tear. As chairman of Searcy's, his defining role, Richard has steered a business from fledgling concept, through an acquisition by the Alternative Hotels Group and latterly an MBO. In both good and bad times Richard has demonstrated a clear set of values, underpinned by a genuine love for his work. In a career spanning more than 30 years, he believes that 'getting down in the trenches' is essential. Richard is one of the true believers in engagement with people and what makes him stand out as a corporate entrepreneur is that he possesses a genuine desire for evolving new concepts and ideas with the support of this team.

Rules of engagement

How is a traditional culture evolved to meet modern-day demands?

The business issues that face ambitious, smaller companies who are focused on taking the leap and securing growth in a competitive marketplace can prove problematic. Competing with larger companies who have greater buying power, strong brand awareness and the infrastructure to control costs and streamline their operations can mean that smaller businesses face the challenge of retaining their core values whilst competing for growth.

Where smaller companies value and promote their 'personal service', how can they retain this approach when there is a need for a greater management structure? Can you truly retain quality whilst expanding your product?

Family-owned contract and event caterer, Searcy's, has undoubtedly faced this challenge as they have sought growth over the past two decades. Established in 1847, the company were renowned for catering for bespoke events and soon became the preferred caterer for London's aristocracy. In 2008, Searcy's catered for the Queen's 80th birthday lunch at Mansion House. From 1990 they have seen a dramatic period of growth. But what was the catalyst that drove this small business into competing with some of the UK's largest contract caterers?

Over the past 20 years, Searcy's annual revenue has grown from £5 million to £35 million and accordingly they are now ranked 12th in their sector in terms of annual revenue. Their core values are simple: 'To deliver the best food with great cooking and great people'. The company exudes their passion, both for the product they produce and the people that work in the business. It's not simply lip service when they speak about inclusion and empowerment. But as the company entered new markets and increased their geographical presence in the UK, have they been successful in sticking to their values?

The catalyst for change in 1990 was the partnership between the two owners and the now Chief Executive, Richard Tear. Their combined entrepreneurial spirit was the vehicle that enabled Richard, alongside brothers Richard and Nigel Goodhew, to take the company from a small, family-run business to a serious competitor in the culture and heritage sector. Yet expansion in the culture and heritage sector can be limited and the need to seek growth in new markets led to their first steps into the business and industry sectors, with contracts including Allen & Overy in London. In addition, their partnership with Richard Corrigan which initially started at the Barbican, also opened the door to the restaurant sector and the company's portfolio now includes the renowned Lindsay House and Bentley's restaurants.

With their next aim to achieve an annual turnover of £50 million, it is in the B&I and restaurant sectors that they will predominantly be seeking their future growth. With such a period of change, the company has needed to adapt in order to balance between achieving growth and not losing sight on what they have always set out to accomplish – the best food with great cooking and great people. Richard is well aware that success can breed contempt and as a company grows, managers can often become distanced from what is truly happening in the business. For such a 'personal' business, they have needed to adapt to having sites that are no longer on their doorstep and a new core team at head office who have introduced systems and procedures in order to increase efficiency. For Richard this period of change has been both an exciting and challenging time. As the company has stepped forward in this journey for growth, what are some of the key elements Richard has adapted and new practices introduced so that the scales stay balanced?

As a small business, the management team had always been able to respond quickly to decision making. Yet, as the company grew and a more refined infrastructure was added, decision making slowed and threatened the company's core values. Frustrated by the change in how the company operated, Richard sought new initiatives to ensure that Searcy's could still have the tools to act swiftly under the new management structure.

'The more senior you become, then the more you rely on people, then the more you rely on information channels and communication flow. Listening to, and engaging your team, are vital.'

Searcy's needed the buy-in from their managers and staff. With a head office tucked away in a discreet corner of south west London, and with a business portfolio that had expanded beyond their traditional units in London to include new contracts in Edinburgh and Bristol, Richard sought to involve his 'people' in all aspects of the business. In order to re-engage managers, they were asked to spend time with the core business team, working alongside the financial director, human resources, sales, purchasing and senior management. They were included in business planning and made to feel part of the company's overall goals and objectives, rather than just a site manager. By knowing that the managers understood the business dynamics, Richard was able to 'let-go' and empower his team, giving him the time to focus on key decision making and strategic planning. Looking outside of the company for new talent was also on the agenda. Richard believed that a company cannot develop right away when you rely only on growing from within. He was passionate about bringing new blood into the business and sought to recruit younger, energetic and passionate people to work with his existing team.

By developing the right people, the company were able to introduce a strong succession planning programme to facilitate growth.

> 'The more you coach people to do better, then the better they will do. By empowering people, both the employer and the employee benefit greatly.'

The company adopted an American style 'internship' programme, allowing graduates and budding junior managers to spend time at head office on project work and shadowing colleagues and senior management. The goal was not only to develop the managers for the future, but by also getting their buy-in, the company benefited from their new and fresh ideas. Searcy's has recorded a low staff turnover in their management team.

Richard was concerned that by becoming more distant from the actual operation, it would be easy to sacrifice the company's core values as the business grows and begins to compete with the bigger players who have greater market share. In order to stay in touch with the business, Richard was not afraid to revisit and question the company's performance and business activity. And having the trust in the team around him was key to maintaining information channels.

Richard blames his poor performance in golf on the fact that this is often his 'thinking time'. In or out of work, the questions that are always on his mind are:

- Are we good enough?
- Are we delivering what people want?
- What are the trends?
- What's the business forecast?
- Do Searcy's know (and understand) what their customers want?
- Can we deliver against all of this whilst still retaining our core values?

As part of their new structure, Searcy's recruited a financial director who introduced new systems, reports and forecasting which was introduced in all areas of the business. Searcy's has by far seen a significant period of change. Richard has led a pivotal role in managing the transformation of this small, independent and family-owned business to a competitive business in the contract catering sector. It's not been an easy journey at times. The maintenance of clear and defined communication channels, which had been established by adapting their approach to operational and people management, has undoubtedly been a catalyst for change.

The seamless relationship between Richard and the Goodhew brothers has ensured a clear flow of information and as such their ability to maintain efficient decision making. The addition of new systems and procedures, alongside fresh initiatives that re-engage the management team in all aspects of the business, ensures that their much desired information channels have remained open. However, this is still a family-run business that revolves around its traditional values. Yet, with the goal of reaching an annual turnover of £50 million, is this going to be enough to ensure its growth in an increasingly competitive market.

(June 2006)

Leisure

Richard Balfour-Lynn

Chief Executive, De Vere Group and Chief Executive, MWB Group Holdings

Richard Balfour-Lynn is a corporate entrepreneur who is the overseer of a number of well-known brands in UK retail and hospitality. By his own admission he sees himself as a catalyst in business, preferring to work in partnership with his leadership teams to stimulate and drive performance. Importantly, Richard regards great brands as crafted by one or two people and he possesses a clear vision of the customer's journey for each of his business entities, this is what drives him as an entrepreneur.

The catalyst

Richard Balfour-Lynn is the integral magnet in a respected house of brands. Chairman of the Alternative Hotel Group (AHG) and Chief Executive of MWB Group Holdings he describes himself as a 'natural interferer'. What does he really mean by this? Where does he believe his role fits in directing the various arms of the business?

FutureShock author Alvin Toffler once said, 'You've got to think about big things while you're doing small things, so that all the small things go in the right direction.' Yet, for many business leaders the balance between macro-and micro-vision is increasingly grey. Where is the market headed? Inevitably the answer to this question requires a discussion of service and customer expectations. Richard has developed a reputation in the industry for his views on these issues, and is something of a controversial figure, often questioning the status quo. He oversees 11 hospitality and retail brands including Malmaison and Hotel du Vin, the De Vere Collection, Liberty and Searcy's of London. Together they employ 20,000 people and he counts some of the industry's most esteemed leaders in his team including Robert Cook, Stephen Carter and Richard Tear. It is a wide scope of influence and accountability, with Richard effectively acting as a catalyst behind the scenes, yet extensively involved with each company to drive vision and delivery.

'In each business I look at everything that touches the brand or customer experience from a micro level, starting from scratch. I always ask: what is the customer journey? I have a very clear vision for each brand, but it's not actually about me. We have a team of people working with me who have been together for 25 or 30 years; they become involved in areas such as marketing, funding and strategy. We operate in partnership with each business and interfere in everything – there is no point otherwise.

'Someone's got to have vision for a brand and great brands are crafted by one or two people. The reason why so many brands fail is that they become corporate and lose their way. My CEOs are bright guys and a fantastic team, yet I expect to know as much as they do about their business. However, unless they respect you, it's not possible to achieve what you set out to do.

'I've been through three downturns, so am used to spotting them and knowing what to do. You have to move fast – speed is vital. The reality is that it's been relatively easy over the past 10 years and lots of leaders cannot get their minds around just how incredibly proactive and determined you need to be. You've got to dust yourself down each day and go out to fight.'

Distinctiveness and creativity are important characteristics of the brands within the AHG/MWB portfolio. They all operate as separate business entities, and while some may appear to be in the same marketplace, such as MWB Business Exchange and De Vere Venues, there are subtle points of difference between each. This means that a single client may be served by different brands, depending on the service required. However, as the economic downturn has progressed, Richard has driven a review of the support services in each business in order to find synergies between each in response to the worsening conditions. So while the individual brand values of each business remain, he has bought CEOs and FDs together to find ways of co-operating in a variety of areas, resulting in the set-up of a group purchasing team and a joint sales and marketing agenda. Richard argues that investment in the latter is crucial and that there is great potential to leverage the strength of a 'house of brands'. This would see the customer base of each business welcoming the chance to access other names in the portfolio, such as clients in serviced offices benefiting from discounted hotel rates. It has been a challenge for all, given that the separateness of each business is also a clear mandate.

'It has been quite hard, as each team has been focused on operating their businesses independently and that is difficult to change. However, in the current climate most companies can cut costs once or twice but no more than that, and my goal has been to force the businesses to start working together and create a group powerbase. The most important thing is revenue generation, and in a shrinking climate you've got to steal market share.'

Intense and charismatic, Richard's approach to leading his business may, at first glance, appear to be a story about directing individual, unique brands and the associated challenges that go with this. There is little doubt that he is a businessman first and foremost. However, the conversation turns to the other major strand of collaboration within the businesses he has driven this year, and this relates to the social role of an organisation. It is an interesting turn in our discussion and a moment for reflection. Could the unification of 11 hospitality and retail brands for a common purpose have been achieved as quickly elsewhere? The initiatives we discuss have all been officially launched within the last 12 business months.

It has been argued that the recession has dampened the appetite for the debate about corporate responsibility, however, Richard clearly disagrees. Across the board, a partnership with the Variety Club has been launched, with employees, customers and suppliers involved in a range of fund-raising activities that have raised nearly £200,000 to date. An Academy for Hospitality to develop recognised qualifications for employees has been launched in Manchester with £2 million of funding, with another planned in the south within six months. Finally a website called 'Keep it Hush' has been created as a portal for employees to access unique discount offers in all brands. This will be progressively opened up to employees of suppliers as well. Richard visibly relaxes when talking about these points and what he sees as the big opportunity offered by his job: the chance to unilaterally make a difference.

'There are 20,000 people working across all of my companies and in an era when salaries are not going up and times are difficult, how else can you offer benefits? My vision is that the 'Keep It Hush' website will be an invitation-only resource with between five and 10 million people registered. So not only are you creating a benefit but an unbelievable marketing vehicle too.

'Customers should enjoy what we deliver and ultimately it's about the interaction between people. You have to make it fun for the people who work for you; all of these initiatives are about raising morale. It's about making people feel that this is not just a job, there is something more fulfilling. This is one of the great things about my job – if I push, it does happen, and once people see the project working they get behind it very quickly.'

So, in a year that has been a real challenge for many, it is evident that Richard has led a path of reinvention within the business, albeit in some subtle and strategic ways that aim to drive competitiveness. He believes successful brands reinvent themselves every seven years as the customer base changes – citing Gucci as an example, following their turnaround in the 1980s. It highlights the influence of his overall vision for a house of brands, and how he can effect change in varying ways. Naturally,

Richard's immediate focus is on supporting each brand through the economic downturn. While he believes that there will be further refinement within the portfolio, including exits or partial exits and reinvestment, he sees opportunities for expansion opening up as the rate of business failures accelerate over the next 12 months, arguing that, to date, banks have been propping businesses up and that this is ultimately unsustainable. As customers become disillusioned with globalisation and corporate brands, he believes growth will be in the leisure market, defined by a return to family values.

'Does anyone believe the next five years will be the same as the last five years? If not, then what is the new buying pattern? What will consumers do differently? It's not that difficult to predict, it just requires a degree of common sense. I take macro themes and adjust my business accordingly. I challenge industry truisms and I love it.'

'You have to make it fun for the people who work for you; all of these initiatives are about raising morale.'

(December 2009)

3 Leaders and Entrepreneurs

'Words are cheap. It is about character, behaviour and deed.'

One of the clear lessons that can be taken from all the analysis and comments is that there is no one way to be either a leader or an entrepreneur. There are no set rules and success comes from within the person. It cannot be easily taught. The golden rule is that there is no set rule. For both groups – leaders and entrepreneurs – it is more about the inner character than skill, intellect or ability. As in all walks of life, there are many very talented individuals who have not fulfilled their potential because, in truth, they have not possessed the inner qualities that are clearly required.

The core lesson is that what lies at the heart of success is a mix of character and vision. There are many common traits between the leader and the entrepreneur but the reality is that are also great differences. A story was told earlier of the entrepreneur and the corporate leader who both wished they could be the other. The truth is that what it takes to be an entrepreneur and what it takes to be an organisation's leader is so very different and requires very different skills. The common traits maybe character and vision but how these traits are used and implemented creates the difference.

The Entrepreneur

The whole concept of entrepreneurship is fascinating as it is not as one would expect – depending, of course, on how it is defined. One of the clear features that comes through is that 'entrepreneurship' is almost a calling.

It happens almost as a matter of course – natural evolution; whether the entrepreneur struggles to be employed by others, or whether they are forced to adapt to a situation or whether they are just 'called' to do their own thing.

One of the common discussions with many large organisations is the need for more entrepreneurial spirit ... though when it is present, the entrepreneur will test the organisation's culture and boundaries.

One of the points that strikes home with the profiles is that the entrepreneurs are driven and genuine. They have all suffered in their own ways in the name of their dream. They believe in their way and there is no room for compromise. They are single-minded, determined and do not possess a fake bone in their bodies. Their genuineness is displayed by their core values and their strength in the belief of their own abilities. They are excited and inspired by their own work. Their traits are so clear:

- **Commitment to their businesses**. They will not shirk the bad times and will face whatever challenge is presented in order to ensure that they can be successful.

- **Commitment to the sacrifice required**. All have gone through some bad times and all have made whatever sacrifice that they have needed to make. There is no room for compromise.

- **Ability to learn and adapt**. The effort required to build a business is immense. There is no room for half measures. Building a company will test a person's character to the full. Every weakness is exposed and the entrepreneur has no choice but to face his or her own weaknesses and failings and learn how to improve. There is no place to hide and it can be absolutely brutal but the true entrepreneur will bounce back, learn and adapt.

  One good example of this is in relation to money. Many entrepreneurs begin a business with not as strong a grasp on finance as one would often expect. They often begin a venture with high hopes and determination but most will have faced a financial nightmare at some point in their careers. Once they have survived, they become very conscious of money issues. Money almost becomes part of their soul – not because they are selfish but because of the fear and horror that financial failure can strike into the heart. Entrepreneurs are often very competitive by nature and the idea of failure – which is reflected by their financial position – is something that they struggle to contemplate. Therefore they come to understand the value of things. Success and failure are very personal to the entrepreneur and therefore, they need to control events.

It is one of life's strange contradictions. Entrepreneurs often begin with idealism and a need to express themselves but the successful entrepreneur is as money-conscious as any banker, if not more so.

- **Ethics and values**. The often-misleading perception of the entrepreneur is that of someone who will 'duck and dive' and yet the profiles show high value and ethical standards. It does not mean that one has to be an 'angel' – most will have their own war stories – but they understand success comes from a culture that is often founded on something greater than can be found in a more corporate organisation. As stated above, building a business is an immense task and it will test one's character the full. Over time, as the company goes through its pains, the entrepreneur will naturally change and adapt through lessons learnt. The challenge of building a business will 'polish' the character far more than anything else as every weakness is exposed. Entrepreneurs come to understand the real meaning of culture, values and standards.

  It is interesting to note that entrepreneurs are clearly very honourable people who will often do business on a handshake. They believe in trust and loyalty to those that display these qualities in return.

- **Commitment to their people**. Entrepreneurs are often viewed as needing to possess high egos but the truth is that they are equally committed and loyal to those that are around them. Entrepreneurs hold trust in very high store. Entrepreneurs understand that their success can only be achieved via people and the culture of the business. Entrepreneurs will often talk far more about culture than the large organizations which will focus more structure, process and systems.

People work for entrepreneurs as the latter will inspire and excite the former. It is common to see real genuine belief in those employed by an entrepreneur for an extended period of time. It goes beyond trust and touches something slightly different – it brings a sense of pride within that person.

- **The downside is that entrepreneurs are often loners** – people who are not natural team players. It is not their fault – they have to travel their own path, it is the way that they are created. What makes them exceptional as individuals is their weakness within a broader sense – an independent thinker will always struggle within a group.

At the same time, their minds are dominated by their work. They often struggle to give enough time to their families and friends. Leisure time is limited. Again, they do not mean to be selfish. It is not that simple. Their principal form of relaxation and pleasure is their work. It is understandable that entrepreneurs struggle ever to retire. We can see many examples of entrepreneurs who even in retirement continue to seek challenges and to relish work. When people discuss the term 'professionalism' with young talent, they would be best served to use an entrepreneur as a role model, for an entrepreneur will work just as well from their kitchen table, their bedroom, the train, car or office. They will not be disturbed by the environment in which they work – they will find the solution.

Could you be an entrepreneur?

That is for you to answer but the one point that should never be underestimated is the personal commitment and sacrifice involved. One entrepreneur used to ask any aspiring talent: 'Do you value your marriage and friendships? For the chances are you may well lose both. Are you prepared for that pain in the name of what you believe?'

Overly dramatic? Maybe. I certainly used to scoff when the comment was made but the great truth is that building a business will test your every essence and the question is whether you are able to handle that. Very few are, but some very people enjoy the challenge that it brings. It is not about selfishness or egotism. It is about something far deeper and something that cannot be avoided.

Leaders

There is much money invested by many organisations into the concept of 'leadership development' and yet the question that has to be posed is whether leadership can be taught?

The one truth that emerges is that no single way to lead an organisation. There are many ways but the common essence is that excellent leaders are of good character. Great leaders give their teams confidence and trust and the result is cultures and teams that grow and excel. It is not rocket science, but is very hard to achieve for the teams and culture need to trust their leader and this is so very rare. It, arguably, makes many leadership theories and textbooks obsolete as they only skim along the surface. As almost every leader and entrepreneur will tell you 'words are cheap. It is about behaviour, character and deed.'

One of the interesting traits of many of the great leaders profiled is that they are often relatively quiet characters. They do not set out each day to command excellence through the strength of their characters. They build excellence very gradually.

As Tim West once remarked to me: 'I never have understood why leaders shout and thump tables. The leader, particularly in times of trouble, should remain calm so that their teams can see that you are in control and understand the situation that is being faced.'

Leadership is not about achieving day-to-day tasks and objectives. It is about setting an agenda or strategy for an organisation to reach and then enabling that the organisation is able to achieve those goals.

Of course, it is so easy to say that character is the be-all and end-all. Not all great leaders are angels: in fact many great leaders have made many mistakes but still emerged to be great leaders. Character takes time to emerge. Leaders make as many mistakes as anyone. The difference is that they learn and amend their behaviour accordingly. A similar point was made in relation to entrepreneurs. The difference is that entrepreneurs are often exposed very quickly as they become leaders by their own making at an early stage. Leaders of organisations emerge over time and the process can be less brutal.

There are many theories that will state that character is formed via one's genes and early environment; that character is formed in the early years of one's life. This may be true and certainly many of the core traits are evident from early on, but those that make good leaders do change and evolve. There are many great leaders who had 'black marks' against their names early in life and yet emerged to prove their doubters wrong. It is too easy to be simplistic about the formation of character. For a leader's character to emerge in someone requires that person to be brutally honest about themselves and to have the courage to learn and make change.

It is an old saying that certain people are 'born to lead'. Clearly this is too simplistic as the skills required to be a leader need – as all the profiles display – high levels of development. The saying almost assumes that people will be influenced by relatively superficial qualities. The reality is that organisational cultures will soon expose a leader's weakness and substance is necessary – especially in this modern age when every word and action is reported. The modern leader needs to be proven.

There was one CEO who will remain nameless who told me: 'When I was first appointed to the board, I enjoyed the power and influence that came my way. I am not proud to say that I had many affairs with ladies and thought that I had made it. Then one day, I was involved in a natural disaster and saw people – people who possessed very little – show more courage and honour than I had ever shown. I knew at that moment that I needed to change if I was ever going to do what I should have done as a leader of an organisation. I walked away with the question: Why should someone respect me and I have attempted to answer that every single day. Can a person change? For sure, they can. I do believe in second chances. People are often too judgemental. They forget that growing up throws up many obstructions and we all fail. Some will fail and learn from their mistakes. They are the people I look out for today for they can really bring an organisation great value. Failure is the greatest teacher so my advice is never to write someone off too quickly. Watch and observe how they react to setbacks and do not be too critical.'

It is a very raw comment but makes a fair point. Building a career takes strength and strong characters will often possess drive, energy and determination. Often in the early years they lack discipline as they are 'over enthusiastic'. As another CEO commented to me: 'It is fair to say that I have polished my character continuously over the years and the person I was just five years ago would have failed in the role I hold today.'

JFK once remarked: 'Courage – not complacency – is our need today. Leadership not salesmanship.'

Good leaders can only achieve success if they are trusted and followed by their teams. This trust does not just come by right. 'Perfect' characters rarely also attract real trust. Trust comes when people view a leader's behaviour in adversity and under pressure. It is an old saying the best teams 'emerge from adversity'.

So what do we learn from the profiles and discussion on leaders? What are the traits required?

One can draw out a number of traits that leaders have in common:

- **Honesty**. They are brutally honest to themselves.
- **Principled**. This does not mean that they take the moral high ground. On the contrary, they are often very understanding of others' failures. They will though possess certain very strong beliefs by which they will stand by and fight for. This can vary from a charitable cause to an initiative to a core belief.
- **Fairness**. Leaders will be objective and broad-minded.
- **A belief in people and training**. It is very common that they believe in the development of their teams and people. They are also team builders who understand that they cannot achieve success alone but via those around them. It is interesting to note that leaders are very loyal to their own. Many have failed by being loyal for too long to their teams. Teams do peak and wane and the leader will understandably struggle to make a tough call on those that stood by them for many years.

  Many years ago, Margaret Thatcher was very loyal to Willie Whitelaw making the comment once that 'Every government needed a Willie'. The point she was making that every team needed someone with experience and knowledge spreading over many years. She was heavily criticised at one point for being too loyal to him in his latter days in government. She valued his contribution and he had helped build a strong government. Of course, it would be difficult to say goodbye to this value. Many sports coaches have lost their positions through being too loyal to a player they trusted but who was not performing. Often the leader can be brutal about themselves but less so about their own.

- **A desire to contribute to the wider community**. The leader will often be seen involved in key projects that have no direct relation to their own business but to the greater benefit of the whole. The leader is often unselfish.

- **A desire to learn**. This may sound strange as most expect leaders to be intelligent and to know the answers but, as with all intelligent people, they understand that the more they know, the more they need to know. They have a willingness to admit mistakes and a desire to learn to ensure that they improve. Good leaders are objective and base decisions on fact and will often bring common sense and simplicity to a problem.

- **Courage**.

- **Competence**. Leaders possess capable, sound business minds.

- **Presence**. A leader needs to have standing in a group and this will not just be about what they say. Their physical behaviour and actions are very important. It is said that people only pick up 20% of the message from what a person says and that 80% is communicated via a person's tone and actions. If this true, how one acts is as important as what is said.

- **Straightforward** with no hidden agendas.

- Clear communicators.

- **Endurance**. A leader will not be a weak character. They will be strong and will be resilient. They have been proven over years and in many situations. Do not expect them ever to back away from a conflict easily.

- **Tact and empathy**. A good leader will be observant and will be able to influence via many methods. They will be tactful and be empathic of the problems that people face.

- **Dependable**. As has written, trust in a leader will often come from how that leader has acted in adversity. They will be dependable characters. It is an old saying that asks; 'Do I want to be in the trench with this person?' With great leaders, the answer is invariably in the affirmative.

- **Vision**. A leader will understand where the end of a journey is situated. Of course, it will move as the journey develops but the leader will understand how and where to.

Many will view the above and believe they possess the above qualities. They may do but do they possess these qualities when it counts in the minds of their teams? That is the essential question. Many believe they are good leaders but fail in the eyes of their people. Great leaders possess these qualities in the eyes of their people.

Once again we return to the story of Tony Blair. Tony Blair was a very successful Prime Minister and leader of the Labour Party. He won three General Elections. He was Prime Minster for over a decade. On that basis, he should be seen as one of the great Prime Ministers, but the truth is that his reputation is tarnished and he does not now carry the respect that he should. Why? For three reasons:

- Iraq is clearly central theme. Many will question whether he lied in the lead up to war.

- Spin. He will always be associated with the 'spin' of facts.

- Many feel let down by him. I recall speaking to one MP who remarked that when Blair came to power in 1997, 'many of us believed that it marked a new era, a time of real change in politics'. Blair was certainly in tune with the country as is best illustrated by his speech on the day of the death of Diana, Princess of Wales. In the years 1997–2001, there was a strong belief in the man. However it wilted and as the MP continued: 'When we realised that it was no new era, we all felt so let down. If I am being honest, I lost belief.'

The key point is that Blair was seen as a great leader through the eyes of others for a number of years, but by the end – and certainly today – he is not perceived in the same way. A leader will always be judged by others. It is very harsh to judge Blair in this way as he was a great leader and the lifespan of most CEOs is very limited. Most great leaders have a lifespan before they lose their aura and ability to lead but the Blair example makes the point. The truth is very few are able to carry teams for long periods of time.

If we look at the Peter Lederer profile, his story is remarkable for the fact that he has been a key leader for over two decades. This is an immense achievement and can only be achieved by the respect he carries through the eyes of his community.

What type of leader would you be? And do you even want to make the sacrifices to become a leader?

Remember that the average lifespan of a CEO is generally so short – an average 32 months. It is worth stopping and considering a few questions at this juncture:

- What leader have you most respect for?
- What leader has inspired you most?
- What have you learnt from the two above that you would use to ensure that you are effective?
- What leadership style would you use?

As has been analysed there is no right or wrong approach. One leading CEO once remarked:

'The person most respected in one's career is the one with conviction who is successful in their journey.'

This is probably true, as those with conviction and who are successful are easy to admire. This often refers to entrepreneurs but leadership is more complicated that just having conviction, as success will often need to be achieved through compromise and influence. The leader will know and understand their team and know when to push and when to hold. The reality is that conviction is just one factor, as any organisation's success needs the leader to have both the right structure in place to ensure successful delivery and employees ready to follow. It is a very subtle, complex and often fickle process and hence the leader needs to be patient and understanding. It is also for these reasons that leaders often invest so much into training and development; to ensure that people are being developed and feel important, and that the relevant skills are possessed within an organisation. This alone illustrates a core difference between a leader and an entrepreneur.

''Leadership is like gravity. You know it's there, you know it exists, but how do you define it?' Former San Francisco 49er tight end, Dr Jamie Williams.

It can be fairly argued that defining good leadership is too subjective. This is fair as the success of a leader depends on the trust and consensus of the organisations and team they lead. But the reality is that leadership excellence comes from qualities that inspire the respect of many, and the ability to communicate to enable action. This requires a very developed skill set, great knowledge, understanding and years of experience. It is very rare and it is to great credit of the hospitality industry that we can illustrate so many.

However, maybe the greatest lesson to take from both leaders and entrepreneurs is that failure is not to be feared: for it is through failure that great leaders and entrepreneurs learn and emerge.

Index of leaders and entrepreneurs

Index of companies